MAINE'S HISTORIC PLACES

D0838065

MAINE'S HISTORIC PLACES

Properties on the National Register of Historic Places

Frank A. Beard & Bette A. Smith

with
Robert L. Bradley & Arthur E. Spiess
of the Maine Historic Preservation Commission

Down East Books
Camden, Maine

Copyright © 1982 by the Maine Historic Preservation Commission
ISBN 0-89272-140-5
Library of Congress Catalog Card Number 82-70900
Design by Nan Kulikauskas
Composition by Camden Type 'n Graphics
Maps by Abbey Williams
Manufactured in the United States of America

Down East Books
Camden, Maine

5 4 3

Contents

MAINE'S HISTORIC PLACES

The National Register

The National Register of Historic Places was created by congressional action in the National Historic Preservation Act of 1966. This remarkable piece of legislation placed the federal government for the first time squarely in the field of historic preservation and created an all-important federal and state partnership in implementing its provisions.

The National Register, administered under the National Park Service, Department of the Interior, is, in essence, a catalogue of those buildings, districts, structures, objects, and sites deemed worthy of preservation for their historic, cultural, or archaeological significance to the American people and to their understanding of their heritage. As such, it is the basis upon which properties qualify for protection — federal matching grants, when available, for preservation and restoration, and tax-incentive provisions for restoration and preservation.

Federal administration of and control over the National Register ensures the uniform application of the criteria for eligibility, which may be judged on three levels: national, state, or local. However — and here is the importance of the partnership — all nominations, with the exception of those made by federal agencies of their own property, emanate from state historic preservation officers delegated by their respective governors, who administer the nomination process within their state. These nominations are screened by state review boards before being submitted to the National Register office in Washington, D.C.

Properties listed in the National Register are afforded a degree of protection from adverse impact by projects funded, licensed or executed by the federal government, since such projects are subject to review by the Advisory Council on Historic Preservation.

Control and authority over the use and disposition of National Register properties remain solely with the owner so long as federal grants or rehabilitation tax incentives are not involved. However, a property that is so altered as to lose its historic, cultural, or archaeological significance will be removed from the register.

The survey of Maine's historic resources and the nomination of those properties deemed eligible to the National Register are carried out by the Maine Historic Preservation Commission and its staff.

This book includes the names, with descriptive information, of all individual properties and districts in Maine that have been listed in the National Register between the origination of the process in 1969 and the end of 1981.

The Maine Historic Preservation Commission

In 1966 Congress passed the National Historic Preservation Act to create a federal and state partnership for the purpose of preserving America's historic, architectural, and archaeological heritage. To implement the program in Maine, Governor Kenneth M. Curtis assigned its functions to the Maine Parks and Recreation Commission in 1969 and appointed its Commissioner, Lawrence Stuart, as Maine's first State Historic Preservation Officer. Mr. Stuart directed that his staff historian John W. Briggs prepare the state's first National Register nominations and grant applications in conjunction with the Commission's Advisory Committee on Historic Sites.

During the late 1960s and early 1970s, support for historic preservation grew dramatically in Maine. This was reflected in the formation of such organizations as Greater Portland Landmarks in 1964, Row House of Hallowell in 1969, and Sagadahoc Preservation of Bath in 1971. In 1970 members of these groups, as well as other preservation-minded individuals, formed a committee that became the organization now known as Maine Citizens for Historic Preservation. Their purpose was to ask the 105*th* Maine Legislature to creat the Maine Historic Preservation Commission in order to accommodate a rapidly expanding federal preservation program at the state level. The Legislature responded favorably to this request, and Governor Curtis appointed the first Commission members in the fall of 1971.

The Maine Historic Preservation held its first meeting in Augusta in January of 1972, at which time Robert W. Patterson of Mount Desert was elected chairman. In April James H. Mundy was chosen as director, and later that year he was appointed as State Historic Preservation Officer. Mr. Mundy hired Richard D. Kelly, Jr., as staff historian in 1972 and Earle G. Shettleworth, Jr., as architectural historian in 1973. Frank A. Beard replaced Mr. Kelly in 1974.

During the Commission's first decade of operation, several individuals have served in leadership and staff positions. Mr. Patterson was followed as chairman in 1973 by David C. Smith of Orono, who was succeeded in 1975 by John D. Bardwell of York. Eugene S. Ashton, has been chairman since 1978. Upon James Mundy's departure to the Maine Legislature in the fall of 19975, Earle Shettleworth became acting director and was appointed as both director and State Historic Preservation Officer in 1976. Mr. Shettleworth hired Robert L. Bradley, an historic archaeologist, to succeed him as architectural historian in 1976. Prehistoric archaeologist Arthur E. Spiess became the final member of the professional staff in 1978. Rita C. Obie served as the Commission's accountant and Sharon L. Morang as its secretary.

When the Maine Historic Preservation Commission was created in 1971, it was an independent agency. As a result of the 1973 state government reorganization, the Commission was placed in the new Department of Educational and Cultural Services for administrative purposes. In 1979 the Commission became a bureau within Educational and Cultural Services, which accorded it with a status equal to the department's three other cultural agencies, the Maine State Library, the Maine State Museum, and the Maine Commission on the Arts and Humanities. The current Commissioner of the department, Harold Raynolds, Jr., has been active in his support of these four agencies.

During its first ten years, the Maine Historic Preservation Commission has established a strong record of achievement in all areas of its state and federally mandated responsibilities. As this publication reflects, Maine now has six hundred entries to the National Register of Historic Places, sixty of which are historic districts with structures ranging in numbers from three to three hundred. Fifty-two buildings and sites have received more than two million dollars in federal assistance which, when matched with private funds, has generated more than four million dollars in preservation work throughout the state. In age these grant projects run from the prehistoric Hirundo and Young Sites in Alton to the Rangeley Public Library of 1909 and in geographic location from the Lady Pepperrell House at Kittery Point to the Acadian Landing Site in Madawaska. The Commission has also funded numerous local and regional archaeological and architectural field surveys and research projects, that have resulted in thirteen publications ranging from *Discovering Maine's Archaeological Heritage* by David Sanger to *200 Years of Maine Housing* by Frank Beard. The most recent dimension to the program is the investment tax credit for the rehabilitation of income producing structures on the National Register. In the last five years, the Commission has processed over seventy applications for these projects, which represent a total of more than thirty-two million dollars in private investment in Maine's historic buildings. With these solid accomplishments to build on, the Commission confidently looks to the next decade in which a growing number of residents and visitors will discover, preserve, and revitalize the cultural resources of this state reflected in the pages of *Maine's Historic Places*.

Earle G. Shettleworth, Jr., Director
Maine Historic Preservation Commission

An Overview of Maine Settlement from Prehistoric Times to the Twentieth Century

Prehistoric archaeology in Maine, which deals with the Indians who inhabited the state for eleven thousand years before the first European visit, demonstrates that the built environment does not long survive above ground in the harsh environment of the Northeast. Maine's prehistoric archaeologists deal with the physical evidence of human habitation as it has been left in the ground. Along the coast, this evidence is often found in manmade accumulations of shell and debris, called shellheaps or shell middens. In the interior, the only overt visual evidence of a prehistoric camp may be a slight darkening of the soil. The most commonly found debris of human occupation in Maine are the stone tools made by native inhabitants, or the flakes of stone discarded during the process of stone tool manufacture. Also common are fire-cracked rocks and cobbles used in fireplaces or in cooking. In the shell middens along the Maine coast, the preservation of bone artifacts and bone tools, and the bone debris of animals used for food, are also common.

The most exciting evidence of prehistoric human settlement in Maine is the recovery of what archaeologists call living floors. In shellheaps, and sometimes in interior sites, we find one or more fireplaces that have been the focus of activity for a short time. Sometimes the fireplaces are associated with a hut or wigwam floor, defined by the dark remnants of postholes from posts used to shore up the walls or of boulders used to support the base of walls.

Living floors, as the archaeological remains of domestic structures, can provide a great deal of insight into past life in what is now Maine. The hearth often associated with a living floor yields charcoal that can be sent away to a laboratory for a radiocarbon date. Along the coast, the foodbone debris and shellfish associated with a living level can tell us whether it was occupied for just one season (and precisely which season) or whether it was occupied year-round. Sometimes the distribution of stone and bone tools gives clues to the activities that took place in a domestic structure, and the distribution of appurtenant features, such as garbage pits around a domestic structure, provide further details.

The earliest period of human occupation in Maine is known as the Paleoindian period, dating from roughly twelve thousand to ten thousand years ago, at the very end of the last ice age. During this time, the first Maine inhabitants lived in an environment with far fewer trees than there are today. Probably the land was covered with a mixture of tundra, grassland, and scrubby tree growth in sheltered places. During this time, men may have hunted the last of the mammoths, wild horses, musk oxen, and bison, and they certainly hunted caribou. Sites of this period in the National Register are the Vail site and some of the sites in the Munsungun–Chase Lake Thoroughfare District.

The last ten thousand years of Maine prehistory, until A.D. 1500, are divided among the Early Archaic, Middle Archaic, Late Archaic, and Ceramic periods.

The division between the Archaic and Ceramic periods is based simply on the beginning of manufacture of clay pottery by Maine Indians about twenty-five hundred years ago. During this time most of Maine's Indians made their living by hunting, fishing, and gathering wild plant foods in a heavily wooded environment. Only during the later Ceramic period did a few Indian groups in southwestern Maine become dependent upon horticulture, growing corn, beans, and squash for a major portion of their diet. But even they retained a great deal of the hunting-gathering way of life. The Indians of the rest of the state did not adopt agriculture until after European contact.

The Early Archaic period in this region, between ten thousand and eight thousand years ago, is very poorly known. We know that this time was one of drastic environmental change: forest tree species migrated into the state from the south, developing the thick forest cover of Maine, and relative sea level fluctuated wildly as an aftereffect of glacial retreat. Beginning in the Early Archaic period, the Indians' use of the interior began to be restricted by the forest to the major inland waterways and lakes. At least, the lakes and waterways became the focus of travel and habitation, while the forest was probably used solely for hunting and other short-term use.

The Middle Archaic period in Maine lasted from about eight thousand years until about six thousand years ago. The Jon Lund site is the only Maine National Register site that primarily dates from this period. Collections of arrowheads and spearpoints from the Androscoggin and Kennebec river valleys show that interior use by Middle Archaic peoples was heavily oriented toward major lake basins and that less use was made of rivers and waterways by these people than by later inhabitants. Isolated point finds from the coast show that the Middle Archaic peoples did live along the coast as well, although coastal erosion has destroyed most site evidence.

The Late Archaic period, from six thousand to roughly three thousand years ago, is a period of major cultural efflorescence. The famous Red Paint (or Moorehead Phase) graves, with their fancy stone-tool grave offerings, are a part of the Late Archaic cultural sequence. Immediately succeeding the Moorehead Phase is the more recently discovered, but also spectacular, Susquehanna Tradition with complex cremation burials. At present it is an unanswered question why earlier evidence of complex cultural practices concerning the dead has not been recovered from Maine, but it is possible that a greater Maine Indian population during the Late Archaic period encouraged greater cultural activity. We have evidence of more intensive use of Maine's interior waterways beginning in the Moorehead Phase (around 4,500 to 3,800 years ago). We surmise that boat transportation improved during this time, and that by the early Ceramic period the birchbark canoe had been invented and developed into a finely tuned transportation mechanism.

Many prehistoric sites in the National Register have components dating to both the Late Archaic and Ceramic periods.

European contact with Maine Indians between A.D. 1500 and 1630 drastically changed prehistoric lifestyles, social organization, and population levels. The Nahanada site has shown that by 1605, well before permanent European settlement, Maine's Indians were heavily involved in trade with Europeans (probably for furs). The historically recorded settlement pattern of spending the summer on the coast trading with Europeans, then dispersing into the interior to go fur trapping in the winter, has been shown by contrast with Ceramic period sites to be strictly a post–A.D. 1500 development. A major epidemic disease of about 1616, with greater than 75 percent average mortality among Maine's coastal Indian bands, began a period of great disruption of Indian life. Later in the seventeenth century, during the French and Indian Wars, surviving Indians essentially became refugees, resettling into the groups we know today as the Penobscot, Passamaquoddy, and Maliseet tribes.

Exploration and Settlement of Maine (through the Revolution)

Although it is just conceivable that the Norse (Vikings) explored the Maine coast in the eleventh century or a bit later, the only proven Scandinavian artifact deriving from an archaeological context is a Norwegian penny minted between 1065 and 1080 that was found in an Indian site on Blue Hill Bay. This coin, however, seems to have been traded from Indian tribe to tribe from the Labrador area where the Norse are known to have been active at various times.

The earliest documented European visits to Maine waters occurred many centuries later, in large part due to the urge to locate a northwest passage to the Orient and its valuable spices. In this context, John Cabot (1497), John Rut (1527), Bartholomew Gosnold (1602), Martin Pring (1603 and 1606), George Waymouth (1605), and John Smith (1614) all sailed under England's colors. In the service of France, Giovanni da Verrazano (1524) and Samuel de Champlain (1604 and

1605) sailed the coast. Estevan Gómez (1524–25) sailed for Spain.

Of course, none of these adventurers found a navigable northwest passage, and none of them found the mythical city of Norumbega with its fabled riches. By the beginning of the seventeenth century, Europeans were admitting that they could not reach China by sailing up the Penobscot River, and that the hills along the coast were not filled with gold and silver. The real wealth of Maine, however, was soon enough recognized — hundreds of safe harbors, almost unlimited timber, lucrative trade with the natives for beaver pelts, and the richest fishing grounds in the Northeast. As the seventeenth century opened, European Maine was about to be born.

The first attempt at a permanent settlement was made by France on St. Croix Island in the summer of 1604, followed by England's Popham Colony in what is now Phippsburg in 1607. The first Maine settlers were not the last summer visitors to pick poor locations for year-round living, and both these earliest colonizing efforts failed within a year, in large part because of Maine's distinctly un-European winter.

The initial failures discouraged both England and France, but valuable lessons were learned. Seasonal fishing and Indian trade accelerated in the second decade of the century, and by the 1620s England in particular began the widespread settlement of Maine. In 1622, the first year-round English fishing station was established on Damariscove Island, and shortly thereafter similar bases were established on the Isles of Shoals, Richmond's Island, Monhegan Island, and numerous other locations.

Many of these fishing stations gave birth to larger settlements on the nearby mainland. Thus, the Monhegan operation, begun in 1623, was moved to Pemaquid in 1625, and thereafter this settlement grew and flourished as England's northeasternmost outpost of the Thirteen Colonies. Archaeological excavations at Colonial Pemaquid have uncovered the remains of more than a dozen early buildings — dwellings, a tavern, a forge, and other community structures. By the 1630s, many other English villages were being founded, particularly on the coast between Casco Bay and the Piscataqua River. But what of the French?

After the abortive St. Croix Colony, France concentrated on settling parts of Nova Scotia, and it was not until 1613 that a mission, known as St. Sauveur, was established on

Mount Desert Island. However, this was destroyed by Englishmen from Jamestown in the same summer. The fact that both England and France claimed much of Maine sowed early and virulent seeds of violent confrontation. In 1635, the French seized a Plymouth Colony trading post in what is now Castine and proceeded to build Fort Pentagoet, an Indian name for the area. This stone fort, which is now the subject of an important archaeological project, was constructed of slate imported from the Mayenne area of France. It immediately became the most important Acadian outpost in Maine.

In the first half of the seventeenth century, English relations with the Indians of Maine were generally good, but, as the century wore on, increasing population pressures strained these relations to the breaking point. One of the root causes was that the native American could not comprehend the European concept of title to specific parcels of land. Thus, many an Indian "deed" was sold for the right to *use* the land, not to *own* it.

In 1675, King Philip's War ravaged Massachusetts, and a year later it spilled over the Merrimack and Piscataqua rivers into northern New England. English Maine was devastated, as virtually all settlements were attacked and many — especially north of today's York County — were completely destroyed. The first of nearly a century of wars between the English and the allied French and Indians had begun, and the early settlement period had come abruptly to an end.

Of the three parties involved — the English, the French, and the Indians — none benefited from the wars. The English ultimately won, but at great cost. The French lost their tenuous hold on Maine forever. Most devastated of all were the Indians, caught in the middle between European rivalries, carrying the brunt of the raids, skirmishes, and battles against the English, and in the end driven north and east as refugees.

As the Indian Wars gradually wound down in the early to mid eighteenth century, much of Maine, particularly the mid-coastal region between Casco and Penobscot bays, became subject to Anglo-American resettlement. Communities like Pemaquid and Sheepscot, abandoned for a generation, were reincarnated as the French and Indian threat receded. Anglo-American settlements slowly penetrated up major waterways like the Kennebec River, invariably accompanied by the construction of stockade forts such as Fort Western and Fort Halifax. With the fall of Louisbourg in 1758 and of Quebec a year later, the French empire in North America collapsed, and Anglo-American settlers must have rejoiced at the prospect of long-term peace.

But it was not to be; a few short years after England and her colonial subjects triumphed over France and her colonies, yet another war destroyed Maine's peace and this time it was a family affair.

Maine is not immediately thought of when pondering the American Revolution. Nonetheless, the war began in Massachusetts, a colony of which Maine was then a part, and this region witnessed some dramatic and tragic events in that long struggle. On the frontier between the Thirteen Colonies and British Canada, Maine was the scene of the first naval engagement of the Revolution, off Machias in 1775. In the same year, one of her principal communities, Falmouth (now Portland), was bombarded and burned to the ground by a Royal Navy squadron. Also in 1775, Maine hosted Colonel Benedict Arnold's heroic march to Quebec — a tactical debacle (Quebec held), but a strategic triumph (Britain's invasion of New York from the north was delayed by a crucial year). Finally, Maine witnessed the worst naval disaster in American history in 1779, when a fleet of forty-four Massachusetts vessels sailed to Castine to dislodge the British from Fort George. The fort was not taken, and not one American vessel survived the Penobscot expedition.

Extended peace, prosperity, and growth at last came to Maine in the years following the Revolution. There were short-term economic and military problems in the early nineteenth century, occasioned by the Trade Embargo of 1807 and the War of 1812 (when the British occupied Castine for one last time). But as the nineteenth century advanced, Maine was to enter the most expansive period of her long history.

Maine History and Architecture: 1750–1910

The economic development that began in Maine following the cessation of the Indian Wars was particularly evident in the southern or western coastal area. There, fishing, lumbering, shipbuilding, and increasing shipping trade made fortunes for a few and improved living conditions for many. Even agriculture, up to that time largely a matter of subsistence, began to produce cash crops as both land and sea access to markets improved.

The increasing wealth of the coastal area as far east as the Kennebec was reflected in the construction of dwellings in the first formal architectural style to appear. Houses of the seventeenth and early eighteenth centuries in Maine were primarily utilitarian in nature, without significant decoration, and loosely grouped under the heading of Colonial architecture. In the 1750s, largely inspired by English plan books, pretentious homes began to be erected in the prevailing fashion of the mother country, referred to as the Georgian style after the second and third monarchs of that name. These grand, solid, formally decorated homes, often with steeply pitched hip roofs and tall chimneys, appeared from Kittery (the Lady Pepperrell House — 1760) to Stroudwater (the Tate House — 1755) to Phippsburg (the McCobb-Hill-Minott House — 1774) on the Kennebec River.

The years following the Revolution, with their even more rapidly developing prosperity, saw the adoption of another somewhat related style, also imported via plan books from England. Inspired in large part by the designs of Robert Adam, the Federal style, a delicate gracile architectural form, was adopted by a new generation of merchants, shipbuilders, sea captains, and lawyers in a much larger area, now reaching as far east as the Canadian border and up the rivers in the newly emerging river ports. On the shore of the St. Croix River, General John Brewer built his "Mansion House" in 1785; Judge Silas Lee in Wiscasset constructed an architecturally outstanding example of the style in 1792; and the stately and formal McLellan-Sweat Mansion was erected in Portland between 1800 and 1801. The Federal style, in fact, persisted into the third decade of the nineteenth century, as exemplified by the magnificent Ruggles House of 1820 in Columbia Falls.

At the same time as Maine achieved statehood in 1820, there began an awakening of American nationalism across the new country and a development of pride in her democratic institutions, which seemed to have proved their worth. In 1821, the Greek war for independence from the Ottoman Empire commenced, and an outpouring of romantic sympathy for the "mother of democracy" was generated among liberals in Europe and most particularly in the United States, where it was felt the ancient Greek political and philosophical traditions had been perpetuated.

The architectural result of this was the development of the Greek Revival style across the young nation, thousands of examples of which appear in Maine. In many ways the most pervasive of all styles in the state and the first to appear in virtually the entire populated area, it persisted from the late 1820s up to 1860 at least. The style itself began as an unabashed attempt to reproduce, as far as was practical given the prevailing climate, ancient Greek monumental architecture on the American landscape. Most of the earliest houses in this style were fairly direct copies of Greek temples, perhaps most notably the Nathaniel Hatch House of 1832–33 in Bangor. Over the years the Greek Revival underwent ingenious adaptations of great beauty, such as the James P. White House (1842) in Belfast, and it was also applied, in modified form, to more modest dwellings, which appear on hundreds of Maine streetscapes. The Greek Revival was also the first style to be extensively employed in the design of commercial and industrial buildings, as Maine's economy became increasingly directed toward business and manufacturing. A handsome example of this in a typical small Maine mill town is the Portsmouth Company Counting House of 1832 in South Berwick. Some of Maine's most beautiful churches, such as the Ellsworth Congregational Church of 1846, owe their design to the Greek Revival.

Although not nearly as extensively employed, another style found its way into Maine during roughly the same years as the Greek Revival. Also born of the romantic tendencies of the period, the Gothic Revival style, an effort to recapture elements of English medieval architecture, achieved limited popularity almost exclusively in domestic architecture. A particularly fine example of the cottage version of this style, with decorative bargeboards and the pointed arch, is the so-called Gothic House of 1845 in Portland.

Increasing industrial activity after 1820 was marked by the development of numerous small mill towns on Maine's rivers and streams producing a variety of products largely for local or area consumption. The advent of railroads in the 1840s stimulated the growth of larger inland manufacturing centers, whose products could now be more widely distributed by rail, to Maine's great seaports in particular. These ports, where shipping and shipbuilding brought rapid growth, provided a major contribution in ships and men to the American merchant marine.

The middle years of the century also saw the advent of

major new industries, such as textile manufacturing and lime burning, and new products, such as the large-scale production of lumber in the watersheds of the Kennebec, Penobscot and other rivers, as well as granite quarrying in numerous coastal areas. As early as 1850, Maine agriculture had begun to decline, and the population had begun to shift to the towns and cities.

All during the century, the growing industrial centers attracted various ethnic groups, so that the population was enriched by the arrival of Irish, Italian, and particularly Franco-American immigrants.

Architecturally, in these years, there emerged what are frequently referred to as Victorian styles. The 1850s marked the advent of the long-popular Italianate style, which saw its most sophisticated development in the nationally famous Victoria Mansion of 1859–63 in Portland, a villa of great opulence. The typical Italianate house, however, tended to be symmetrical in form and ranged from modest homes to the impressive houses of the rich, such as the Porter-Bell-Brackley House of 1866 in Strong. This style also found expression in industrial architecture, such as the Pejepscot Company Cotton Mill (1868) in Topsham, and in commercial buildings such as the Elias Thomas Block of 1860 in Portland. Churches, and particularly schools in great number, were designed in the Italianate style.

Following closely on the heels of the Italianate came the Mansard, or Second Empire, style made popular by the double-pitched roof form employed by Napoleon III in his extension of the Louvre in Paris. High-style Mansard houses, such as the 1858 Blake House in Bangor, reflected newly acquired industrial wealth, although the style was at times applied to humbler dwellings. Commercial architecture, as in the handsome Woodman Building in Portland, was strongly and handsomely affected by the Second Empire influence.

Two styles of the post–Civil War period almost exclusively restricted to commercial or public buildings were the High Victorian Gothic and the Richardsonian Romanesque. The former finds expression in the highly decorative and vertically oriented Belfast National Bank of 1879, while the latter appears with its heavy rounded arches in Augusta's 1896 Lithgow Library.

The culmination of Victorian complexity in architecture arrived in the 1880s with the Queen Anne style, employed most frequently in the design of residences. Featuring an asymmetrical assemblage of projecting gables, corner towers, decorative chimneys and ornate filigree, these houses employed a variety of surface treatments, from decorative shingles to clapboards to half-timbered portions. The general appearance could be somewhat exotic, as seen in the Straw House (ca. 1885) in Guilford.

The last three decades of the nineteenth century saw the beginning of what was to become a vital part of the Maine economy, the advent of the summer visitor and summer resident. For the former, summer hotels, such as the Claremont (1883) in Southwest Harbor, sprang up in large numbers along the coast, on many lakes, and in the western mountains. For the latter, a new style of summer-cottage architecture was developed that was also adopted for year-round residences. Designed to blend both design and materials with the natural surroundings, the Shingle Style featured expansive, all-encompassing roof lines and stone and shingle wall surfaces. The C.A. Brown Cottage of 1886 on Cape Elizabeth is a notable example of this naturally oriented style.

The first years of the nineteenth century saw a return to earlier American architectural styles. Drawing on elements of both the Georgian and Federal styles, the Colonial Revival was widely exemplified in all types of buildings, typical of which are the White Memorial Building of 1903 in Houlton and the Security Trust building of 1912 in Rockland.

The nearly two hundred years beginning in 1750 saw Maine's emergence from a struggling colony, through a period of rapid growth, to a relatively stable state, whose economic base has changed but whose environmental qualities have largely been retained. The period is marked by great architectural variety and vitality, the evidence of which is still with us and richly deserves to be preserved.

A Guide for Using this Book

In order to facilitate the use of this book, a brief explanation of its plan seems appropriate. For the sake of geographical convenience the state of Maine has been divided into seven regions, in most, but not all, cases along county lines. Maps of each region are provided. Within these regions, the towns have been arranged alphabetically. Under each town's heading, every National Register district or individual property has been listed with the districts first, alphabetically, followed by the individual properties, chronologically. A description, and sometimes a photograph, is included for every Maine listing in the National Register of Historic Places.

Those sites marked with asterisks have been approved by the Maine Historic Preservation Commission for nomination to the National Register. Their inclusion in the register should have been finalized by the time of publication.

Several buildings, although included in the register, have also been recognized as having outstanding national significance. They have been designated as National Historic Landmarks and are marked accordingly with the letters "NHL."

The index includes only the names of towns and properties; thus, if one knows the name of the town or the property, but not its region, it can still be found easily.

The Regions

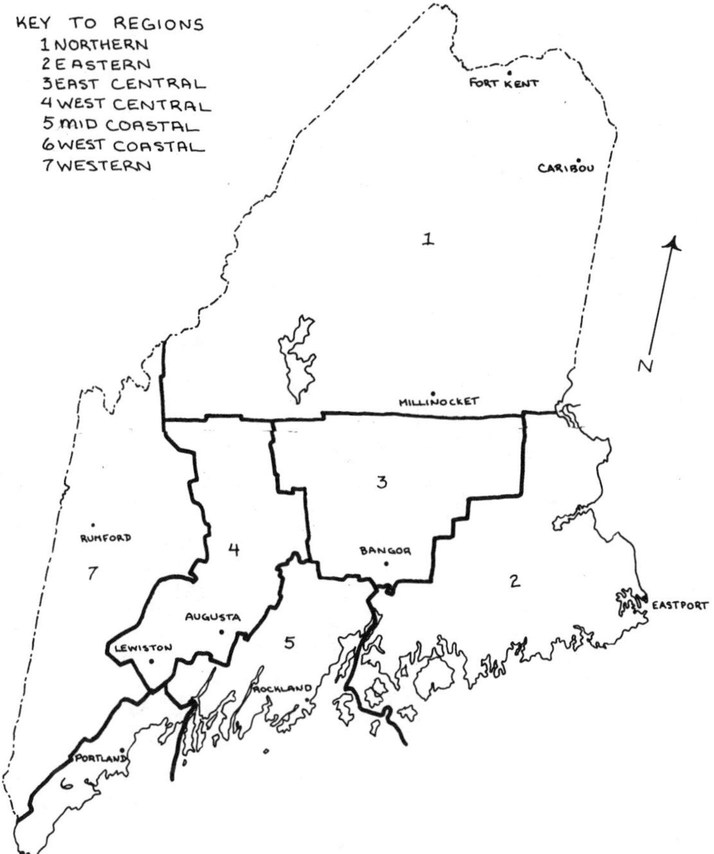
KEY TO REGIONS
1 NORTHERN
2 EASTERN
3 EAST CENTRAL
4 WEST CENTRAL
5 MID COASTAL
6 WEST COASTAL
7 WESTERN
FORT KENT
CARIBOU
1
N
MILLINOCKET
3
RUMFORD
4
BANGOR
7
2
EASTPORT
AUGUSTA
5
LEWISTON
ROCKLAND
PORTLAND
6
KITTERY

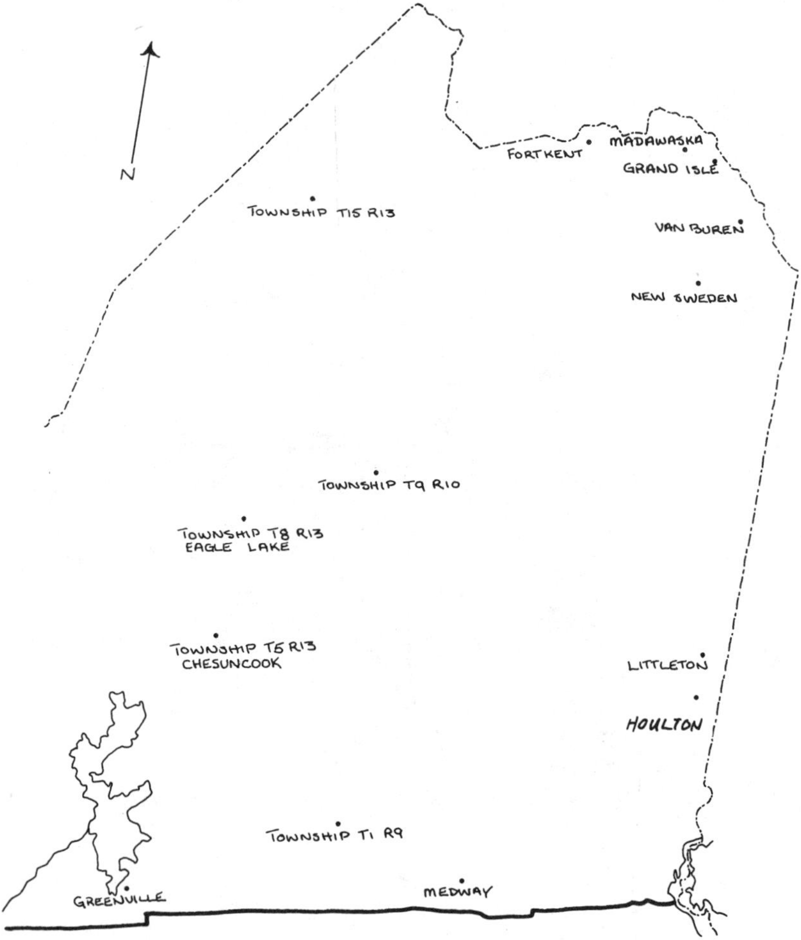
N
FORT KENT
MADAWASKA
GRAND ISLE
VAN BUREN
NEW SWEDEN
TOWNSHIP T15 R13
TOWNSHIP T9 R10
TOWNSHIP T8 R13
EAGLE LAKE
TOWNSHIP T5 R13
CHESUNCOOK
LITTLETON
HOULTON
TOWNSHIP T1 R9
GREENVILLE
MEDWAY

Northern Region

AMBAJEJUS LAKE

Ambajejus Boom House, Township, T1, R9 — 1830, 1907

There has been a Boom House at the head of Ambajejus Lake since 1835; the present building was constructed in 1907 and used until 1971. The simple, 1½-story structure is the only surviving building that was connected with the west branch log drives that made the Penobscot River and Bangor famous nationwide.

CHESUNCOOK VILLAGE

Chesuncook Village, Township T5, R13

Chesuncook, locally referred to as "Suncook," is one of the last surviving Maine woods frontier settlements that served the people who worked in the lumbering industry and then dwindled away when lumbering techniques changed. Begun as a wilderness outpost in the early nineteenth century, Chesuncook increased in size and activity during the log-drive era to the point that it was expected to become a city! The twentieth century brought many changes to the village; it now has only two year-round residents and is used mainly by sportsmen.

EAGLE LAKE

Tramway Historic District, Township T8,R13, Between Eagle and Chamberlain Lakes—1902, 1927

The Tramway, a remarkable engineering feat, was constructed in 1902 to transport logs across a 3,000-foot-wide neck of land from Eagle Lake, at the head of the Allagash waterway, to Chamberlain Lake and the east branch of the Penobscot River. From there the logs could be sent to the great mills on the lower Penobscot and the resulting lumber shipped by sea to worldwide markets. Chamberlain Lake itself had originally been part of the Allagash River system, but, in an incredibly ambitious undertaking, its waters had been diverted in 1841 into the Penobscot by means of dams and excavation. By the turn of the century, however, the areas around Chamberlain had been largely cut, and new timber was sought from Eagle and Churchill lakes.

The Tramway consisted of a 1⅓-inch-diameter steel cable, 6,000 feet long, made into an endless loop. Trucks were attached to this at intervals of 10 feet and consisted of a steel saddle with teeth and two 11-inch wheels that ran on tracks with a 22-inch gauge. Two sets of tracks, one directly above the other, were mounted on a heavy wooden framework. These carried the loaded trucks (one log spanning two trucks) on the upper level and the returning empty trucks upside down on the lower. Halfway between the trucks, steel clamps were attached to the cable, and these, as well as the trucks, fitted into a 9-foot sprocket wheel at the Chamberlain (delivery) end of the Tramway. This wheel was turned by a steam engine. Today virtually the entire system remains intact, except for the wooden frame that supported the tracks and some sections of the track itself, which have been carried off for scrap.

Tramway Historic District, Township T8, R13

The Tramway ceased operation as the result of the invention of the Lombard steam log hauler in 1907 by Alvin O. Lombard of Waterville, Maine. This huge machine, with caterpillar drive in the rear and runners in front, could haul eight sleds at a time, averaging forty thousand board feet per load. Later models were gasoline powered.

Between 1926 and 1927, a railroad 18 miles long was constructed between the Tramway site and Umbazooksus Lake so that logs could be introduced into the west branch of the Penobscot and driven to the pulp mills in Millinocket.

From 1927 to 1933, during the summer only, the so-called Pulpwood Express ran several trips a day over this isolated, junctionless 18-mile railway in the Maine wilderness. Each train consisted of ten to twelve cars, and an average work week saw 6,500 cords hauled by the two locomotives.

When the line ceased operation in 1933, the engines were stored in a shed at the Eagle Lake terminal, never to run again. The shed was later burned, leaving these monuments to the logging industry surrounded by the wilderness in which they had run during their last years of operation. The remaining log cars were also burned, leaving little but their trucks as remains.

Thus ended a century of logging history, during which the Tramway district had been at the center of activity. Today the Tramway is part of the Allagash Wilderness Waterway, a state park administered by the Maine Bureau of Parks and Recreation.

FORT KENT

Fort Kent — 1838–39 (NHL)

Fort Kent was constructed between 1838 and 1840 as a result of the northeast boundary controversy between the United States and Great Britain. The controversy, which began at the Treaty of Paris in 1783, was finally resolved by the Webster-Ashburton Treaty signed in Washington in 1842. In the intervening years, however, a combination of resentment remaining from two wars with Britain, trespassing by both sides onto disputed territory, an awareness of the Aroostook Valley's timber and land resources, greed, chicanery, and political maneuvering led to the bloodless

Fort Kent Blockhouse

Aroostook War of 1838–39 and a possibly explosive diplomatic issue on the northeast frontier.

Fort Kent Blockhouse, named in honor of the governor of Maine, was built by members of the Maine militia under Captain Nye who were sent to prevent Canadian lumbermen from trespassing onto claimed state territory.

The blockhouse, a two-story structure with walls of hand-hewn cedar timber, some squaring over 19 inches, was set on a shale rock foundation about 1½ feet off the ground to protect the lower timbers from ground rot. The base is 23 feet, 5 inches square, while the second story has an overhang of approximately 15 inches on each side.

In 1858, the blockhouse was sold into private hands but was reacquired by the state in 1891, with the intention that it be preserved as a historic monument. For nearly sixty-eight years, Fort Kent was neglected by the state, until local interest was focused on it in 1959. Since this time Maine's

Department of Parks and Recreation has maintained the site and blockhouse as a state memorial.

GRAND ISLE

Our Lady of Mount Carmel Catholic Church, U.S. Route 1 — 1893–1903

This large, Romanesque-style, clapboard church is significant in the St. John River Valley both architecturally and historically. Built between 1893 and 1903, it is a monument to the years of struggle for parish status by the Grand Isle Catholics.

GREENVILLE

Lake Boat *Katahdin* — 1914

One of the few remaining lake boats once so common on Maine inland waters, the *Katahdin* was the last and biggest steam vessel operated by the Coburn Steamboat Company on Moosehead Lake, where such service began in 1836. Built at Bath Iron Works in 1914, she was delivered in sections at Greenville on August 20, where she was assembled for service the following year.

The vessel, affectionately called the "Kate," operated between various points on the lake, carrying passengers and freight. She was especially popular among the summer visitors at such famous hotels as the Mount Kineo House, who were in the habit of using her for excursions around the lake.

Because of changing modes of transportation, particularly the increasing use of the automobile, the *Katahdin* gradually ceased to be economically feasible. On September 11, 1938, she made her last run as a passenger boat, carrying 300 people on a special farewell excursion to Seboomook and back to Greenville.

The *Katahdin* was purchased in 1940 by the Hollingsworth and Whitney Paper Company and converted into a towboat for hauling pulpwood booms on the lake. This company was absorbed by Scott Paper Company, which continued this use until 1976 when she was finally laid up.

The "Kate" is now owned by the Moosehead Marine Museum, which plans to restore her to her earlier configuration although not to run her on the lake.

HOULTON

Market Square Historic District

This district consists of an extremely homogeneous and cohesive grouping of twenty-eight architecturally significant structures dating largely from 1885 to 1910. The district spans both sides of Market Square, an impressive open space, and runs two blocks east on Main Street, as well as entering side streets. All major styles of the period are represented, with a number of the buildings having been designed by the noted Bangor architect, Wilfred E. Mansur (1855–1921). The buildings are well maintained, with less than the usual amount of modern first-floor overlays than is usually found in older commercial areas.

Although one of the early towns in Aroostook County, having been settled in the first decade of the nineteenth century and incorporated in 1831, Houlton grew very slowly and in 1870 had a population of less than two thousand. Yet in the 1890s, when the rest of the United States was ex-

French Block, Market Square, Houlton

Market Square, Houlton

periencing the worst depression in its history and while labor unrest, radicalism, and controversy over the money system had the nation in a turmoil, Houlton experienced its biggest boom and by 1910 boasted a population of nearly six thousand.

Houlton was already the market town for the area, especially since the arrival of the New Brunswick Railroad (CPR) in 1870, and the years since then had been good years. But that was nothing compared to the burst of enthusiasm, business and building that accompanied the construction of the Bangor and Aroostook Railroad to Houlton in December 1893 and of the Aroostook Valley Railroad the following year. The end result was that the Houlton of today took shape in wood, brick, and steel in 1894 and 1895. Large, attractive, and expensive structures demonstrated local confidence that prosperity had come to stay.

This district still retains almost undisturbed its architectural flavor of three quarters of a century ago.

Black Hawk Putnam Tavern, 22 North Street — 1813

This structure is the oldest surviving house in Aroostook County and must have loomed immense at the time of its building in what was then a frontier town. Quite naturally, it became an inn or tavern, providing shelter for passing travelers or temporary quarters for new settlers moving into the area.

White Memorial Building, 109 Main Street — 1903

The finest residence of its style and period in Houlton, this Colonial Revival house was built by Mrs. John C. McIntyre on land originally acquired in 1843 by her grandfather, an early settler in the area. It is now the home of the Aroostook Historical and Art Museum.

First National Bank, Market Square — 1907

One of the last, and most successful, designs of Maine architect George M. Coombs, the First National Bank of Houlton is a fine example of turn-of-the-century financial buildings. The gray granite façade of this neo–Greek Revival building makes the bank unique in this late-nineteenth-century business district.

LITTLETON

Watson Settlement Bridge—1911

This 150-foot-long bridge spans the Meduxnekeag Stream and is supported by two abutments and a central pier made of rubble. Designed on the Howe truss system, this bridge was constructed before there were any approaches to it.

MADAWASKA

Site of Acadian Landing, St. David Village—1785

In 1710, that part of Canada now called Nova Scotia, but then known as Acadia by its French population, came under British rule. For a time the Acadians were allowed to continue their former existence, but they declined to take a full oath of allegiance to the British Crown. At the outbreak of the French and Indian War in 1755, this issue became critical. The combination of their questionable loyalty to the Crown and their Roman Catholicism made the Acadians unwelcome in their own land. They were taken prisoners by the King's army and were deported to Louisiana, Bermuda, points along the Atlantic Coast, and even England. Some Acadians, forewarned of the plans, fled to New Brunswick and Quebec.

Loyalists who sought refuge in Canada during the American Revolution brought new trials to the Acadians still in New Brunswick. Much of their land was confiscated, but a sympathetic governor granted them land along the upper St. John River. In June 1785, the Acadians again abandoned their homes. Several families left Fredericton in canoes and finally settled on the southern shore of the St. John River in the region of Madawaska. At the landing place, their leader, John Daigle, erected a cross in thanksgiving for their arrival in their promised land. The area, however, almost became a battleground during the border disputes of the

Acadian Village, Madawaska

Acadian Village, Madawaska

early 1800s. Finally, in 1842, the Webster-Ashburton Treaty brought calm to the land of the Acadians.

The present cross is of little historic significance; it is not even a replica of the original cross. The site it marks, however, represents the wellspring of Franco-American culture in the St. John River Valley, which has provided ethnic enrichment to the area and to the state of Maine.

St. David Catholic Church, U.S. Route 1 — 1911–1913

Construction of this imposing brick and granite church began in 1911; the first mass was said in 1913. Another example of the Romanesque style so typical of the St. John River Valley, St. David is a visible result of the transferral of area Catholics to the jurisdiction of an American diocese.

MEDWAY

Congregational Church of Medway, Routes 11 and 157 — 1874

This structure is of particular importance because of its remote location. Built when the town was little more than a resting place on the great Penobscot log drive, it is an unorthodox but compellingly straightforward building, which remains a landmark in what is still a largely wild and untamed region.

NEW SWEDEN

Timmerhuset, Jemtland Road—1870–75

In the 1870s, a new group of immigrants came to Maine. Having been recruited in northern Sweden, these settlers began to make a future for themselves in the woods of northern Maine. The log cabin, Timmerhuset, was constructed in the same manner as cabins in Sweden and is the only one of the pioneer cabins that still exists.

TOWNSHIP T9, R10

Munsungun–Chase Lake Thoroughfare Archaeological District—Prehistoric

The Munsungun–Chase Lake Thoroughfare Prehistoric District holds the key to understanding human occupation of the far northern Maine woods. Chase and Munsungun lakes were apparently created by dams of glacial ice or glacial moraine debris at the close of the last ice age. Their shorelines were occupied by Paleoindians with a fluted-point technology soon after their creation, probably around eleven thousand years ago. The lakes' outlet stream slowly cut down through the glacial dam, and the lake level gradually drained, leaving a series of shorelines analogous to the rings on a dirty bathtub. The lakes reached their modern level about four thousand years ago. There are series of occupations on most of the shoreline at the Thoroughfare that date between four thousand and ten thousand years ago, as well as some on the modern shoreline. Some of these occupations contain types of stone tools that are very rare in the Northeast, representing poorly known cultures.

Moreover, adjacent to the Thoroughfare is Norway Bluff, which is a major chert outcrop that has been used as a quarry for stone tool material since Paleoindian times. Thus, the area not only contains rare periods of occupation, but the data needed to investigate prehistoric procurement of stone material and changes in procurement strategy over time.

TOWNSHIP T15, R13

Big Black Site—4,000 B.C.–Twentieth Century

The Big Black site is the largest and best preserved prehistoric site on the upper St. John River. It covers a large terrace near the confluence of the Big Black and St. John rivers and apparently holds key evidence for deciphering Indian use of the upper St. John over the last three centuries or longer. Most importantly, evidence from the site can be used to reconstruct contact between prehistoric inhabitants of the Bas Saint-Laurent (Quebec), the Lower St. John in New Brunswick, and the Allagash and other drainages in Maine.

VAN BUREN

Acadian Historic Buildings, U.S. Route 1

Descended from the hardy Acadians who, driven out of Nova Scotia in 1855, settled first in New Brunswick and then in the St. John Valley, present-day residents of the area are intensely proud of their heritage and traditions.

Although this district contains structures moved from other locations and also buildings that are contemporary reconstructions of earlier styles, it is strongly felt that, because of the unusual circumstances and conditions that prevail, this grouping represents the best testimony to the quality and style of earlier days in the valley. Because of the remoteness of the region and its unique ethnic and historic background, preservation of this heritage is both difficult and important. Because of the relatively limited economic resources in the region, there appears to be no other way in which these buildings can be protected from decay and, eventually, total disappearance. A way of life found nowhere else in Maine is represented here. The loss of these tangible remains would be irreparable.

The stated purpose of L'Héritage Vivant, a non-profit historical society incorporated in 1973, is to foster, promote, and encourage interest in the history of the regions of Van Buren, Grand Isle, Hamlin, and Cyr Plantation, and the surrounding communities in the St. John Valley. The Acadian Village is the result of dedicated, self-generated effort on the part of the people and local organizations of the valley. The ambition and spirit of the earlier pioneers in the face of great obstacles still rest in their descendants.

Violette House, 464 Main Street — 1850s

Though humble in appearance, this simple 2½-story house of the mid nineteenth century loomed large among the single-story log cabins occupied by the majority of Acadian loggers and rivermen who inhabited the area. Though this building, too, was of log construction, with beams supported by ship's knees, it was sheathed with clapboards and shingles.

It stands today as a reminder of the staunch French and Acadian culture, which left so strong a mark in this region of Maine.

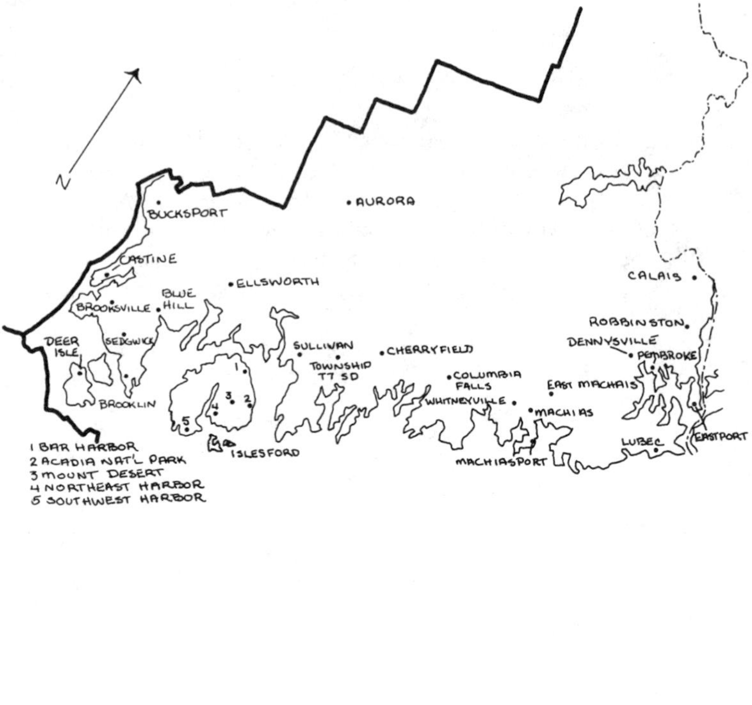
N
BUCKSPORT
AURORA
CASTINE
ELLSWORTH
BROOKSVILLE
BLUE HILL
DEER ISLE
SEDGWICK
BROOKLIN
SULLIVAN
TOWNSHIP T7 SD
CHERRYFIELD
COLUMBIA FALLS
WHITNEYVILLE
MACHIAS
EAST MACHAIS
MACHIASPORT
ISLESFORD
CALAIS
ROBBINSTON
DENNYSVILLE
PEMBROKE
LUBEC
EASTPORT
1 BAR HARBOR
2 ACADIA NAT'L PARK
3 MOUNT DESERT
4 NORTHEAST HARBOR
5 SOUTHWEST HARBOR

Eastern Region

ACADIA NATIONAL PARK

Carriage Path System — 1920s

Between 1905 and 1910, permanent and summer residents of Mount Desert Island fought, respectively, to admit or to ban automobiles from the island. Automobiles were ultimately admitted, and in response, John D. Rockefeller, Jr., set about building a 57-mile network of carriage paths through the hills in the vicinity of Jordan Pond. There was some opposition to this construction, led by Senator George W. Pepper of Pennsylvania, who summered at Northeast Harbor, but by the late 1920s the completed Carriage Path System extended from Paradise Hill on the north to the Day Mountain area at the south.

The Carriage Path System is unique in blending with its surroundings and affording hikers, horseback parties, and others the opportunity to explore the area. The twelve bridges constructed from native granite to span streams and other features are impressive in their own right. Bridge builders of today would do well to study this blending of structure with environment.

AURORA

Brick School House, Route 179 — 1827

This fine, late Federal neighborhood school is considered to be the oldest standing public brick building in Hancock County, despite its very remote location. It reflects a determination on the part of the early settlers of this region to provide an educational facility of exceptional quality.

BAR HARBOR

West Street Historic District

Located in one of the few areas totally spared by the forest-fire holocaust of 1947, the West Street Historic District, though limited in area, provides a remarkable microcosm of Bar Harbor's emergence from a small rural village called Eden into a playground for the wealthy.

Bar Harbor's scenic beauties were first discovered by artists in the 1840s, most notably Thomas Cole, founder of the Hudson River School, who introduced friends and associates to its natural splendor. By 1855, a number of local residents had begun to open their homes to summer boarders, or "rusticators," as they were frequently called. In this same year, the Agamont House was opened in Bar Harbor at the foot of Main Street, the first inn devoted solely to that purpose.

"Petunia Cottage" of 1877, the first to be erected in the West Street area (the street itself was not laid out until 1886), was soon rented to vacationers and represents the next step in the development of the resort. Beside it, the "Foster Cottage" of 1878, while built as a local family house, was bought by a summer resident. "Petunia Cottage" was also acquired quickly by an off-islander, the social lion, S. Weir

"La Rochelle," West Street Historic District, Bar Harbor

Mitchell, who, having moved from Newport, Rhode Island, placed high society's stamp of approval on Bar Harbor.

The laying out of West Street in 1886 was followed by a building boom the following year, when five large summer houses were constructed, all but one of which were on the north side of the street and had extensive lawns sloping down to the waters of Frenchman Bay. These were really the first of the so-called cottages, a term applied by the wealthy summer residents to their spacious houses. It is significant that three of these houses were designed by Rotch and Tilden, an extremely prominent Boston architectural firm. The other two were by William A. Potter of New York, also well-known among the social elite. That they were designed by such notable practitioners indicates the coming of age of Bar Harbor as a fashionable watering place soon to rival Newport, Rhode Island.

From a stylistic point of view, these first cottages are not easy to pinpoint. Their very size militates against the adoption of the standard residential styles. Although elements of the Shingle Style, for example, appear on many of them, the basic form of the style was too limiting to be applied in the traditional manner.

Houses in this same scale continued to be built on West Street through the turn of the century, and, in 1903, "LaRochelle" was constructed — a massive French Renaissance chateau, which represents the culmination of Bar

Harbor's development as a spa for society's highest level. This huge and ornate structure joined others like it, many of which were destroyed in 1947, to make the Mount Desert area a fashionable summer showplace unequalled elsewhere in Maine.

"Redwood," Bayberry Lane—1879

Designed by the distinguished architect William Ralph Emerson, this spacious summer cottage is recognized as one of the earliest, if not the first, true Shingle Style houses in America. Magnificent in its concept, "Redwood" was built for C.J. Morrill, a wealthy Bostonian, and symbolizes an era in the evolution of Maine coastal living.

Sproul's Café, 128 Main Street—1880

This well-preserved Mansard style commerical building was erected by Elihu T. Hamor for Mr. and Mrs. Robert Sproul. After twenty-three years of business, the Sprouls sold the building to a Mr. Franklin who remodeled the structure into a "first class department store."

The success of the original restaurant is recalled in the *Bar Harbor Record* of March 11, 1903: "Being the only place of the kind in the village, its fame spread. Season after season saw its opening, each year added another gem to its crown of prosperity. When the young bloods of the town wanted a late dinner in thoroughly good style, the went to Sproul's and nothing was ever lacking."

"Reverie Cove," Harbor Lane—1895

This early and elegant Colonial Revival cottage was the work of Fred L. Savage, a local architect who designed a large number of these ambitious summer residences, including "Highseas." Built for Dr. John Davies Jones, a prominent agriculturist, the design, with modifications, was probably based on the Taylor House in Newport, Rhode Island. Significant architecturally and socially, it is mentioned in Cleveland Amory's *The Last Resorts*. Now privately owned, "Reverie Cove" has been restored and carefully looked after for the last twenty years.

"The Turrets," Eden Street — 1895

This imposing granite Chateauesque home overlooking Frenchman Bay is an important relic from Bar Harbor's heyday as a fashionable turn-of-the-century resort that rivaled Newport in opulence and social distinction. The immense cottage was designed by Bruce Price and built by J.J. Emery in 1895.

"The Turrets," Bar Harbor

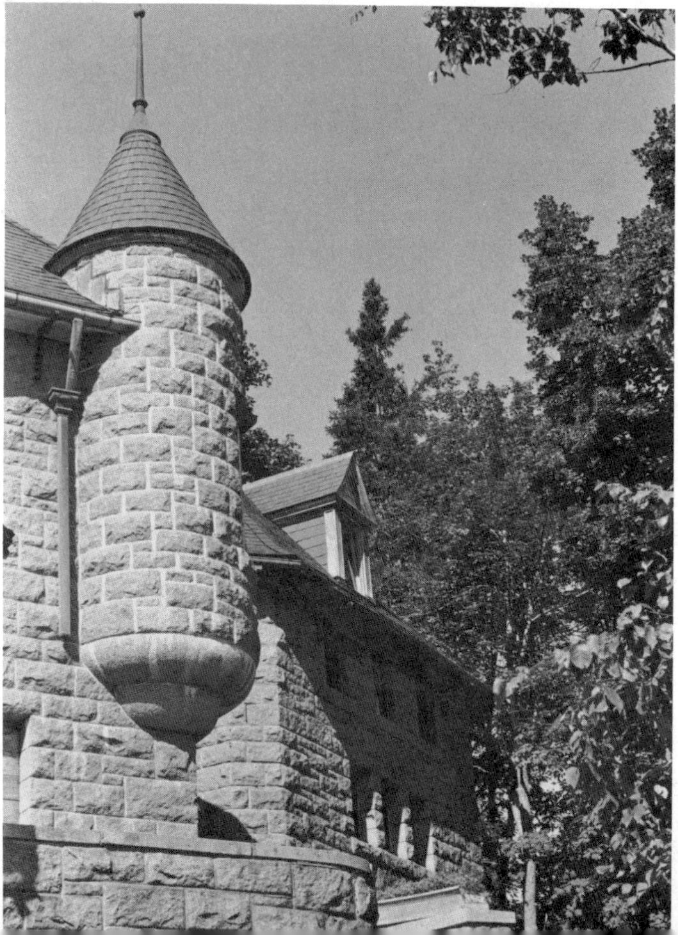

Emery was a typical late-nineteenth-century financier with diverse business involvements. He and his brothers had made their father's lard and candle business into the largest such industry in the country. Price had shown his versatility as an architect by designing buildings in the Shingle, Beaux Arts, and Chateauesque styles.

The "great freedom and intelligence" of Price's design remains intact on the interior. Even though the splendid furnishings are gone, the elegant spaces remain on all four floors.

"The Turrets" is a survivor of a lost segment of the American social scene, but it is also a part of a promising educational experiment. The cottage is now used by the College of the Atlantic, an institution dedicated to environmental studies.

"Eegonos," 145 Eden Street—1910

This Mediterranean, Second Renaissance Revival mansion with Beaux Arts overtones was designed by Guy Lowell, the well-known architect of the Boston Museum of Fine Arts and the Cumberland County Courthouse. Built as a summer home for Mr. and Mrs. Walter G. Ladd of New York, the estate later became a summer French language school for young men and women and was renamed the Ecole Arcadie. It is now owned by a consortium of individuals.

"Highseas," Schooner Head Road—1912

This massive and dramatic example of Colonial Revival architecture in a remarkable oceanfront setting was designed by local architect Fred L. Savage. The exterior is enhanced by the use of a tapestry brick finish. The building is now owned by the Jackson Laboratory.

Criterion Theatre, 35 Cottage Street—1932

The Criterion Theatre in Bar Harbor is one of only two Art Deco movie theatres extant in Maine, the other being the State Theatre in Portland. In its day an avant-garde style, one might wonder at the appearance of Art Deco in Bar Harbor, until one remembers that in 1932 this community had reached its height as a summer playground for the very rich. Attuned to the latest fashions, they were captivated by the new designs that emanated from the "Exposition des Arts Décoratifs et Industriels Modernes" held in Paris in 1925. The attempt to achieve modernity by uniting the decorative arts and industry, and the resulting emphasis on geometric patterns in design, proved immensely popular. In America it gave form to a sentiment that modernity could be achieved by means of decoration.

Most of the typical Art Deco themes are present in the Criterion Theatre, such as the emphasis on the rectilinear, with curves playing a secondary role within rigid patterns. Common motifs include fluting, reeding, chevrons, zigzags, and various frets. Typically, highly emphatic polychromatic effects are everywhere present.

The Criterion Theatre opened on Monday, June 6, 1932, with two performances combining movies and vaudeville, to a capacity, standing-room-only audience totaling over two thousand. Originally, there was a change of shows four times a week, including a regular picture, short subjects, and an orchestra, with five acts of first-class R.K.O. vaudeville.* There were three shows a day, except on Sunday. Movies are still shown at the Criterion during the summer season.

This rare and almost totally unaltered Art Deco movie palace deserves recognition as an example of its style and because of its place in the social evolution of this remarkable summer resort.

BLUE HILL

Blue Hill Historic District

Blue Hill survives remarkably unspoiled as a nineteenth-century Maine coastal community, containing excellent examples of prevailing architectural styles of the period. The district is comprised of over seventy historically significant

---

*R.K.O. stands for Radio Keith's Orpheum, a national vaudeville production agency.

Holt House, Blue Hill Historic District

buildings — residential, commercial, and public, located at the head of Blue Hill Harbor.

Originally settled in 1762 by settlers from Andover, Massachusetts, Blue Hill emerged in the nineteenth century as a thriving diversified community with important maritime ties. With the arrival of its first settled minister, the remarkable Jonathan Fisher, in 1796 and the chartering of Blue Hill Academy, the community early became a remarkably cosmopolitan center in a then remote area.

Lumbering became the first major industry following the erection of the earliest sawmill in 1765, and easy access to the sea resulted in large-scale export of the product to Boston and other ports. Shipbuilding was also an important part of the economy for almost exactly a century between

Pendleton House, Blue Hill Historic District

1792 and 1891. The early nineteenth century saw the development of varied industries along Mill Brook, and granite quarrying for export began in 1816.

In 1876 copper was discovered in the area, and a mining boom of significant proportions began, with many companies formed and large numbers of outside workers brought in. Joseph Holt's early brick block was refurbished as a mining exchange and fine hotel called the Pendleton House. Speculation was rampant; the boom collapsed in 1881 because of unstable copper prices and poor management.

Against this economic background stands today's Blue Hill, with many fine residences reflecting commercial and industrial prosperity as well as some belonging to the numerous sea captains produced by this active port. Since the 1870s, Blue Hill has lured large numbers of summer visitors and residents who have built homes largely along the shore. The intellectual tradition of Blue Hill has been carried on by individuals such as composer Ethelbert Nevin, who built a summer house in the area, and noted Maine author Mary Ellen Chase, who was born in the Chase House.

Parson Fisher House, Route 15 — 1814

Parson Fisher built this two-story, four-room house in 1814, largely by himself. Harvard-educated, he came to Blue Hill in 1796 as the first settled pastor of the Congregational Church. Fisher was a linguist, printer, inventor, artist, architect, teacher, poet, botanist, and father of nine children. For forty-one years he ministered to Blue Hill Congregationalists; for fifty-nine years he kept a journal, which scholars in many fields have come to admire.

"Barncastle," South Street — 1884

This unique and eccentric variation on the Shingle Style was built by Effie Kline, wife of John D. Rockefeller's chief attorney, over and completely surrounding an 1834 Cape where she was born. The house is filled with wonderful architectural flights of fancy.

The Ward Hinckley House — 1916

A rare New England example of the early Prairie-style house in the manner of Frank Lloyd Wright, the Hinckley House was designed in 1916 by Wallace Hinckley for his distant cousin Otis Ward Hinckley, who made his fortune in the Chicago bottling business. One of only two Prairie-style houses in Maine, the Hinckley House is more closely related to Wright's style than is the Graves house in Kennebunkport, which is a more modified example.

BROOKLIN

The Goddard Site — Prehistoric Seventeenth Century

The large and important Goddard site occupies a hayfield on a point of land extending into Blue Hill Bay. It contains the highest concentration of artifacts of any known prehistoric site in Maine, and it has been carefully excavated by both amateur and professional archaeologists for over twenty years. Sporadically occupied since at least eight thousand years ago, there are two occupations whose physical evidence quantitatively overwhelms all the rest. The first major occupation of the site occurred during the Moorehead Phase between roughly four thousand and thirty-six hundred years ago. At this time the site occupants made their living by hunting swordfish and deer. They left behind many stone tools, including ground slate points, similar to those found in the famous "Red Paint" cemeteries.

The later major occupation occurred between A.D. 1,100 and 1,400 during the later Ceramic period. This major Ceramic period occupation was seasonal in nature, limited to March or April through October or November of every year. The Indians made their living during the warm-season occupation by hunting seals and sea birds like great auks and guillemots, taking a few moose, bear, beaver, and other furbearers, and fishing for sturgeon.

Most important, the Ceramic period occupation at the Goddard site contains much physical evidence of trade between the Indians of Maine and Indians further east in the Canadian Maritimes. Raw materials such as copper and chert come from Nova Scotia and as far away as the north coast of Labrador. Moreover, there is a Dorset Eskimo stone artifact, which must have come from Newfoundland or Labrador, and a Norwegian silver penny minted around A.D. 1080, which must have come from Norse contact with Newfoundland or Labrador native Americans.

The site yielded evidence, in the form of postholes and hearths, that the Ceramic period Indians were living in long wigwam structures with multiple hearths, rather than the oval or round single-family structures recorded for the area at the time of European contact. It is entirely possible that the Ceramic period occupation at the Goddard site represents a major summer population gathering, coupled with major trading activity, perhaps a local "trade fair." The Goddard site is on private property, not accessible without permission.

BROOKSVILLE

"Topside," off Route 176—1920

Construction on this log and stone summer home began in 1918, just after the Armistice. Really three buildings in one,

Topside was designed by William Crutchfield and built by local shipbuilders and ship carpenters.

BUCKSPORT

James Emery House, Main Street — ca. 1855

This 1855 cottage is a delightful example of the eclectically designed residence of the mid nineteenth century. Greek, Gothic, and Italian features combine to make the house one of the more unusual of Maine's cottages. The upper stage of the tower has been removed, but otherwise the appearance of "Linwood Cottage," as it is also known, remains unchanged since the 1850s.

Bucksport Railway Station, Main Street — 1874

This building is characteristic of good nineteenth-century American commercial architecture, combining compact utilitarianism with pleasing exterior design. The rectangular frame building with a granite foundation is now a historical museum and the headquarters of the Bucksport Historical Society, Incorporated.

CALAIS

Calais Historic District

This district comprises two blocks on the south side of Main Street facing the St. Croix River and several buildings extending up Church Street and North Street. The majority of the buildings were constructed after the 1870 fire of Calais, though a few date back to the mid nineteenth century.

Calais was incorporated as a city in 1850 with a population of 4,749. Situated at the head of tide water on the St. Croix River twelve miles from the Passamaquoddy Bay, it was an excellent port for shipbuilding and the lumber industry as well as an ideal site for water-powered mills. The quarrying of granite was another source of income that drew settlers to the area. These industries were at their peak by the end of the nineteenth century, and the border city had continual traffic up and down its wharves.

In August of 1870, a major fire destroyed much of the downtown area. Construction was resumed immediately following the fire, and all new building was done in brick.

Calais was able to rebuild much of its downtown area within one year of the fire due to the ample supply of carpenters and builders from its shipbuilding industry. The Main Street Historic District is comprised of buildings both architecturally and historically significant to the period when Calais was a leading saltwater port.

St. Croix National Monument, Red Beach — 1604–5 (NHL)

In the summer of 1604, a party of Frenchmen, under the leadership of the Sieur de Monts and Samuel de Champlain, attempted to establish the first permanent European colony in North America north of Florida. The site selected for this very early settlement was a small island, which became known as St. Croix, lying off the modern city of Calais in Washington County.

This was not to be the last time that summer visitors to Maine picked a poor location for year-round living. Choosing an island for a colony may have been wise for security reasons, and in July the Maine coast could be a delightful place. But St. Croix was bitterly exposed in the harsh months following autumn. Champlain sadly noted in his diary, "There are six months of winter in this country."

Compounding the colony's problems with a North American winter (a constant surprise to Europeans in the early years of settlement), St. Croix Island was very cramped and had no supply of drinking water. Most devastating of all was the scurvy that swept through the colonists' ranks, killing more than half of the population.

Champlain published a delightful drawing of the St. Croix colony in 1613, a drawing which may have been more wistful than candid. Although the seeds of an early-seventeenth-century French village were sown here, the harvest was a failure. In the summer of 1605, the settlement was dismantled and the survivors moved to Nova Scotia.

Archaeological excavations in 1950, and again in 1968–69, uncovered rough stone footings for several buildings, as well as the graves of many of the men who were sacrificed in this ill-conceived venture.

Gilmore House, 316 Main Street — ca. 1850

Built by Alexander Gilmore, an Irish immigrant who became a highly prosperous merchant, this intricately detailed Gothic Revival house reveals a sophistication most unusual in view of the fact that Calais in this period was a frontier town just emerging as a commercial and industrial center.

George Washburn House, 318 Main Street — 1855

The Washburn House is an excellent example of vernacular Gothic Revival style. Built on the banks of the St. Croix River, the house offers a fine view of the Canadian shore. The Washburn House is all the more notable because of its location in what was at the time of its construction a rather unsophisticated and remote industrial community.

Thomas Hamilton House, 78 South Street — 1856

This very unusual Italianate style house was built for a modestly successful businessman. It was an extremely pretentious home for its location, probably reflecting ambitious and extravagant character flaws of its first owner. The local landmark is still known as "Hamilton's Folly," since its expensive construction contributed to the bankruptcy of the unfortunate owner.

First Congregational Church, Calais Avenue — 1871–73

A large and dramatic example of Italianate ecclesiastical architecture, this ornate church building was designed by John Stevens of Boston. Of particular interest is the Stevens tracker organ dating from the construction of the church and one of the largest extant instruments of its kind.

CASTINE

Castine Historic District

The town of Castine consists of a cross section of late eighteenth- and nineteenth-century architecture. There are early Capes, several magnificent Federal-period houses, an abundance of Greek Revival structures, and several elaborate summer houses of the late nineteenth century. Intermingled with these are a variety of historic sites: a British fort from the Revolution, the site of the French Fort Pentagoet (ca. 1635–75), the site of the greatest naval defeat in American history, and even the very visible remains of a canal dug by British troops in 1779.

Established as early as 1630 by the Plymouth Company as a fortified trading post, Penobscot or Pentegoet, as it was then variously called, passed back and forth over the next forty years between the English and French and was even occupied by the Dutch for two years. It prospered under the leadership of Baron de Saint Castin, who gave it its name,

Johnson House, Castine Historic District

but it was virtually abandoned by 1774. Fort Pentagoet is now a remarkable archaeological site.

Resettled by the English in 1760, the town was taken over by American revolutionaries in 1775, only to fall to a British squadron in 1779. To defend the town, the British constructed Fort George. An attempt to dislodge them by a fleet of forty-four vessels and an army from Massachusetts resulted in America's greatest naval defeat — the loss of every ship! Though the British surrendered it following the war, they again seized Castine in 1814 and occupied it until 1815.

Following the War of 1812, Castine prospered and became one of the wealthiest towns of its size in New England. It is from this period and the later development of summer resort living, that many of its greatest architectural monuments derive their origins.

John Perkins House, Perkins Street — 1765–83

Castine's only pre-Revolutionary dwelling is an excellent example of Colonial architecture. When it was built in 1765, it was one of the first frame houses in the area. It survived the bombardments of the Revolution and the War of 1812 and was used to quarter British officers during both those wars.

John Perkins House, Castine

Fort George Memorial — 1779–1815

"The most regularly constructed and best finished of any in America." So wrote George Washington of Fort George, built by the British in the summer of 1779 when they occupied Castine in order to dominate strategic Penobscot Bay during the Revolutionary War.

The American response to this invasion was immediate. Massachusetts assembled a fleet of forty-four vessels and sailed to Castine with some two thousand men. Among the leadership, Paul Revere was commander of artillery.

Upon arrival at Castine, the American force delayed for four days before landing troops and undertaking an uncoordinated siege and bombardment of Fort George. The 750 British regulars simply waited for an assault that never happened, while the hundreds of American naval guns remained silent.

Two weeks later, six British ships sailed up Penobscot Bay. The American expeditionary force immediately embarked and fled northward. In the worst naval disaster in American history, not one vessel survived the action, as all were scuttled by their crews or captured by the British. In 1814, the British once again occupied the fort for a short period.

Fort George is today a prominent square earthwork with 200-foot sides and "arrowhead" bastions. Elaborate brick powder storehouses have been excavated and restored by the State Bureau of Parks and Recreation as a public memorial to an important but little-known episode in American history.

Adams-Cate House, Court and Pleasant Streets — 1815

The Cate House is a large Colonial-style home, built in 1815 for Thomas and Jane Russell Adams. Their granddaughter, Anna Cate, was raised in the house and there married Sanford Dole, the only president and first governor of Hawaii. The home is still in excellent condition. Of special note is the hall with its curved door and stairway.

CHERRYFIELD

General Alexander Campbell House, Campbell Hill—1790

A large Federal house impressively sited on a hill in Cherryfield, the General Campbell House has passed through a series of stylistic changes, alterations, and additions. Its builder and first owner was a leading figure in military operations in eastern Maine during the Revolution, a member of the Massachusetts Senate, and one of the original overseers of Bowdoin College, who was considered "the most distinguished man of his time in eastern Maine."

Cherryfield Academy, Main Street—1850

Cherryfield Academy was begun in 1829 and held in a restored meeting house for ten years. The school then languished for a decade until it found a new home. This building was erected in 1850. The first floor was used as a town hall and for public entertainments; the second story was for school. Serving as a free high school from 1875 to 1895, it returned to its academy status and remained such until 1964, when the regional high school is constructed.

Patten Building, Main Street—1865

The Patten building was erected in 1865 by Frank W. Patten to be used "as a boot and shoe store and manufactory." Over the years, this building has, at one time or another, served as a meat market, a pool hall, a photography shop, and a barber shop. By providing the home for so many varied businesses, the Patten building itself became important to the people of Cherryfield and ranks as a local landmark.

This structure is a charming example of a rural store built in the Italianate style. To find such a sophisticated piece of commercial architecture in such a remote location is remarkable.

The building belongs to the Cherryfield-Narraguagus Historical Society and is being restored for use as a museum.

Colonel Samuel Campbell House, Route 1—1883

Charles A. Allen of Cherryfield, an architect and builder, was responsible for this home built by the grandson of General Alexander Campbell, whose house next door is also on the National Historic Register. The Samuel Campbell house ranks among the finest of its period in eastern Maine. This impressively large and handsomely detailed Queen Anne style structure employs both Stick Style and Eastlake elements, and is situated on a hill overlooking the town. Colonel Campbell was prominent in the Narraguagus Valley lumber trade and in local politics.

COLUMBIA FALLS

John Bucknam House, U.S. Route 1—1792

The Captain John Bucknam House is significant as an unusually large and well finished eighteenth-century home for its location in the state. Its builder, Captain Bucknam, served as an officer in the Revolution.

The Ruggles House, U.S. Route 1—1820

The Ruggles House was built by Aaron Sherman of Duxbury Falls, Massachusetts, for Thomas Ruggles, a wealthy lumber dealer, store owner, post master, militia captain, and justice of the court of sessions. The house was completed in 1818, but the interior woodwork was three years in the making. An English woodcarver was hired to decorate the interior. With his penknife he carved such delicate and beautiful designs that the villagers believed that his knife was guided by the hand of an angel. He was paid over $3,000 for the parlor carving alone.

Another impressive part of this small Federal-style house is its "flying staircase." Noted architects say that it is the only flying staircase of its period anywhere that has never needed repairs or reinforcement and that the Ruggles House is one of the amplest and most spaciously planned small houses in the world.

In 1949, the Ruggles House Society was formed to restore the house. The main section has been well renovated, but

Ruggles House, Columbia Falls

an ell containing the kitchen, dining room, and three bedrooms could not be saved. The Ruggles House is open as a museum during the summer months.

Samuel Bucknam House, U.S. Route 1—1820–21

This is one of the finest and most ornately finished Federal Capes in Maine. The delicate woodcarving, which distinguishes both exterior and interior, was done by Alvah Peterson, who also did similar work on the magnificent Ruggles House across the street. Beautiful original wallpaper further enhances the dignity and charm of the interior. The house was built by the grandson of John Bucknam, one of the earliest settlers in the region.

DEER ISLE

Pond Island Archaeological District

The Pond Island Prehistoric District comprises all of Pond Island in Central Penobscot Bay. The island is the location of two major Ceramic-period clamshell middens, both located adjacent to a marshy lagoon, which is protected by a sand barrier beach. The presence of the lagoon and sand barrier beach is a unique ecological feature. As well as providing a freshwater source and perhaps some sort of attraction to waterfowl, the barrier beaches and marsh are providing natural erosion protection, a rare phenomenon on the Maine coast. From test excavations at the site, we suspect that both sites were occupied roughly between 300 B.C. and A.D. 1,000.

Peter Powers House ("Range 7"), Sunshine Road—1785

In 1785, the First Congregational Church of Deer Isle, which had originally gathered in 1773, issued a call to Reverend Peter Powers of Newbury, Vermont, to become its first settled minister. Powers, New Hampshire–born and a Harvard graduate, had been among the founders of Dartmouth College in 1769. The call included an offer of £ 100 annual

Peter Powers House, Deer Isle

stipend, 100 acres of land from the 400-acre ministerial grant established by the General Court of Massachusetts, together with a house 20 feet by 32 feet, to be built thereon "in such manner as such buildings are commonly finished in country towns."

Mr. Powers, a strong and outspoken supporter of independence, who had largely alienated himself from his predominantly Tory parish in Vermont, accepted with alacrity. He moved into his snug new house and served his Deer Isle flock faithfully until his death in 1800.

This small dwelling, the oldest house in Deer Isle that has survived intact, is particularly unusual in having a gambrel roof, rare in Maine and especially on a Cape. The extreme simplicity of the interior attests to its authenticity as an early rural abode.

Squire Haskell House, Route 172A — 1793

This unusually large and impressive gambrel-roof house was built by Squire Ignatius Haskell, who came to Deer Isle from Newburyport in 1778 with his father and brother. The Haskells established a number of successful business enterprises, including grist and saw mills, house construction, shipping, and shipbuilding. Haskell built this spacious home for his second wife, Mary Stickney of Newburyport, who requested a house of the generous proportions she had been used to in Massachusetts.

Frederick Law Olmsted Summer Home, Sunset—1897

The summer home of Frederick Law Olmsted, America's greatest landscape architect of the late 1800s, was built in the Shingle Style in 1897 as a retirement home for the ill and aging designer. Innovative architect William Ralph Emerson drew the plans for "Felsted," which was intended to be a cottage where Olmsted could recuperate; unfortunately, his mind failed to such an extent that his family was forced to commit him in 1898.

Resting half on the top of a cliff's edge and half on stone walls, this warm, earthy, and protective home seems rooted in its place. It is a magnificent example of the popular Shingle Style and shows that a manmade object can be blended successfully with its natural and picturesque surroundings.

Olmsted's early background in engineering and farming and his dabbling in home landscaping were of major significance in preparation for his career as a landscape architect. Beginning in 1857, when he was thirty-five, Olmsted spent forty years designing landscaping for parks (including New York's Central Park), schools, and communities, as well as for private residences. The home that was built for him is entirely in keeping with his own sensitivity in design. It is unfortunate that he spent only one summer at "Felsted," where he would have flourished.

"Felsted," Deer Isle

DENNYSVILLE

Dennysville Historic District, Main Street and the Lane

The Dennysville Historic District comprises a cohesive and homogeneous grouping of nineteenth-century buildings, largely residences, but including also a church, library, former academy, legion hall, and former inn. The district runs along the west shore of the Dennys River about two miles above its entrance into Dennys Bay, a tidal estuary and an arm of Cobscook Bay that empties into the Atlantic Ocean. The village, located in a fairly remote part of Washington County, has undergone very little change within the last hundred years and retains its nineteenth-century flavor both in architecture and in the generous spacing of the buildings. The structures are generally in good to excellent condition.

Dennysville was founded by General Benjamin Lincoln, who received the sword of surrender at Yorktown on behalf of General Washington, after a survey trip to the area in 1784. His son, Theodore, Dennysville's first permanent settler, built a large frame house in 1787 on the bank of the Dennys River just north of this district. Most of the early settlers were artisans and farmers from Hingham, Massachusetts, General Lincoln's home.

The early years of the settlement were especially difficult because of its extremely remote location, but in the early years of the nineteenth century the area's plentiful timber started being cut and reduced to lumber in mills along the river. Easy access to the sea made the lumber trade highly successful, and Dennysville prospered by mid-century, as witnessed by the homes, the academy, and the handsome church built during this period.

In the early years of the twentieth century, virgin timber resources began to diminish in the region, which had already been damaged by the famous Saxby Gale of 1869 and serious forest fires the following year. In the 1930s, the mill dam on the Dennys River was destroyed. Increasing numbers of Dennysville wage earners had to seek employment in the surrounding area.

During the nearly two centuries of its history, Dennysville grew from a small settlement to a prosperous community and then, with the decline of the lumber industry, became a largely residential area. Most of the original frame houses still stand and are still occupied by descendants of the early settlers. It is only within the last several years that new families, attracted by the natural beauty of the area, have moved into the town. This trend has resulted in the construction of new houses, largely on the perimeter of the community, leaving unspoiled this nineteenth-century village.

Lincoln House — 1787

In addition to its importance as a colonial residence and a well-restored country inn, the Lincoln House of Dennysville possesses a unique and important history.

The original grant of ten thousand acres around Dennysville was held by proprietors in Massachusetts, one of whom was General Benjamin Lincoln of Hingham, Massachusetts, a major general during the Revolutionary War.

In 1786, General Lincoln sent his son, Theodore, to lead a group of colonists to the tract of land that became Dennysville. Artisans from Hingham, led by master builder Joshua Chubbock, built the first frame house in Dennysville for Theodore Lincoln in 1787.

Judge Lincoln, as he was known during later life, was also a friend of naturalist John James Audubon. Before leaving for Labrador in 1822, Audubon visited the Lincolns. Thomas Lincoln, Theodore's son, then went with Audubon to Labrador, while Mrs. Audubon remained at the Lincoln's home in Dennysville. It was in honor of Judge Lincoln's family that Audubon named a new species discovered in Labrador the Lincoln Sparrow.

EASTBROOK

Eastbrook Baptist Church and Eastbrook Town House, Route 200 — 1860, 1880–81

Architecturally these buildings are of great interest, as they demonstrate the persistence of a particular style in a remote region long after it had been supplanted elsewhere. The church is a simple, pure, and very late example of the Greek Revival. The town house, built to conform to its partner, carries the style twenty years beyond its time.

EAST MACHIAS

East Machias Historic District

This rural historic district is situated along the east banks of the East Machias River approximately four miles from the county seat of Machias. It runs south on two streets from the Pope Memorial Bridge for about one mile.

Although not permanently settled until 1763, the area now known as Machias, East Machias, and Machiasport had attracted the interest of settlers since 1633 and was early settled by the French. In 1688, a census was taken of all settlers living between the Penobscot and the St. Croix rivers. According to the tally, there were nine French settlers living at Machias. This small settlement was finally abandoned by the French and settled by the English in 1763.

In 1770, the Commonwealth of Massachusetts granted a

Congregational Church
East Machias Historic District

township, which included Machias, East Machias, Machiasport, Whitneyville, and Marshfield. On May 12, 1784, Machias was incorporated and in 1790 was divided into four school districts, the present town of East Machias being one of them.

From the time of its establishment as a village in 1763, the town of East Machias has been a thriving little community and remains so today. The nineteenth-century economic base of East Machias, its lumber mills and shipyards, are gone, but the village remains as a reminder of the early pioneers who carved their homes out of the Maine wilderness.

Site of Fort Foster, "The Rim" — 1775–77

After capturing the *Margaretta* in the "First Naval Battle of the Revolution" in 1775, the people of Machias decided to fortify "the rim" of Machias Bay. In 1776, they constructed a boom across the narrows, a breastwork on the south side, and a fortification (Fort Foster) on the rim itself. In August 1777, another battle took place in Machias and the townsmen were victorious. The site is largely grown over at this time.

EASTPORT

Todd House, 11 Capens Avenue — ca. 1781

The Todd House is judged to be the oldest frame house in Eastport and is very likely one of the very first to have been built on Moose Island. In 1801, the easternmost Masonic lodge in the United States was instituted in this house.

Fort Sullivan, Moose Island — 1808

Built in 1808, occupied by the British from 1814 to 1818, and deserted in the late 1800s, Fort Sullivan draws its historic significance from the War of 1812. In capturing the fort during that war, the British hoped to be able to claim the territory between the Penobscot and St. Croix rivers and create the province of New Ireland, whose population would be made up of Loyalists expelled during the Revolution. Only the Powder Magazine remains of the original buildings on the site.

Central Congregational Church, Middle Street—1829

This charming, clean-lined Federal-style building of 1829 is one of the earlier churches in this down-east corner of Maine. Designed by architect-builder Daniel Low, it is an area landmark and one of the finer provincial churches in this style in the state.

EAST SULLIVAN

"Wickyup," Admiral Richard E. Byrd Estate, off Route 183, Township T7, SD—completed 1929 (NHL)

This large log residence built by Florida millionaires in the late 1920s became the base of operations for Admiral Richard E. Byrd, the polar explorer. Byrd explored or directed the exploration of more previously unseen lands than any other individual in the twentieth century. He bought "Wickyup" in 1937 for use as a summer home and as a place to plan his Antarctic expeditions of 1937, 1946, and 1955; it was there that he wrote his last book, *Alone*, and drafted the Antarctic Treaty of 1959. Unchanged, the residence remains in the hands of the Byrd family.

A native of Virginia, Byrd graduated from the Naval Academy, then entered the naval flying school in 1917. He pioneered in the development of aviation during World War I and was instrumental in the establishment of the Naval Air Reserve and the Naval Bureau of Aeronautics. In 1926, Byrd flew over the North Pole, and in 1927 he carried the first air mail and freight from New York to Paris. His exploits in the air made him a national hero.

In 1928, Byrd conducted his first Antarctic expedition. On November 29, 1929, he made the initial flight over the South Pole. Byrd was involved in five more explorations of the Antarctic Continent.

Colonel Black Mansion, Ellsworth

ELLSWORTH

Colonel Black Mansion, West Main Street, Route 172 — 1824–27

Shortly after the Revolutionary War, William Bingham, a banker in Philadelphia, bought a large tract of land in Maine and employed General David Cobb as his agent to sell land to settlers. Cobb went to Gouldsborough in 1795. During the panic of 1792, Bingham sold half his Maine holdings to Hope and Company of London. This firm employed an English boy, John Black, then only eighteen years old, to be Cobb's assistant. Black arrived in Gouldsborough in 1799.

Black eventually married the General's daughter Mary, moved to Ellsworth, and in 1824 began construction of a combined office and residence on a 300-acre plot, a gift from his father-in-law. The resulting edifice, a brick Federal country house, took three years to build. The bricks came from Philadelphia and the workmen from Boston.

The home and grounds, now operated as a museum, are in excellent condition, virtually unchanged from the nineteenth century. Entering the house is like stepping back a hundred years in time, for the furnishings were not changed by the three Black generations who occupied the home.

Colonel Meltiah Jordan House, State Street — 1817

In 1817, Colonel Jordan constructed this frame, Federal-style building for his eldest son, Benjamin. In 1897, the house was remodeled to serve as a public library. The present library, besides being a fine example of the Federal style, is also an excellent case of a residence converted to a practical use for public enlightenment as well as aesthetic enjoyment.

Old Hancock County Buildings, Cross Street — 1834, 1838

In 1834, the first of this handsome pair of 1½-story, Greek Revival, municipal buildings was built as a town hall. In 1837, Ellsworth became the shire town of Hancock County, and the structure became the courthouse. In the following year, the second building was constructed for additional space. Both buildings were later used for many years as the Ellsworth High School.

Ellsworth Congregational Church, State Street — 1846

The Ellsworth Congregational Church is an impressive Greek Revival structure well sited on a raised platform of

Ellsworth Congregational Church

ground on the side of a hill. The large scale and boldness of its detail are appropriate to a building of such size. Rising from the hill, the church is a focal point of an architecturally rich district in the center of Ellsworth.

The church was designed and built in 1846 by Thomas Lord, a carpenter-designer of Blue Hill, Maine. Lord built several churches in Hancock County and in 1856 renovated the Blue Hill Baptist Church.

Stanwood Homestead ("Birdsacre"), Bar Harbor Road — 1850

This typical Cape Cod–style homestead is maintained very much as it was when built. The owner and builder of the house was Captain Roswell Stanwood. His first daughter, Cordelia, born in 1856, became Maine's pioneer ornithologist. This self-educated naturalist contributed greatly to the study of the distribution, migration, and abundance of North American birds. Her home, now the Birdsacre Sanctuary, was her outdoor workshop during her many years of research. The Homestead is now a museum operated by the Stanwood Wildlife Foundation.

ISLESFORD

Islesford Museum and Blue Duck Ships Store, Little Cranberry Island — 1928, 1870

William Otis Sawtelle of Bangor spent his summers on Little Cranberry Island and built up a collection of documentary and physical material relating to the islands. Through his efforts, funds were raised to erect a fireproof museum building to house his collection. Opened in 1928, the neo-Colonial, or Georgian Revival, building still serves as a museum and library.

The Hadlocks operated a store on Little Cranberry Island for three generations. The store, built in 1870, handled general merchandise and ship supplies; the upper story was used for storage and sailmaking. Later the building served to house Sawtelle's collection for a time, but it is now used for storage and public restrooms.

West Quoddy Head Light Station, Lubec

LUBEC

West Quoddy Head Light Station, West Quoddy Head — 1808, 1858

West Quoddy Head Light Station, first authorized in 1808 and rebuilt in 1858, is one of the earliest such installations on the Maine coast and the first east of Penobscot Bay. It is also the easternmost light in the United States. In 1869, West Quoddy was one of the first two stations in the country to be equipped with a steam-operated horn to replace the old fog bell. Picturesquely sited with a magnificent view across Quoddy Roads to the palisades of Grand Manan Island, West Quoddy Head Light, with its red and white stripes, is an internationally known landmark and a favorite tourist attraction.

MACHIAS

The Burnham Tavern, Main Street — 1770

The Burnham Tavern was constructed in 1770, seven years after the first settlers came to Machias. It is the only building

The Burnham Tavern, Machias

in eastern Maine directly connected with events of the American Revolution. The men of the town met at the tavern to discuss the recent news of the battles at Concord and Lexington. They resolved to erect a liberty pole on the village green and made plans to capture the British vessel *Margaretta*, then in the harbor. They were successful and this encounter in Machias Bay is considered to be the first naval battle of the Revolution. The wounded sailors of the *Margaretta* were cared for at the Burnham Tavern, where the east room was turned into a hospital.

Beginning in September 1787, the local Masons met at the Burnham Tavern; it was also an informal gathering place for the townspeople. During World War I, the house was the center of activity for the Machias branch of the Surgical Dressing Work.

Centre Street Congregational Church,
Centre Street — 1837

The Centre Street Church is of architectural importance as one of Maine's rare examples of an early Gothic Revival church. Designed in 1836, the building has remained the architectural focus of this northern coastal community since its completion.

The Locomotive "Lion," Machias

The Locomotive *Lion*,
University of Maine at Machias — 1840

The lines of this particular locomotive may not be beautiful, but the construction is rugged, especially when one considers that the *Lion* was in actual operation for fifty years and no serious replacement was ever made. This oak and iron steam locomotive and its duplicate, the *Tiger*, were built expressly for the Whitneyville and Machiasport Railroad Company, the second steam railroad in Maine. The road was constructed between 1840 and 1842 for the sole purpose of transporting lumber from Middle Falls to Machiasport or to the tide water. When the *Lion* was retired in 1896, the Sullivan family of Whitneyville became its owner. Through the efforts of the Sullivans and Alderman Rounds of Portland, the *Lion* now belongs to the University of Maine at Machias, where it rests in its own building to give future generations a taste of early steam locomotion.

Washington County Courthouse, Court Street — 1853–54

Designed by the noted architect Benjamin S. Deane of Bangor, this Italianate building was the first brick structure in

Machias and remains a landmark to this day. It is remembered as the scene of the famous 1864 trial of three Confederates found guilty of the attempted robbery of the Calais Bank. The fact that the convicts were treated as common criminals rather than as prisoners of war attracted national attention.

Clark Perry House, Court Street — 1868

Built for one of Machias' most successful nineteenth-century entrepreneurs, this unusual and ornate Italianate dwelling is a remarkable architectural achievement reflecting rare imagination in design. It is without question the most ambitious house of its period in Machias and probably Washington County.

Machias Post Office and Custom House — 1872

Built to satisfy the increasing need for a federal building in this important eastern Maine community, this simple but impressive Italianate structure was designed by the Treasury Department's architect, Alfred B. Mullett. It is an important link in the development of Maine's federally financed public architecture.

Porter Memorial Library, Court Street — 1893

This small but dignified, Romanesque Revival structure was designed by George A. Clough of Boston. The building honors both Rufus K. Porter, a prominent Machias attorney, and his son, H.H. Porter, who became a successful railroad magnate in the Midwest and donated the funds to construct the library.

MACHIASPORT

Fort O'Brien (Fort Machias) — 1775–1865

On June 12, 1775, the first naval engagement of the American Revolution took place, as Machias area rebels siezed the

British ship *Margaretta*. Anticipating rapid retaliation, the local residents quickly erected an earthen gun battery on the Machias River below the community to protect eastern Maine's most important settlement of the time. This work, supervised by Jeremiah O'Brien, has become known as Fort O'Brien.

Although the British soon returned and drove away the defenders, Fort O'Brien was thereafter strengthened, and it protected Machias for the duration of the war.

In 1814, the British again attacked the fort and burned it after removing the guns. The site was to remain unfortified until 1863, when a large battery of five guns was built to protect the river from attack by Confederate raiders during the Civil War.

Today Fort O'Brien is administered for the public by the State Bureau of Parks and Recreation as a memorial to fortifications of three wars.

The Gates House, Route 92 — 1807

The Gates House is significant as the first Federal-style residence in this area of the state. The site of the Gates House is of commercial interest as the nineteenth-century terminus of the Machias–Whitneyville Railroad. Once an important part of the region's economy, this line transported lumber to the piers for loading on coastal schooners.

Libby Island Light Station — 1822

By order of President James Monroe, this granite lighthouse was constructed in 1822; the keeper's house, a 1½-story woodframe, in 1824; and the other outbuildings of wood and masonry, in 1856. Only fifteen lives were lost during the thirty-five shipwrecks in Machias between 1856 and 1902 due to the efficiency and valor of the lighthouse crews.

Liberty Hall, Route 92 — 1873

An excellent example of Italianate-style public architecture executed in wood, Liberty Hall was designed by Andrew R. Gilson and was his most important work up to that time. Older residents recall that there was some public function or entertainment in the building almost every night. This important local landmark has long been a source of pride to the community.

MOUNT DESERT

Somesville Historic District

The striking and singularly beautiful island known as Mount Desert was one of the earliest landmarks noted by explorers of the Maine coast. To Somesville falls the distinction of being the first permanent settlement in this now popular resort area, site of New England's only national park.

At the behest of Governor Bernard of Massachusetts, Abraham Somes, who had visited Mount Desert in 1759, established a home for himself, his wife, and four daughters in what is now Somesville in 1761. There he built a rude log cabin a little to the east of the present Somes House. He was

Lewis Somes House, Somesville Historic District

shortly joined by James Richardson, who built the first mill in 1763, and these two large families (Somes had thirteen children and Richardson eleven) were influential in almost all aspects of the early development of the community.

Somesville, at first known by the picturesque name of Betwix't the Hills, became part of Mount Desert Plantation, which was incorporated in 1789.

Records of 1836 indicate that there were nine families living in Somesville. Evidently this small population was, nevertheless, extremely active, for the town contained "one small store, one blacksmith shop, one shoemaker's shop, one tan yard, two ship yards, one bark mill, one lath mill, one shingle mill, one gristmill and one schoolhouse in which schools and meetings were held."

Besides the modern dam at the outlet of Somes Pond, there are clearly evident remains of several mill sites along Somes Brook. Shipbuilding, which became the most important nineteenth-century industry, was carried on along the shore of landlocked Somes Harbor, although few traces of it remain.

Somesville is also notable as an early artist's mecca and perhaps the first place visited by the early "rusticators," the progenitors of the legions of summer folk who have made Mount Desert a legendary summer resort. Prominent nineteenth-century artists, such as Thomas Cole and Frederick Church, were drawn to the unusual scenery of the area as early as the 1840s.

Although the architecture of the area ranges from Colonial to late-nineteenth-century Victorian, it retains a cohesive homogeneity in an idyllic setting. Painted a uniform white, these buildings reflect a quiet simplicity expressive of the slow-paced growth of this serene unspoiled community nestled at the headwaters of majestic, fjord-like Somes Sound.

NORTHEAST HARBOR

Daniel Coit Gilman Summer Home, Huntington Lane — 1880s (NHL)

"Over Edge," a 3-story Shingle-Style structure, was constructed in the late 1880s as a summer cottage for Daniel Coit Gilman. Situated on a high bluff overlooking Northeast

Harbor, this cottage offers an excellent view from its front veranda.

Gilman, a native of Connecticut and graduate of Yale, is recognized for making graduate education a recognized university responsibility in America. As first president of Johns Hopkins University, Gilman elevated pure research to a pre-eminent position. To ensure unrestricted research, he stressed the necessity for academic freedom and quality teaching. The university created fellowships to attract the best students and was, at Gilman's insistence, nonsectarian.

PEMBROKE

Charles Best House, County Road — 1845

This Greek Revival residence was the home, until his departure for college in Canada, of Dr. Charles H. Best, co-discoverer with Sir Frederick Banting of insulin and its practical application in the treatment of diabetes. It is the only home ever occupied by Dr. Best in the United States.

ROBBINSTON

The General John Brewer House, U.S. Route 1 — 1790–1810

This large Federal-style mansion is a great and lasting monument to the enterprise and prosperity produced by the development of the important shipbuilding industry on the western shore of Passamaquoddy Bay. General John Brewer, a leading Federalist, was one of the most active shipbuilders in the area. James Shepard Pike, who bought Brewer's mansion, was one of the leaders of the antislavery movement. In 1970, the house was winterized, but the improvements in no way changed its appearance.

SEDGEWICK

The First Baptist Church, Route 172 — 1837

The First Baptist Church of Sedgewick is possibly the finest example of classic Greek Revival church architecture on the

Maine coast. Its elevated site, together with its monumental Ionic portico, resembling a Grecian temple façade, and its stately belfry, make a powerful stylistic statement.

The church was designed by Benjamin S. Deane, a distinguished architect who came to Bangor in the 1820s. Deane designed many Greek Revival churches in Maine, deriving the Sedgewick church design in 1837 from drawings by Asher Benjamin, a noted American architect.

This classic piece of architecture is not only a tribute to Deane and Benjamin, but remains as a significant and important part of our nation's architectural history.

SOUTHWEST HARBOR

Fernald Point Site — Prehistoric

The Fernald Point Site is the best preserved and best understood shell midden in Acadia National Park. It has been excavated by the University of Maine at Orono, which recovered a series of occupations of the last three thousand years at the site. Data from other coastal sites in Acadia National Park, with Fernald Point, will provide a glimpse of life in the Mount Desert Island region during the Ceramic period of pre-history. An effort has been made to protect the site from erosion by the emplacement of large boulder rip-rap. Decisions about protecting other Maine coastal sites will be made following our experience with this erosion-control effort.

Claremont Hotel, Claremont Road — 1883

The Claremont Hotel stands as one of the last reminders of Maine's early summer resort period of the 1870s and 1880s. In an era still unaffected by the rush and bustle of modern transportation and tourism, areas such as Mount Desert became summer meccas for those with sufficient means to leave the sweltering cities. Arriving by train with numerous trunks and other baggage, families would spend the entire summer ensconced in the comforts of luxurious hotels like the Claremont. Each such establishment became for a season a kind of community unto itself, a home away from home, with quiet pastimes like picnicking, fishing, hiking, and occasional excursions taking up the passing days.

Overlooking Somes Sound and what is now Acadia National Park, the Claremont is significant both on its own merits and as a reminder of a prosperous, relaxed, and seasonal way of life that no longer exists.

SULLIVAN

Granite Store, U.S. Route 1—1835–50

The Granite, or Old Salt, Store is an unusual commercial structure built in vernacular Greek Revival style out of rough, irregular blocks of locally quarried granite. In its early years, its principal function was to supply salt for preserving the catches of the Grand Banks cod fishermen and heavy winter clothing to protect the dorymen from the North Atlantic winters.

WHITNEYVILLE

Whitneyville Congregational Church, Main Street—1869–70

An elaborate and impressive example of the Italianate style in a rural setting, this building was constructed by William Bowker, a master builder, probably employing plan books of the period.

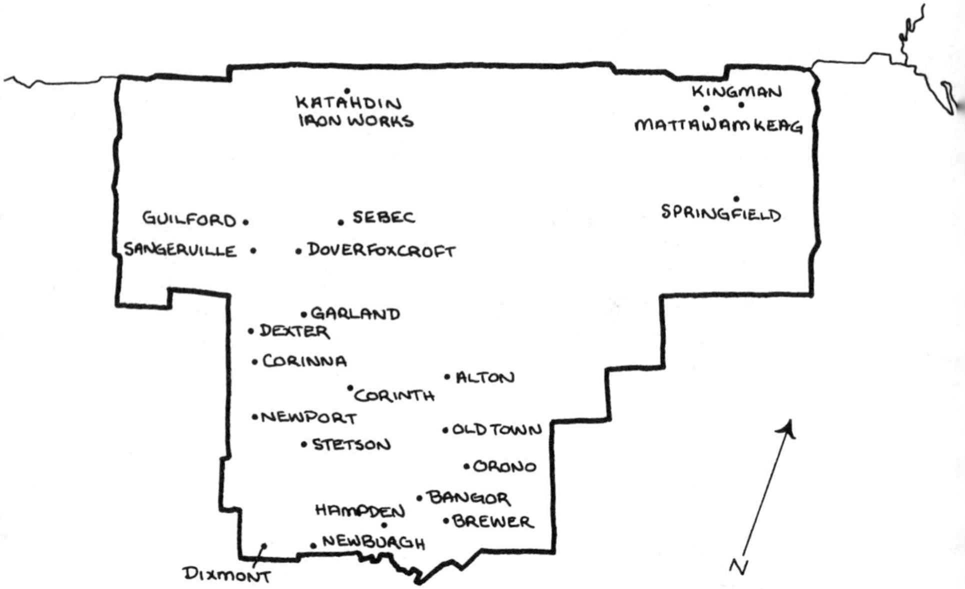

KATAHDIN IRON WORKS
KINGMAN
MATTAWAMKEAG
GUILFORD
SEBEC
SPRINGFIELD
SANGERVILLE
DOVERFOXCROFT
GARLAND
DEXTER
CORINNA
ALTON
CORINTH
NEWPORT
OLD TOWN
STETSON
ORONO
BANGOR
HAMPDEN
BREWER
NEWBURGH
DIXMONT
N

East Central Region

ALTON

Hirundo and Young Sites — Prehistoric

The Hirundo and Young sites are sister sites immediately adjacent to a set of rapids in Pushaw Stream, which is a tributary of the Penobscot River. Both sites have been extensively excavated by the University of Maine at Orono and have yielded evidence of use over at least the last six thousand years. Occupation II at the site, which may date around six thousand years ago and which is characterized by Otter Creek–style spearpoints, represents a culture not often found along the Maine coast. The Hirundo-Young sites are similar in physiographic location to the Cobbossee Outlet sites, and it is surmised that the occupants were heavily dependent upon seasonal anadromous fishing. The presence of the Otter Creek occupation at the Hirundo-

Young site may hold some clues to an inland versus coastal cultural division during that period, which should be further investigated.

A Susquehanna Tradition cremation burial, without preserved human remains but with many burned and cracked stone artifacts, was also recovered at the Young site. The Hirundo site is on the Hirundo Wildlife Refuge. Public access is allowed with permission from the refuge.

BANGOR

Bangor Theological Seminary Historic District

The seven buildings that comprise this district date from 1828 to 1959 and hence represent styles ranging from the Federal through the Greek Revival, Italianate, Queen Anne, and Romanesque Revival to the contemporary. All are restrained and dignified and continue to serve the purposes for which they were designed.

The Bangor Theological Seminary, one of the five oldest institutions for the training of ministers, missionaries, and Christian educators in the United States, is significant as being the first such school in Maine. At its founding in Portland in 1811 and its incorporation in 1812, it was, besides Bowdoin College, the only other educational institution above the academy level in northern New England.

Bangor Theological Seminary Historic District

Founded primarily to prepare men in the gospel ministry in what was then the Province of Maine, The Maine Charity School, as it was first called, was chartered in 1814 and accepted its first students in 1816. Temporarily located in Hampden, near Bangor, it was moved to its present location in 1819 and graduated its first class the following year.

Always recognizing its primary function of Christian education, Bangor Theological Seminary offered pre-theological courses for those students who had had irregular preparation. This later developed into the "Bangor Plan," designed to accommodate students of varied age and background in preparation for the ministry. This plan has been increasingly adopted by similar institutions in other areas.

Approximately 650 ministers, educators, and other Christian workers trained at Bangor are at present serving in forty-six states and several foreign countries.

Broadway Historic District

The district, with Broadway at its center, is bounded on the north by Garland Street, on the east by Essex Street, on the south by State Street, and on the west by Center and Park streets.

Broadway Historic District, Bangor

The Broadway area of Bangor is a classic example of an upper-class residential section in mid-nineteenth-century New England. The district displays a variety of architectural styles, although it is predominantly Greek Revival in character. The architectural composite is made up of Federal, Greek Revival and Second Empire residential structures, with some designed as individual family dwellings and others as duplexes.

To Bangor's merchant princes, Broadway was "a little bit of Boston" transposed into the center of a rough frontier boom town of the mid nineteenth century. If prosperity was gained from the stands of white pine on the branches of the Penobscot River, at least some of the profits were lavished on the street "that lumber built."

It was only natural that the leading citizens of Bangor would ape the styles of Boston, for that city was the source of most of their imports in both the material and cultural sense. Broadway became the showplace for Bangor's elite — a symbol of the "Queen City's" faith in a future of continued economic and cultural progress.

Mt. Hope Cemetery Historic District

The rural cemetery movement in the United States began in 1831 with Mount Auburn Cemetery in Cambridge, Massachusetts. Before that urban cemeteries had been situated in the midst of the towns and cities and were often crowded and virtually grassless. With increasing urbanization, city dwellers began to be concerned about the need for natural beauty. A romantic landscape was sought as a counterbalance to the disturbing aspects of the cityscape.

At Mt. Auburn, a large tract of land was converted into a romantic park with ponds, bowers, grottoes, and great variety in planting. It was consciously designed for the living as well as the dead.

Bangor was not long in following suit. Many people were dissatisfied with the old, small, crowded cemeteries and, in 1834, the Bangor Horticultural Society was formed to purchase a fifty-acre lot on the outskirts of the city. To design a layout following the style of Mt. Auburn, Charles G. Bryant, a noted local architect, was retained. Bryant probably left a stronger mark on Bangor's architectural tone than any other man. His plan for Mt. Hope divided the land into two areas, one for burials and the other for horticultural purposes.

The Mt. Hope Cemetery Corporation laid out the cemetery according to Bryant's plan, and it was consecrated on July 21, 1836.

Mt. Hope Cemetery ranks among the earliest American garden cemeteries, following Mt. Auburn by only three years and predating both Philadelphia's Laurel Hill of 1836 and Brooklyn's Greenwood of 1838. Its larger importance lies in its reflection of a new mood abroad in America, a disenchantment with the already burgeoning urban centers and a desire to provide a romanticized rural atmosphere within reach of the city dweller. It was not long before the next step was taken — the laying out of the great city parks typified by Central Park in New York City.

West Market Square Historic District

The West Market Square Historic District is a single block consisting of six mid-nineteenth-century buildings and one

West Market Square Historic District, Bangor

West Market Square Historic District, Bangor

building of the early twentieth century, all commercial in nature, which are in an excellent state of preservation. All are survivors of the disastrous fire of 1911, which gutted most of the commercial area of downtown Bangor. In 1968, much of what was left was destroyed by urban renewal, leaving this small cluster as the best of the remaining nineteenth-century downtown. The district is located on the south side of State Street and to the east of Main and Broad streets.

West Market Square, originally known as Market Square, was the first open area market place in Bangor. As far back as 1834, at the incorporation of the city, the corner of Main and Broad streets was listed in the *City Directory* as West Market Square to distinguish it from its new counterpart at the corner of Central, Harlow and Park streets, which was known as East Market Square.

West Market Square remained the central focus of all business activities through most of the nineteenth and twentieth centuries. The occupants of its buildings read like a "Who's Who" of Bangor's leading and most prosperous citizens. It was the location of doctors, attorneys, dentists, druggists, bookkeepers, booksellers, grocers, confectioners, jewelers and merchants of all kinds. At one point during the latter part of the 1800s, West Market Square was the location of at least four individual banks.

This single block is the only grouping of buildings remaining intact that conveys the ambiance and scale of West Market Square as it existed in the nineteenth and early twentieth centuries.

Site of Penobscot Expedition July and August 1779

Most of the American fleet of some forty-five vessels, which sailed from Massachusetts to Castine in 1779, lie buried beneath the waters of the Penobscot River. The Penobscot Expedition was designed to dislodge a force of British regulars who had seized Castine and built Fort George. Due to a lack of coordination between the naval guns and landing parties, the American attack was a failure, and, in the worst naval disaster in American history, the entire fleet was scuttled or captured when a small Royal Navy squadron arrived to relieve the fort.

General John Williams House, 62 High Street — 1822–25

This is one of the very few Federal houses in Bangor and almost certainly the oldest brick residence in the city. Its first owner, General Williams, was a leading military and business figure in the early history of the city and one of the original incorporators of the Bangor Mechanic Association.

Nathaniel Hatch House, 123 Court Street — 1832

Built between 1832 and 1833 from plans by Charles G. Bryant, with a wing added in 1846 from plans by Isaiah Rogers, the Nathaniel Hatch House is one of Maine's grandest Greek Revival, temple-style homes. Its amphiprostyle conformation, with a portico at either end, is extremely rare

Nathaniel Hatch House, Bangor

in the state. Although the building has undergone some alterations, it is basically intact.

Nathaniel Hatch, a prominent Bangor attorney, had the house built in 1833, but sold it only three years later. Samuel Farrar moved into the residence in 1836 and lived there until 1857. Farrar had been trained as a lawyer but ill health forced him to give up his studies. Upon returning to Maine, he began to work for his father in the mill and lumber business. Throughout the 1840s and 1850s, Farrar was a successful businessman; unfortunately, in 1857, his enterprises failed and he was forced to sell his property. Broken by his losses, he removed to Wisconsin, where he died suddenly in 1862.

Now owned by the Pentacostal Assembly in Bangor, the Hatch House presents a most impressive statement of Greek Revival, temple-style architecture in Maine.

Zebulon Smith House, 55 Summer Street — 1832

This Greek Revival temple–style home was built in 1832, the same year as the Clapp House in Portland. These two buildings are among the earliest Greek Revival residences in Maine. The 2½-story wood and brick building still retains most of its Greek Revival details. Like the Clapp House in southern Maine, the Smith House played an important role in introducing the temple style to Central Maine.

Bangor House, 174 Main Street — 1833–34

Flushed with the profits of speculation in timberlands and enthusiastic over the extension of steamship service that tied Down East to the port of Boston, merchants and speculators turned to the development of the town of Bangor as one additional means of consolidating their social and economic position. In January 1833, under the leadership of William Emerson, a joint stock company was formed to construct a modern "public house." Construction of the "Bangor House" began the next spring.

Modeled after the Tremont Hotel in Boston and designed by Charles G. Bryant, the Bangor House opened on Christmas Eve, 1834. The craftsmanship of the building and the luxurious furnishings that the proprietors had installed in the public rooms and private chambers impressed a great

Bangor House, Bangor

many individuals. The fame of the Tremont aided in the success of its smaller-scale sister. The exterior design and interior arrangement of the palatial Tremont were carefully reproduced for the Bangor House. Now a senior citizens' residence, it is the only remaining example of the early, so-called palace hotels built in this country.

The Jonas Cutting–Edward Kent House, 48-50 Penobscot Street — 1836–37

This excellent Greek Revival–style house is unique in New England, as the building was constructed as a double residence for Edward Kent, later governor of Maine, and his law partner, Jonas Cutting, later named to Maine's supreme court.

Designed by Bangor's erratic genius, Charles G. Bryant, the house is one of exceptional beauty. It was in this style that Bangor's influential lumber aristocracy lived in the 1830s. Governor Kent, a Whig, lived among them and shared their tastes, their style, and their views.

Jonas Cutting–Edward Kent House, Bangor

Kent practiced law in Bangor and was its mayor during 1836 and 1837; he then served two terms as governor in 1838 and 1840. From 1849 to 1854 Kent served as U.S. consul in Brazil. Upon his return, he was named to the Maine supreme court, where he served as an associate justice from 1859 to 1877.

Grand Army Memorial Home, 159 Union Street — ca. 1840

This impressive Greek Revival–style building was constructed in around 1840 from designs by Richard Upjohn. Although the interior was altered somewhat in 1952 to accommodate the Bangor Historical Society collections, the exterior has been restored recently and is in fine condition.

Originally constructed for Bangor businessman Thomas A. Hill, the residence was later used by Bangor's first mayor, Allen Gilman, and by Mayor Samuel H. Dale. Three generations of Dale descendants occupied the house, but in 1944 the Sons of Union Veterans acquired title and currently hold the building in public trust.

Grand Army Memorial Home, Bangor

Symphony House (Isaac Farrar House), 166 Union Street — 1843–45

The Symphony House was the first Maine commission of architect Richard Upjohn. Well-known for his Gothic designs, Upjohn began his career working in the Greek Revival style. Handsomely proportioned and boldly detailed, this home, designed in 1833 for Isaac Farrar, reflects Upjohn's remarkable talents. The Symphony House, built between 1843 and 1845, today retains many of its original features.

The first owner, Isaac Farrar, was a lumberman, merchant, and president of the Maritime Bank of Bangor. Charles B. Sanford, proprietor of Sanford Steamship Lines, occupied the house from 1865 to 1878, and Owen Davis, owner of the Katahdin Iron Works, lived in the home from 1882 to 1888. The final owner, Isaac Merrill, made extensive changes to the exterior in 1893 and 1894. Wilfred Mansur, Bangor's premier architect of the period, oversaw these renovations.

From 1911 to 1929 the building was used as a dormitory by the University of Maine Law School. Beginning in 1929, it became the Bangor Symphony's Northern Conservatory of Music — thus its common name, "Symphony House." At present it is owned by the Bangor YWCA.

Symphony House, Bangor

Doghouse at Godfrey–Kellogg House, Bangor

**Godfrey-Kellogg House,
212 Kenduskeag Avenue — ca. 1847**

The Godfrey-Kellogg House was built in about 1847 for John Godfrey as a summer residence for his family. It is one of the finest surviving examples of Gothic Revival cottage architecture in the state.

Situated high on the cliffs overlooking Kenduskeag Stream, the estate consists of a main house with attached barn, a carriage house, a smaller barn, and even a doghouse — all executed in the same Gothic Revival style. All of the buildings are finished in a combination of clapboard, matched boarding, and board and batten, and decorated very lavishly with Gothic trim. The exterior has not been altered and the interior, with much of the original furniture designed especially for this house, is intact.

Hannibal Hamlin House, 15 Fifth Street — 1848–51

Though the birthplace of Hannibal Hamlin in the Paris Hill Historic District survives, this is the house that he purchased in 1862 while vice president of the United States and that remained his home in Maine until his death almost thirty years later. Originally a flat-roofed, 2-story, Italianate dwelling built in 1851 by William T. Hilliard, Clerk of Courts and later Deputy Collector of Customs, it was altered in 1870 by Hamlin with the addition of a Mansard roof, effectively adding a third story.

Born in Paris Hill, Maine, on August 27, 1809, Hamlin was educated locally and, after brief periods as a surveyor, newspaper printer, and schoolteacher, took up the study of law in a Portland office. On winning admission to the bar in 1833, he began practice in Hampden, Maine, and soon became active in politics, serving in the legislature from 1836 to 1841. In 1842, he was elected as a Democrat to the House of Representatives, where he remained until 1847; after another term in the legislature in that year he was elevated to complete an unexpired term in the Senate in 1848, returning to the seat for a full term in 1851. He became gradually more and more outspoken in his dislike of slavery, and he opposed in particular the Kansas-Nebraska Bill of 1854; finally, two years later, he broke with the Democrats and joined the Republican party. In 1856, he was elected governor of Maine, the first Republican to hold the office; early in 1857 he left the Senate to assume the governorship but resigned a few weeks later to return to the Senate. His position as an easterner and a former Democrat made Hamlin a strategic choice for the Republican vice-presidential nomination in 1860 on the ticket headed by Abraham Lincoln. Although he sided more often than not with the Radical wing of the party, he remained throughout his term in office on close terms with President Lincoln. Failing to be renominated in 1864, he was appointed collector of the port of Boston in 1865, but he gave up the post a year later in protest against President Andrew Johnson's Reconstruction policies. After two years as president of a small Maine railroad, he ran successfully for the Senate in 1868 and remained there for two terms, supporting radical Reconstruction and serving for a time as chairman of the Committee on Foreign Relations. On leaving the Senate, he served as U.S. minister to Spain for a year, between 1881 and 1882. Hamlin then retired to Bangor, where he lived, still an influential figure in state Republican affairs, until his death on July 4, 1891.

In 1933, Hannibal E. Hamlin, son of the vice-president, donated the house to the Bangor Theological Seminary as a residence of its president.

St. John's Catholic Church, York Street — 1855

St. John's Catholic Church was built in 1855 from designs by a Mr. Keeley, under the direction of Father John Bapst, a Jesuit priest. The church was to become a symbol of the Irish community of Bangor. The builders of St. John's were conscious of the need to establish roots, having seen an earlier generation of Irish immigrants burned out and driven from the city by roving gangs of sailors and lumberjacks in the 1830s. Two years before, their own priest had been ridden out of Ellsworth on a rail, complete with a suit of tar and feathers.

In 1855, Bangor was experiencing the height of the Know-Nothing movement, with a Know-Nothing city council and a Baptist minister for a marshall. The marshall had been appointed to end the trade of the predominantly Irish-owned grog shops on the waterfront and was carrying out his work with great zeal. While the church was being constructed, Irish laborers stood guard against the threats of the Know-Nothings to burn it to the ground.

The church stands in what was once the heart of the Irish community in Bangor. It remains a symbol to many of the old Irish families of a way of life that has largely disappeared. The Irish immigrants survived famine, riot, and hatred to erect the edifice that would become a curious combination of America and Ireland and a continual reminder of an all but forgotten part of the city's history.

Joseph W. Low House, 51 Highland Street — 1857

Designed by Harvey Graves and built by Fogg & Benson in 1857, the Low House is one of eastern Maine's finest Italianate residences. Low had his house built of wood in the Thomas Hill area where the Mayor of Bangor had instituted a tree planting and housing development project. Situated on this picturesque spot, the house remains one of the finest examples of architecture from Bangor's halcyon days before the Civil War.

W.A. Blake House, Bangor

W.A. Blake House, 107 Court Street—1858

This handsome residence is the finest of its type in Bangor and possibly the state of Maine. Designed by Calvin Ryder for his brother-in-law, W.A. Blake, it epitomizes the lifestyle of the pre–Civil War period when the "Queen City" reached the pinnacle of a lumber-based economy. Ryder designed a Second Empire house with Italianate influences and a sweeping concave Mansard roof pierced by dormers with arched hoods. The semi-circular bay on the east side is a later addition, which in no way detracts from the grandeur and formality of this remarkable house.

Wheelwright-Clark Block, 34 Hammond Street—1859

The Wheelwright-Clark Block was Maine's first Mansard commercial building. Erected in 1859 from designs by the prominent local architect Colonel Benjamin S. Deane, the building survived both the Bangor fire of 1911 and urban renewal in 1968 and has become a major landmark in the city's business district.

Located on a corner lot, the building possesses a modified "L" shape. On the first story, a cast-iron arcade originally surrounded the façade. This series of handsome cast-iron arches, which enclosed shop windows and entrances, was replaced by modern storefronts. The fifth story, a Mansard roof that was once sheathed in slate and pierced by dormers, is now covered with sheet metal, and only one dormer remains. Fortunately, a recent rehabilitation has restored the arcade.

The architect, Benjamin S. Deane, was a major designer and builder in nineteenth-century Maine. His career stretched from the Federal period through the Greek and Gothic revivals to the Italianate and Second Empire periods. He practiced during a time when professional architects in the state numbered less than a dozen.

Bangor Children's Home, 218 Ohio Street — 1868–69

The Bangor Children's Home, designed by Henry W. Hartwell in the Stick Style, is evidence of the social and humanitarian concerns of mid-nineteenth-century America. First incorporated in 1839, the Home was endowed by Sarah Pitcher in 1865, and the present building was constructed with facilities for boys and girls. The Bangor Children's Home continues to fulfill its original purpose more than a century after its construction.

The Adams-Pickering Block, corner of Main and Middle Streets — 1871

This block is a rare survivor of downtown Victorian Bangor, as well as being architect George W. Orff's most distinguished remaining commercial work in the city and the state. Designed in the Mansard style in 1871, the building is a 4-story double block with a granite foundation, brick construction, and a granite façade.

Morse Bridge, Coe Park–Kenduskeag Stream — 1882

Maine's largest covered bridge is 212 feet in length and is probably the only such bridge in the Northeast located within the city limits. Spanning the Kenduskeag Stream, this bridge, with a truss designed by William Howe, was moved downstream — granite abutments and all — in 1965 for pedestrian use.

Morse & Company Office Building, Harlow Street — 1895

Constructed in 1895, this 2-story building served two functions: it was both an administrative center and a showplace for representative lines of Morse & Company goods. Morse & Company was Bangor's outstanding industrial commercial conglomerate of the late nineteenth century. For nearly a century the company was Bangor's largest firm; with its liquidation in 1948, another era in the history of Bangor ended.

The Bangor Standpipe, Jackson Street — 1898

The Bangor Standpipe is really two structures in one. The standpipe itself consists of steel plates and is 75 feet in diameter and 50 feet high. The building enclosing it is 80 feet in diameter and 110 feet high. Along the inner wall of the building is a winding stairway that leads to the promenade deck, which entirely circles the building. Constructed in 1898 in the Shingle Style, the Bangor Standpipe was intended to be an observatory from which to view the entire city.

The standpipe was built to be a landmark in its own time, dominating the skyline of the city. It is an outstanding relic of a time when people believed that even so functional a structure as a standpipe should be aesthetically pleasing as well.

The Bangor Standpipe

BREWER

Penobscot Salmon Club and Pool, North Main Street — 1887–94

In the 1880s, the Bangor Salmon Pool, a stretch of shoal water unusually productive of large specimens of this species of game fish, was discovered. At this spot a clubhouse was erected in 1887, and the Penobscot Salmon Club organized in 1894. This distinguished holdover of a nineteenth-century gentlemen's sporting club still retains its tradition of presenting the first salmon caught by a member each year to the president of the United States. The present clubhouse was built in 1923.

CORINNA

Stewart Free Library — 1895–98

Twenty-five miles west of Bangor lies the small wool-manufacturing town of Corinna with a population of approximately two thousand people. A single-industry town of this size in Maine is not unusual, but the fact that the town is visually dominated by a refined late Victorian town hall and library of the architectural integrity and proportions of the Stewart Free Library is unusual indeed.

Adding to the unique character of the Stewart Library is the fact that it was designed by a Midwestern architect from Minneapolis, William Harrison Grimshaw. Grimshaw was commissioned by Levi M. Stewart, a Minneapolis millionaire who was a native of Corinna.

Stewart started his career as a teacher and then became a fisherman. After saving enough money, he put himself through Dartmouth and Harvard Law School. In 1858, Stewart moved to Minneapolis, where he became involved in real estate speculation, as well as pursuing his law career. It is thought that the fortune he gained amounted to between $12 million and $30 million.

In 1895, he began work on the free library as a memorial to his parents. By the time it was finished, "The Pride of Corinna" cost $65,000. Stewart donated and bequeathed a total of 13,000 volumes to the library, along with a $50,000 trust fund.

The library stands today as a well-preserved monument to late Victorian architecture, to the philanthropy of Corinna's financially most successful son, and to the interrelationship of rural Maine and the Midwest as created by William Grimshaw and Levi M. Stewart, "The Elder" of Corinna.

CORINTH

Skinner Settlement Historic District, West Corinth

The life of most nineteenth-century farming frontiers centered around a loosely defined crossroads village within a decade of settlement. These rural hamlets effectively met the trading and social needs of the pioneer society and grew in size and complexity with the changing needs of the totally agricultural society.

The Skinner Settlement on the Kenduskeag–Exeter Mills Road in West Corinth began with the arrival of Daniel Skinner as the first permanent settler in the town of Corinth in 1793. The growth of the settlements followed the usual pattern. Skinner opened a tavern in his log dwelling shortly after coming to Corinth. Isaac Hodsdon, subsequently the commander of the Maine Militia in the Aroostook border difficulties, became the first resident blacksmith in the settlement a decade after Skinner's arrival. Before Hodsdon's immigration, residents in the Skinner Settlement had to travel to neighboring settlements for blacksmithing. There is no record of the first store in the Skinner Settlement, it is likely that the Skinner Tavern doubled in that capacity or that Hodsdon maintained a small store before he built a larger store in about 1830. The Hodsdon store survives very much in its original condition. The first schoolhouse was built in the settlement in 1811, with Hodsdon serving as the first schoolmaster. The present one-room schoolhouse was built later in the century and is a few hundred feet removed from the original site. The Methodist Meeting House in the Skinner Settlement was dedicated in 1849, a product of the revival movement that swept through Maine in the 1830s and 1840s.

The meeting house and store have remained in use until

the present time, although the volume of traffic in both has declined. Six dwelling houses remain occupied, two less than in the previous century. The Skinner Settlement is still a cohesive community with virtually the same boundaries and external appearance as a century ago.

Robyville Bridge, Robyville Village — 1876

Spanning the Kenduskeag Stream in the village of Robyville, this 76-foot bridge was built of wood using the Howe Truss system. The last of the many bridges on this site, it is probable that construction took place in 1876.

DEXTER

Dexter Gristmill — 1854

During the eighteenth and nineteenth centuries, the gristmill was a feature of most rural Maine communities. Approximately a half dozen of these mills survive, including the Dexter Gristmill. The mill was established in 1802, the present building was constructed in 1854, and the mill operated until 1967. The miller's house, built in 1838, served as the miller's residence until the late 1940s. The town of Dexter and its historical society have preserved these buildings as a regional museum, which now serves as a valuable landmark to a vanished rural industry.

Abbott Memorial Library, Route 7 — 1894

This remarkably fine example of Renaissance Revival architecture is particularly notable in view of its location in a small and rather remote industrial town in Maine.

Money for both the purchase of the land and the erection of the library was provided by George Amos Abbott, a leading figure in Dexter and owner of Amos Abbott and Company, a woolen mill founded by his father. Some claim that this mill is the first of its kind in Maine. On Christmas Day, 1894, Abbott deeded the building to the town for one dollar. The gift was unanimously accepted by the community the following day.

Abbott Memorial Library, Dexter

DIXMONT

Louis I. Bussey School, Dixmont Corner — ca. 1808

Built through the generosity of the original town proprietor, Dr. Elijah Dix, grandfather of Dorothea Lynde Dix, this simple structure, with its later, Greek Revival, templelike portico, symbolizes the early recognition of the importance of education in even the smallest emerging Maine communities.

DOVER–FOXCROFT

James Sullivan Wiley House, Main Street — 1849

This handsomely proportioned, Greek Revival, temple-style house, unusual for a then remote section of Maine, was built by James Sullivan Wiley, A Demogratic member of the House of Representatives in the Thirtieth Congress.

GARLAND

Garland Grange Hall — 1891

Located in the center of a northern Maine community, the Garland Grange is typical of the many late-nineteenth-century grange halls that once dotted Maine's rural landscape. Built in 1891, it is one of the oldest surviving examples of this type of structure. The hall has both Greek Revival and Italianate elements, and, in its forthrightness and simplicity, embodies the character of the people and the region that created it.

GUILFORD

H. Hudson Law Office, Hudson Avenue — 1867

Of the small professional buildings in Maine, none are more interesting than the local law offices that sprang up in many communities during the nineteenth century. Almost al-

H. Hudson Law Office, Guilford

ways of superior design, they represent most of the major styles of the period.

No other, however, can be said to equal the H. Hudson Law Office in Guilford in terms of scale, neatness, and sophistication. It exists as a tiny, ornate Mansard jewel.

Henry Hudson, who built this office at the height of his career, was born in Canaan, New Hampshire, in 1824. He was admitted to the Piscataquis Bar in 1849 and was in active practice in Guilford until his death in 1877. He gained a reputation as one of the ablest lawyers in eastern Maine. His son Henry, also a lawyer, continued practice in the same office until his retirement in 1919.

Since that time, the building has undergone various uses but has returned to its original function with the present owner.

Straw House, Golda Court — ca. 1885

This marvelously ornate Queen Anne house, painted to show off its architectural detail, was built by David Robinson Straw, Jr., a leading member of the bar and insurance executive. Its highly ornate external surface treatments of gables and tower rival any building of the style in Maine. Now operated as an inn, this large structure is beautifully sited on the crest of a hill overlooking the town.

GUILFORD-SANGERVILLE

Low's Bridge over Piscataquis River, off Route 6 — 1857

Resting on granite abutments, this 125-foot, wooden covered bridge was built using the Lang Truss system. It spans the Piscataquis River, joining Guilford and Sangerville.

HAMPDEN

Hampden Academy, Route 1A — 1842–43

This brick and granite building is representative of educational buildings erected in small Maine communities before the Civil War. Exterior and interior details, designed by Stuart and Wallace, are in simple Greek Revival style. The Academy was incorporated in 1803, and the present building constructed in 1843. Today it is a flourishing public school that has expanded beyond its original facilities yet has preserved its first building, now used as the music department.

KATAHDIN IRON WORKS

Katahdin Iron Works, Township T6, R9

Moses Greenleaf, a famous Maine geographer, discovered iron ore on what is now known as Ore Mountain in 1843. Two years later, Katahdin Iron Works was incorporated, and until 1890 "K.I." operated continuously, except for the eight years between 1865 and 1873. Up to 2,000 tons per year of raw iron were produced.

From 1872 to 1890, K.I. employed 200 workers and owned several homes, two large boardinghouses, a town hall, a school, a post office, a company store, a photo salon, and two farms to produce hay for the horses. There were fourteen charcoal kilns (beehives) providing fuel for the blast furnace. Attached to the blast furnace was the casting room.

A railroad was built to Katahdin Iron Works from Bangor in 1882. The community already required 10,000 cords of wood a year to make charcoal for the blast furnace; the extra 4,000 cords needed to fire the Black Maria, the railroad's

Kiln, Katahdin Iron Works, Township T6, R9

Blast furnace, Katahdin Iron Works, Township T6, R9

locomotive, put a great strain on the economy of K.I. With the competition from the new Mesabi Range ore fields, K.I. was forced out of business.

Only one of the beehives and the blast-furnace tower remain. They were thoroughly renovated by Roland Robbins in 1966.

KINGMAN

Romanzo Kingman House, Main Street — 1871–72

Located in what is now a tiny rural community in remote Penobscot County, this finely detailed Italianate residence was built by a founder of the great tannery that once gave strong commercial impetus to the town and region.

MATTAWAMKEAG

George W. Smith Homestead, Main Street — 1874

A handsome Italianate residence, almost completely unaltered, this house is a local landmark that stands out in a remote community without other buildings of architectural significance. Built by a successful local entrepreneur, it is notable for its pristine condition.

NEWBURGH

Jabez Knowlton Store, Route 9 — 1839

Beyond its interest as an early-nineteenth-century rural commercial structure, the fixtures and contents of this general store represent an amazing turn-of-the-century survival. Untouched since its abrupt closing in 1910, it is an absolutely authentic period piece.

NEWPORT

Hexagon Barn, Spring and Railroad Streets — 1850

Attached to a Greek Revival Cape, this barn is apparently unique in Maine. There are, in fact, no other polygonal agricultural structures known to exist in the state.

OLD TOWN

St. Anne's Church, Indian Island

This mission to the Penobscot Indians was established by French priests in 1688; the present St. Anne's is the third church building to be constructed on this site. It is one of the oldest Catholic churches in New England, and nearby is New England's oldest Catholic cemetery. The simple, vernacular structure was altered at the turn of the century, but the chapel has remained an important landmark for over 150 years.

St. James Episcopal Church, Centre Street — 1892

One of four buildings designed by noted Gothicist Henry Vaughn, St. James Church was built of wood on a granite foundation. The church is basically unchanged from Vaughn's design, with only interior colors differing. Although modest in size, St. James's distinctive architecture makes the building a focal point in a community with few surviving local landmarks.

ORONO

Orono Main Street Historic District

The Main Street Historic District, lying between Maplewood Avenue and Pine Street, is composed of a remarkable collection of nineteenth-century and turn-of-the-century buildings, covering all of the major styles: Federal, transitional Federal–Greek Revival, Greek Revival, transitional Greek Revival–Italianate, Italianate, Gothic Revival, Queen Anne, and Colonial Revival. All of the buildings are presently used for their original purposes. The residential environment has been completely preserved.

First settled in the 1770s, this community was originally called Stillwater after the western channel of the Penobscot River, which sets off part of the town as an island. Its present name, adopted at the time of its incorporation by the Massachusetts General Court in 1806, was chosen to honor Joseph Orono, chief of the Penobscot Indian tribe who died in 1801. Orono was instrumental in keeping the Indians of eastern Maine favorably disposed toward the colonists during the Revolution.

The town grew very slowly at first, with only 77 inhabitants in 1800 and 415 by 1820. Conditions were primitive. After 1820, however, rapid growth took place largely because of a dramatic boom in the lumber industry. Between 1820 and 1840, the largest population growth in the town's history took place, and by the latter date it had become a thriving community including numerous professional men and prosperous mill owners and merchants.

The Main Street Historic District clearly reflects the prosperity created during the era of the great Penobscot River log drives and the lumber boom. The McRuer, Baxter, and

McRuer House, Orono Main Street Historic District

Ricker houses were built by the first doctors in the community. Israel Washburn, Jr., one of the first lawyers in Orono and later governor of Maine, built an impressive house. The Ludo Thayer and Babcock houses were the homes of lumber-mill owners.

Main Street is primarily significant as it reflects Orono's emergence as a prosperous thriving community in the first half of the nineteenth century. These generous homes mir-

Governor Israel Washburn House, Orono Main Street Historic District

ror the achievement of dignity and permanence by what had been little more than a hardscrabble frontier village two decades before the great years of the log drivers.

University of Maine Historic District

The ten buildings selected for inclusion in the University of Maine at Orono Historic District represent the earliest structures remaining on this first, and principal, campus of the state university.

Founded as a result of the Morrill Land Grant Act of 1862, the Maine State College of Agriculture and Mechanic Arts opened its doors to students for the first time on September 21, 1868. At that time there were only two professors and twelve students.

Although not executed exactly as conceived, the original plan of the campus was drawn by the preeminent landscape architect Frederick Law Olmsted, who also drew up a proposed curriculum and statement of educational philosophy for the college.

The earliest building within the district, Fernald Hall, was constructed with student labor between 1868 and 1870. Originally called Chemical Hall, the building was one of the early chemical laboratories for undergraduates in the United States.

Carnegie Library, University of Maine Historic District, Orono

Lord Hall, University of Maine Historic District, Orono

Holmes Hall, built in sections between 1888 and 1913, and Coburn Hall, built between 1887 and 1888, were both designed by Frank E. Kidder, a Boston architect and 1879 alumnus of the college. Kidder attracted national attention in 1885 as the author of *The Architects' and Builders' Pocket Book* which, having passed through many editors, is still in use as a reference work. Of particular note is a plaque in Coburn Hall commemorating the founding of Phi Kappa Phi, now a national honor society, there in 1897. This society is the equivalent of Phi Betta Kappa for students in courses of study other than liberal arts.

The Carnegie Library, built between 1905 and 1906, is of interest in that, although Andrew Carnegie donated money for literally hundreds of municipal libraries, this building is one of only two that he funded for colleges.

William Colburn House, 91 Bennoch Road — 1780

Revolutionary War soldier William Colburn was the architect and the builder of this 1½-story Cape Cod–style farmhouse. The interior of the house contains the original wide softwood flooring and wainscoting. Fireplaces and chimneys are intact, as are the original six-over-six windows. This fine dwelling is one of the few eighteenth-century Cape Cod–style houses that exist in this region.

Nathaniel Treat House, 114 Main Street — 1830s

Built in the early 1830s, this brick house represents the transition from the Federal to the Greek Revival style. The interior is as lovely as the exterior, with its curved flying staircase, hand-tooled woodwork, Indian shutters and original fireplaces. Nathaniel Treat built the house and lived in it for almost thirty years. Treat was owner of several dams and sawmills and was also selectman of Orono for many years.

Governor Israel Washburn House, 120 Main Street — 1840

This home is a classic example of the Greek Revival style. Built in 1840 for Israel Washburn and his bride, the house remains basically unaltered and in excellent condition. Israel Washburn, one of the seven famous Washburn brothers, was a congressman and governor of Maine, who played an important part in the formation of the Republican party and in the antislavery movement.

SANGERVILLE

Robert Carleton House, North Main Street — 1815

One of the oldest dwellings to survive in the northern Maine county of Piscataquis, this house, with its military connections with the Aroostook War, is a valuable example of provincial Federal architecture in the context of a then largely unsettled region.

SEBEC

Burgess House, Sebec Village — ca. 1816

This remarkably early building for its remote location was built by Icabod Young at the outlet of Sebec Lake, the site of numerous mills in the nineteenth century. The most important feature of the house is the extensive and well-preserved stencil and fresco work attributed to Rufus Porter and his associate, Moses Eaton, Jr.

SPRINGFIELD

Springfield Congregational Church, Route 6—1852

Though relatively small, this church building is a remarkably sophisticated and well-conceived example of Gothic Revival architecture, particularly within the context of its extremely remote location.

STETSON

Stetson Union Church, Route 22—1831

Stylistically excellent and sophisticated, this Greek Revival church in a remote rural community was probably designed by Benjamin S. Deane. Deane exerted a wide influence in central Maine and is well known for such commissions as the Pierce-Giddings House and the Wheelwright-Clark Block in Bangor, as well as the magnificent First Baptist Church in Sedgwick, all on the National Register. The building was a gift of Amasa Stetson of Massachusetts, founder of the town.

BINGHAM
NEW PORTLAND
SOLON
EMBDEN
MADISON
PITTSFIELD
SKOWHEGAN
NORRIDGEWOCK
MERCER
CLINTON
FAIRFIELD
VIENNA
OAKLAND
WATERVILLE
WINSLOW
SIDNEY
LIVERMORE
VASSALBORO
READFIELD
MANCHESTER
CHINA
WAYNE
AUGUSTA
WINTHROP
HALLOWELL
TURNER
FARMINGDALE
CHELSEA
MONMOUTH
PITTSTON
LEWISTON
POLAND
LISBON
AUBURN
DURHAM
N

West Central Region

AUBURN

Edward Little House, 217 Main Street — 1827

This Federal house in Auburn was the home of Edward Little, who may reasonably be called the "Father of Lewiston-Auburn." Little inherited from his father, Josiah Little (the last clerk of the Pejepscot Company), vast land holdings, including most of present day Lewiston and Auburn as well as Greene, Leeds, Mechanic Falls, Poland, and Minot. After moving to Auburn from Newburyport, his birthplace, he largely subsidized the first church, founded the academy, which later became Edward Little High School, promoted industry, and sold his water power rights at low price to secure the introduction of outside capital.

High Street Congregational Church, High Street — 1858

The High Street Congregational Church is a major work by the mid-nineteenth-century Boston architect Harvey Graves, a Bowdoinham, Maine, native. Italianate in style, the church has a tall spire that is the most prominent feature on the Auburn skyline.

Frank L. Dingley House, 291 Court Street — 1867

An unusually impressive example of the Second Empire style, this house was built and lived in for the last half of his life by Frank L. Dingley, a founder and editor of the Lewiston Journal (as a daily) for fifty-seven years. In an era noted for personal journalism, Dingley, because of his wit, zeal for righteousness, and longevity, became a dean of American newspaper editors by the end of his career.

Roak Block, 144-170 Main Street — 1871–72

At the time of its construction, this immense Mansard-style, commercial-industrial structure was the largest such building in Maine. Designed by Stevens and Coombs, it came to be known as "the cradle of the Auburn shoe industry." It has recently been beautifully rehabilitated.

The Roak Block was the brainchild of local businessman Jacob Roak, who brought in eight other partners connected with the shoe industry. Each owned a separate vertical section in what became a virtual "row factory." For nearly ninety years the Roak Block served the shoe industry, and it still stretches for 270 feet along Auburn's Main Street.

Barker Mill, 143 Mill Street — 1873

Architecturally, the Barker Mill is one of the best-proportioned of the relatively few Mansard-roofed mills in Maine. Although, by their very nature, late-nineteenth-century textile mills tended to be stark and rather drab, this particular structure, even with the loss of the top floor of the tower, possesses an unusual stylistic dignity and extensive decorative detail.

The Barker Mill was designed by Charles F. Douglas, whose brief but meteoric career included such outstanding

Barker Mill, Auburn

works as the impressive Continental Mill in Lewiston, the Somerset County Courthouse in Skowhegan, and the Glover House in Rockland.

This mill was for a long time Auburn's one major venture in the textile industry. It was the enterprise that gave the New Auburn section its favorable start as a business center.

First Universalist Church, Elm and Pleasant Streets — 1876

Designed by John Stevens of Boston, this building, like his Italianate First Congregational Church in Calais, is the outstanding representative of the High Victorian Gothic style in the city.

The Engine House, Court and Spring Streets — 1879

This substantial brick structure, with its interesting bell tower designed in the Stick Style, is the last in a series of such buildings on this site. Fire protection in Auburn dates from 1849 with the founding of the Lewiston Falls Village Corporation, which was chartered by legislative action for this purpose. The history of this service is unusually well documented and is symbolized by the Engine House.

Holman Day House, Auburn

Charles A. Jordan House, 63 Academy Street — ca. 1880

The most ornate Victorian house in the Lewiston-Auburn area, this wooden, Second Empire–style mansion was designed and constructed by local architect Charles Jordan for himself. A handsome array of wooden details makes this 1880s house an impressive architectural example.

Charles L. Cushman House, 8 Cushman Place — 1889

This unusual architectural specimen in the Queen Anne style was designed by George M. Coombs, a noted Lewiston architect, and executed in fieldstone. It was built for Charles L. Cushman, son of Ara Cushman, founder of one of the largest shoe manufacturing complexes in New England.

Holman Day House, 2 Goff Street — 1895

The Holman F. Day House is unquestionably one of the finest Queen Anne–style wooden residences in the state. This is so not only in terms of the quality of its construction, but also in terms of its architectural detail. The interior is similarly of high style. The magnificent residence was a gift from Day's father-in-law.

In addition to its value as an outstanding example of the Queen Anne style, the Holman Day House is rich in its association with this famous Maine author. Remembered for their colorful Maine characters and accurate depiction of Maine customs and life, the works of Holman F. Day are an important part of the literary heritage of Maine.

Born in 1865 in Vassalboro, Day long served as a newspaper correspondent in the state. He was eventually retained by the Lewiston *Journal* to cover the Maine Legislature.

In 1898, still reporting for the *Journal* and also filing special articles with the Boston *Herald* and *Globe* and the New York *Tribune,* Day began writing a daily column of poetry. Called "Up in Maine," this column was carried by newspapers across the country for six years. These poems were collected as Day's first book, also entitled *Up in Maine.* Two more books of catchy verse were printed in the next four years, and the three entertained more than thirty thousand readers. He wrote at least eighteen novels in his lifetime; his first, *Squire Plum,* was also made into a play. His most famous novel was *King Spruce,* which became a prototype for books about Maine lumbering. This book firmly established Day's reputation as a novelist and delighted President Theodore Roosevelt so much that he invited Day to the White House.

Day's interest was early directed to the infant motion-picture industry. Beginning in 1918, he and his associates made two-reel pictures in Augusta, often dramatizations of his own stories. Day then moved to the West Coast to become a scenario writer for the Hollywood film community, while he continued to write novels. Later, he also went into radio broadcasting as "The Old Salt," a portrayal of a Maine deep-sea fisherman.

Holman Francis Day died in Mill Valley, California, in 1935.

Horace Munroe House, 123 Pleasant Street — 1899–1900

This architecturally complex but beautiful Queen Anne–style house is outstanding even in a city with numerous fine examples of the style. It was built by Mrs. Noble Munroe, widow of one of the founders of an early Auburn shoe manufacturing company.

Horatio G. Foss House, 19 Elm Street — 1914

This impressive Colonial Revival mansion was built by Horatio G. Foss, a highly successful Lewiston industrialist and self-made man. Designed by Eugene J. Gibbs and Addison Pulsifer, it stands as a reminder of the rewards that could be reaped by the ambitious son of a shoemaker in the nineteenth-century industrial world.

AUGUSTA

Kennebec Arsenal Historic District, Arsenal Street — 1828

In 1827, an act was passed enabling the United States government to build an arsenal in Augusta for the protection of the northeastern frontier. Maine, at that time, was considered likely to become the stage for war with England in the northeastern boundary dispute. Construction commenced on June 14, 1828.

The forty-acre lot was enclosed by a heavy iron fence, which encompassed fifteen buildings (ten of unhammered granite), wharves, and even a trout pond. The arsenal produced a large quantity of ammunition during the Mexican War, and in the Civil War the demand for ammunition was so great that temporary wooden buildings were erected to house the manufactories of paper cartridges. Supplies were provided by the arsenal at the time of the Spanish-American War as well.

The arsenal was abandoned in 1903, and in 1905 the property was transferred to the state for public purposes. The ten granite buildings are still in use by the state.

Kennebec Arsenal Historic District, Augusta

Fort Western, Bowman Street — 1754 (NHL)

Fort Western in Augusta, built in 1754, is one of the oldest and best preserved colonial buildings in America. Recognizing this, the Department of the Interior has designated it a National Historic Landmark.

Although there are extensive archaeological remains beneath today's city streets and replica blockhouses have been erected on the site, the only original component of the fort that survives above ground is the main building, which functioned as officers' quarters and a trading post. This building is constructed of shingle-covered sawn logs forming a rectangular block 100 feet long by 32 feet wide. Four massive internal brick chimneys stand astride the gable roof.

The fort was built for the Kennebec Proprietors by Boston housewright Gershom Flagg to defend Anglo-American

Fort Western, Augusta

settlements in the southern Kennebec Valley from attack by the French and Indians and to provide logistical support for Fort Halifax. In 1775, it was an important staging-point for Benedict Arnold's march to Quebec. In the nineteenth century, however, it survived only because of its adaptive reuse as a tenement.

In the early 1920s, the main building was extensively restored by the Gannett family and given to the city of Augusta. Today Fort Western is a museum open to the public each summer. As a rare survival from the period of the French and Indian Wars, Fort Western is an important reminder of the hostile environment facing central Maine's settlers in the mid-eighteenth century.

Tappan-Viles House, 154 State Street—1816, ca. 1865, ca. 1915

Built by the Reverend Benjamin Tappan of South Parish Church, this began as a fairly traditional square hip-roofed home. Sold to Colonel Alanson B. Farwell in 1862, the structure was brought up-to-date in the Italian style, with the addition of an ornate lantern, brackets, and quoins. In 1915 the third owner, Dr. William Graves, chose Maine architect John Calvin Stevens to revitalize the building. By applying the then-popular Colonial Revival features, the architect further enhanced the house's charm. The surprising result of this architectural melange is a structure of impressive dignity and style.

Kennebec County Courthouse, 95 State Street — 1829

The Kennebec County Courthouse is especially significant for its architecture. The building was among the earliest Greek Revival structures to appear in the state and only the second with a temple front.

In December of 1827, the Court of Sessions of Kennebec County decided to erect a new courthouse and appointed a building committee to obtain a plan with an estimate of expense. The committee reported in February of 1828 that the county commissioners should erect a courthouse of "split stone." The report and its attached plans by James Cochran were accepted. The present site was purchased in January 1829, and the cornerstone was laid in May. James Cochran and Robert C. Vose oversaw the construction of the building, which was completed in the spring of 1830 and occupied for the first time on June 1 of that year.

Maine State House, Capitol Street — 1829–32

Any understanding of the State House must take into account the history of its physical development. When Maine separated from Massachusetts and became a state in 1820, Portland was selected as the temporary capital. A modest 2-story state house (since destroyed) was erected at Congress and Myrtle streets to accommodate the government. Though Portland was the largest and most prosperous of Maine's municipalities, there were many who felt that the permanent capital should be located in a geographically more central and more easily defended place. After careful consideration, the legislature chose the Kennebec River community of Augusta, and Governor Enoch Lincoln signed the bill into law on February 24, 1827.

Appropriately, General William King, the champion of statehood and Maine's first chief executive, was chosen as commissioner of public buildings in 1828. King turned for assistance to the great New England architect, Charles Bulfinch, who was then at work on the United States Capitol in Washington, D.C. Largely through King's influence, Bulfinch responded in 1829 with a set of drawings for the new Maine state house. These survive today in the collection of the Maine State Library. Concerning this last major work of his career, the architect wrote:

The Maine State House, Augusta.
(From an engraving in the November 19, 1853 issue of Gleason's Pictorial Drawing Room Companion.*)*

I have endeavored, while preserving the general outline of the Boston State House, to prevent its being a servile copy; and have aimed at giving it an air of simplicity, which, while I hope it will appear reconcilable to good taste, will render it easy to execute in your own material.

Fittingly the "material" was granite from nearby Hallowell, and Bulfinch's design was a striking transformation of his brick Federal-style Massachusetts capitol of thirty years before into a bold statement of the Greek Revival.

Under the keen eyes of William King, construction of the State House began at "Weston Hill" in Augusta on July 4, 1829. Subsequent commissioners William Clark and Reuel Williams saw it to completion during January 1832. In terms of advanced design and careful workmanship, Maine now boasted of having one of the most beautiful and modern capitol buildings in the nation.

The Maine State House today

Well into the twentieth century, nearly all government offices, including the museum, the library, and all of the departments, were housed in the State House itself. As state government grew in scope and size, changes in the building became necessary. The first of these changes was a remodeling of the interior, made at a cost of several thousand dollars in 1857. Need for space increased thereafter, and, while two expansion plans were considered, they were not funded. In 1889, approval to enlarge the building was granted. Between 1890 and 1891, Boston architect John Calvin Spofford's design for a 3-story rear wing was carried out. The wing was constructed of matching granite, and its restrained neo–Greek Revival lines were designed to harmonize with Bulfinch's original concept. By 1907, the inadequacy of the State House interior working space again became painfully apparent. This time another Boston architect, G. Henri Desmond, was selected to undertake the final expansion.

Desmond's plans radically altered both the outside and inside of the State House. Using matching granite, Desmond more than doubled the length of the building by adding large wings to the north and south sides. To compensate for this horizontal expansion, he replaced the low saucer dome with one of copper-covered steel that rises 185 feet. Atop this was placed a gold-covered figure representing

Wisdom, executed by the Gardiner sculptor, W. Clark Noble. Executed between 1909 and 1910, these changes mark the final architectural evolution of the Maine State House. The only Bulfinch features to survive the Desmond expansion are the impressive portico and front wall behind and adjacent to it. In all, any contemporary consideration of the capitol must recognize it as a fine public building reflecting the interior and exterior aesthetics of 1910. Virtually no permanent physical changes have occurred since that date.

James G. Blaine House,
Capitol and State Streets — 1830s (NHL)

Captain James Hall of Bath began building what is now the governor's official residence while the State House was being erected across the street. Hall, a retired master mariner, completed his home in 1833, a year after the Bulfinch capitol was finished. In every sense, the two structures were born and brought up together. In its original form, Hall's house was a square, hipped-roof structure with a handsome colonnaded porch. Captain Hall eventually added an ell to his retirement home. On November 20, 1862, J. Rufus Child, a subsequent owner, conveyed house and land to James G. Blaine for the sum of $5,000. At that point, the building entered the mainstream of state and national history.

Congressman Blaine presented the deed to his wife, Harriet Standwood Blaine, as a birthday present, and the family of five moved in. As the politician's family and career grew, so did the shape and size of the house. The Blaine addition, a smaller replica of the old "Hall House," was erected at the end of the ell. It featured a porch and entrance which led to the "Plumed Knight's" study and much prized billiard room. Other changes included the addition of cupolas, the changing of porch styles, and the lowering of chimneys. By 1872, the interior and exterior architecture bore little resemblance to Captain Hall's late-Federal-period mansion.

The family also had a cottage at Bar Harbor and a mansion in Washington, D.C., but the house in Augusta was always "home." Here Blaine mapped his political strategy, relaxed on the lawn, and entertained. In 1879, the house was the site of an aborted assassination attempt against the con-

James G. Blaine House, Augusta

gressman. Blaine's years of residency in Augusta were tumultuous. When he bought the property, he had just won election to Congress after having been editor of the *Kennebec Journal* and having served in the Maine legislature and as chairman of the Republican state committee. He subsequently rose to become the Speaker of the House, a United States senator, a Republican presidential candidate, and the secretary of state under Presidents Garfield and Harrison. A statesman of rare ability, James G. Blaine, who died in 1893, was by all accounts the most prominent Maine political figure of the nineteenth century.

In 1915, the Maine legislature required the governor to have an official residence in Augusta. The legislature considered buying the Blaine House for such a purpose. Mrs. Harriet Blaine Beale, daughter of James G. Blaine, however, chose to present the property to the state of Maine in the name of her son, Walker Blaine Beale, and as a memorial to her father. A noted architect, John Calvin Stevens, was engaged to design major interior and exterior alterations. A new wing was added to the rear for service functions, the "Sun Room" replaced the old veranda, and the house was modernized in keeping with its historic character.

Lot Morrill House, 113 Winthrop Street — 1830s

This early Greek Revival–style home was built of brick in the 1830s and has been occupied by several famous men. Lot Morrill, an influential politician during the mid nineteenth century, lived here while he was a state legislator, state governor, United States senator, and secretary of the treasury. A Democrat who turned Republican, Morrill was very active in the Abolition and temperance movements and initiated what proved to be the first civil rights measures. John Nelson, representative from 1921 to 1933, and his son, Charles Nelson, representative from 1947 to 1959, were also occupants of this forthright Greek Revival dwelling.

Dr. J. W. Ellis House, 62 State Street — ca. 1855

An exceptionally finely detailed and impressive example of formal Greek Revival architecture, this house, built by a prominent local physician, is particularly notable for its uniquely designed doorway. Its only rival for ornamentation is the Charles Pond House in Bangor.

South Parish Congregational Church and Parish House, Church Street — 1865, 1889

The South Parish Congregational Church is significant as one of the most important ecclesiastical works of Francis H. Fassett, Maine's leading mid-nineteenth-century architect and as a dominant landmark on the Augusta skyline. Its attached parish house is a notable representative of the Stick Style, examples of which are comparatively rare in Maine.

All Souls Church, 70 State Street — 1879

Designed by Thomas W. Silloway of Boston, this is one of the finest and most elaborate Stick-Style churches in Maine. The Stick Style is quite rare, therefore this church is an important specimen. Silloway, the architect of over 300 churches as well as other public buildings, also created the impressive state capitol at Montpelier, Vermont. At the age of 34, he was ordained as a Universalist minister and wrote a number of books on both theology and architecture.

United States Post Office, Augusta

United States Post Office, Water Street — 1886–90

The U.S. Post Office and Courthouse in Augusta is a massive granite building in the late-nineteenth-century Romanesque Revival style. Constructed of Hallowell granite between 1886 and 1890, the building is the most monumental example of its architectural style surviving in Maine. Originally designed with the tower at the corner of the building, the building was given a wing identical to the southern section of the north side within a few years, making it symmetrical.

The U.S. Post Office building was utilized into the 1960s, when it was replaced by a larger federal building. Fortunately, the government located the new structure on another site and sold the old post office as surplus property to a private interest, which has successfully adapted it for a bank, a restaurant, and offices. Thus, the exterior integrity of this magnificent landmark has been preserved, while the interior continues to serve the community of which it has so long been a part.

Algernon Bangs House, 16 East Chestnut Street — 1892

Although not an aesthetic masterpiece, this imaginative Queen Anne house reflects the forthright spirit of its builder, a lumber baron who believed, in the 1890s, not only in women's suffrage but also in the future of commercial air travel! A native of Farmington, Maine, Mr. Bangs began as an apprentice and rose to the position of an independent manufacturer. Entering the lumber business in 1868, he settled in Augusta in 1881 and founded Bangs Brothers, builders of doors and windows.

Probably designed at least in part by Mr. Bangs himself, the building's astounding variety of decorative features reflects the eclectic mood of the late nineteenth century. The house was eventually purchased by Augusta General Hospital. Renamed St. Catherine's Hall, it served as a nurses' residence. It was an apartment complex from 1953 to 1980, and is now being rehabilitated as a medical professional building. It has been beautifully restored and painted in period colors to show off its elaborate details.

The Lithgow Library, Winthrop Street — 1894–96

Like so many small public libraries in Maine, the Lithgow Library was the outgrowth of a nineteenth-century private library organization. Endowed by Lewellyn Lithgow and Andrew Carnegie, the organizers were able to construct a permanent library on a corner lot purchased in 1888. The cornerstone was laid on June 14, 1894, and the building was dedicated on February 3, 1896.

The building reflects as direct an inspiration from the work of H.H. Richardson as any building in Maine. Richardson's Romanesque Revival–style architecture of the 1870s and 1880s was used by architect Joseph Ladd Neal as a source for the design of the building, along with the Beaux Arts influence inside with dark Colonial Revival woodwork in the hall and stack room, and with white and gold French Renaissance decor in the reading room. The beauty of its exterior Romanesque Revival design combined with the richness of its interior make it the most important library executed in the Richardsonian manner in Maine.

Lithgow Library, Augusta

Governor John F. Hill Mansion, 136 State Street — 1901

This magnificent Colonial Revival mansion, dominating the central section of State Street in Augusta, epitomizes the career of its first owner, a highly successful turn-of-the-century entrepreneur and politician. Designed on the grand scale by Maine's most noted architect, it is a symbol of stability and achievement.

John Fremont Hill was born in 1855 in Eliot, Maine, and was a descendant of prominent founders of the community. After attending various private academies, he attended Bowdoin College and received an M.D. from the Maine Medical School in Brunswick. After practicing medicine for a short time in Boothbay Harbor, he found himself increasingly drawn to the world of business and in 1879 joined Peleg O. Vickery in the publishing house of Vickery and Hill in Augusta.

In the 1880s and 1890s he also became politically active and served several terms as state representative and state senator and one term on the governor's executive council. In 1900, he became the Republican candidate for governor

Governor John F. Hill Mansion, Augusta

of Maine and was elected by a large majority. He was re-elected in 1902 by a significant margin. During his tenure in the governorship, there being then no executive mansion, he decided to erect a suitably impressive home and chose the most prominent architect in the state, John Calvin Stevens, to conceive the design. The Hill Mansion is possibly Stevens' most distinguished work in the Colonial Revival style.

BINGHAM

Bingham Free Meeting House, South Main Street—1835–36

This Federal-style building with tastefully blended Gothic Revival elements was built between 1835 and 1836 and was the first church building used by the first religious organization north of Caratunk Falls on the Kennebec River. Originally designed to accommodate the variety of denominational persuasions in the area, fifty-two pews were installed, and the owner of the appropriately numbered pew on a given Sunday might choose the form of service and the preacher. The Congregational Church, however, being the only organized body, soon took over the building and installed the first permanent minister.

CHELSEA

Governor's House, The National Home for Disabled Volunteer Soldiers, Togus—1869 (NHL)

At the close of the Civil War, Congress passed an act to establish a national asylum for disabled volunteer soldiers. The home was to be open to "any worthy soldier . . . if suffering under such a degree of disability that the privileges and comforts of such a home as this would be convenient to him." The first veterans to be cared for under this act were received in October 1866 at the "Eastern Branch," located on what was then known as the Togus Springs Estate, five miles east of Augusta.

In 1858, a Rockland granite dealer named Horace Beals had purchased the 1,900-acre tract and erected a 134-room hotel surrounded by a racecourse, bowling alleys, bath house, and other recreational facilities. Beals had intended to create a second Saratoga, but after three seasons his enterprise closed. After Beals's death in the Civil War, his widow sold the property to the federal government.

The resort was converted into the national asylum, and a building program was launched. Unfortunately, a fire in January of 1868 made it necessary to rebuild the entire plant. During a relatively short time, every building from the 1860s had either been burned or demolished, except the governor's house, which stands today almost perfectly preserved. Completed in 1869, the Director's Quarters, as the building is now called, is typical of the style of all the early buildings at Togus. The twenty-two-room, Mansard-style home has not been changed on the interior, and only the replacement of the open veranda with a narrower enclosed porch has altered the outside.

Only three other nineteenth-century buildings survive at Togus; all others were constructed in this century. The Director's Quarters, the oldest and most elegant building on the property, commemorates the founding of this significant institution, the first of its kind in the United States.

CHINA

China Village Historic District

The area that became the town of China was first surveyed between 1773 and 1774, and the first settlers arrived in the

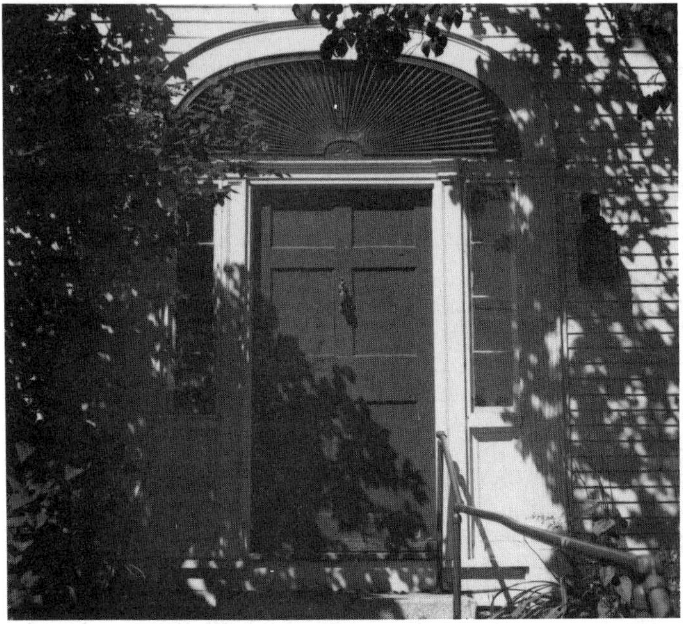

Albert Church Brown Memorial Library, China Village Historic District

summer of 1774. The farmlands around the head of China Lake and the brooks falling into it were soon made productive. By 1784 there was a primitive grist mill, and the first general store opened in 1804. When it was incorporated in 1818, China had another gristmill, a sawmill, a potash works, two general stores, and a tavern.

In the 1820s and 1830s, China Village had a sudden spurt of growth, which established it as a trading, manufacturing, and cultural center for the surrounding countryside. By 1827, the main road from Portland to Bangor ran through China Village, and throughout the mid nineteenth century the village flourished. Cabinetmakers, chairmakers, shoemakers, blacksmiths, millers, and tanners were among the tradespeople who were located in China.

China Village today, although many of the commercial and industrial structures are gone, retains the atmosphere and air of self-sufficiency of a prosperous nineteenth-century rural community. It transmits a feeling of unity and permanence typical of the region and period.

Dinsmore Grain Company Mill, Branch Mills — 1914

Built after the disastrous fire of 1908 on the site of mill operations dating back to the very early nineteenth century, this combination grist- and saw-mill is one of the few water-powered mills remaining in the state. Although not operating at present, all the machinery and appurtenances are present, and plans are under way to operate it as a working museum.

CLINTON

Brown Memorial Library, Route 11 — 1899–1900

The Brown Library is of architectural importance as one of the finest libraries designed by John Calvin Stevens of Portland, Maine's leading turn-of-the-century architect. Richardsonian-Romanesque in style, the Brown Library ranks in quality of design with two other contemporary buildings, the Lithgow Library in Augusta and the Lawrence Library in Fairfield.

DURHAM

Shiloh Temple, off Route 125 — 1897

Shiloh Temple was built in 1897 as a bible and missionary training school. Erected by Reverend Frank W. Sandford and his disciples, the building is a dramatic and unusual statement of late-nineteenth-century vernacular architecture. Its surrounding porch and Mansard roof give it the appearance of a summer hotel, while the shingled tower surmounted by a coronet is reminiscent of a church.

Although several buildings were constructed at Shiloh at the turn of the century, only this one survives. The builders were members of a religious movement known as "The Kingdom" or "The Holy Ghost and Us Society." For twenty-three years, continuous prayers for the evangelization of the world were said in the tower of the temple, and a group of believers undertook a missionary cruise around the world. The voyage ended in disaster. Reverend Sandford, who had consistently refused aid, was found guilty of man-

Shiloh Temple, Durham

slaughter, and the sect began to weaken. "The Kingdom" still exists, however, and the temple, though rarely used, still functions as a forum for Sandford's interpretation of Christianity.

EMBDEN

Hodgdon Site — Prehistoric, 1600–1699

The Hodgdon site is the location of a riverbank bedrock ledge covered with Indian rock carvings, or petroglyphs, and an adjacent associated small campsite. Excavations at the site have shown that its primary use occurred after A.D. 500, continuing through the seventeenth century. The petroglyphs, as well, contain such historic subjects as European-style buildings. From the archaeological evidence at the small site, we conclude that petroglyph production was not part of large-scale ceremonial activity, that it was probably seasonal in nature, and that it continued into the early eighteenth century. Public access to the site is by permission of the landowner only.

FAIRFIELD

Connor-Bovie House, 22 Summit Street — 1856–58

This late–Greek Revival residence has some Italianate details because it was built in the years when both styles were popular. The interior and exterior are in almost original condition. William Connor, nineteenth-century lumber baron, and William T. Bovie, twentieth-century surgeon and inventor of surgical equipment, occupied the house during the active years of their lives. In 1888, the Connor-Bovie House became the first in Fairfield to be electrified.

Lawrence Public Library, Lawrence Avenue — 1900–1901

Successful lumberman Edward J. Lawrence gave the funds necessary for the construction of Fairfield's public library. The plans for the Romanesque Revival–style stone building were drawn by William R. Miller, a prominent Lewiston architect. Like the exterior, the interior retains much of its impressive original appearance, so that the building is a community landmark.

L.C. Bates Museum, Hinckley School, Route 201 — 1903

Designed by William R. Miller of Lewiston in the Romanesque Revival style, this building bears witness to the vision of George Walter Hinckley, founder of the Good Will Home and School for homeless children. A selfless worker and gifted fundraiser dedicated to the welfare of underprivileged youth, Hinckley built from humble beginnings an institution of national distinction, which still serves those in need.

Amos Gerald House – "The Castle," 107 Main Street — 1910–13

The Amos Gerald House in Fairfield is important for at least three reasons: it was built by the first and foremost pioneer in the development of the once vast trolley-car system in Maine; it is designed in a rare vernacular architectural style derived from the medieval castle; and it is very possibly the first residence ever constructed of cement blocks in Maine and perhaps New England.

Born in Benton in 1841, Amos Gerald launched his business career in 1868 with the manufacture of a curtain fixture of his own invention. He also invented a successful drophead sewing machine.

After a brief sojourn in New York City in the early 1880s, he returned imbued with ideas of establishing a Waterville-Fairfield street railway. At first horse-drawn, it was electrified in 1890. It was the first of a dozen trolley systems that Gerald built, many of which were much longer. He also was involved in the successful consolidation of several groups of local lines into larger, more efficient systems.

In order to popularize trolley use and also to provide public recreation, Gerald developed a number of amusement parks, skating rinks, bandstands, and the like along various routes in scenic locations. He also built the famed Casco Castle, a medieval-style summer hotel in South Freeport and the Hotel Gerald in Fairfield, which is topped with three golden domes and known for its luxurious interior and fixtures.

On the day of his funeral in September 1913, every trolley car throughout the state stood still for three minutes.

FARMINGDALE

Peter Grant House, 10 Grant Street — 1830

Its construction date of 1830, ascertained from Hallowell tax records, places this house among Maine's earliest examples of Greek Revival, temple-style architecture as applied to a private dwelling. Its builder, Peter Grant, was a self-made man who, at his death in 1836, left an estate of over $100,000 (very large for the time), including a shipyard in Farmingdale, half ownership in four good-sized vessels, and large real estate holdings in the area. His social position is indicated by the fact that one of his sons married a daughter of Dr. Benjamin Vaughan, the patriarch of Hallowell.

GARDINER

Gardiner Historic District

The Gardiner Historic District lies along both sides of Water Street and is comprised of forty-seven architecturally significant, primarily commercial buildings dating mostly from the nineteenth century. While a number of the buildings have suffered from cosmetic façade remodeling, the basic fabric remains underneath in most cases and a move toward rehabilitation is well under way. All major styles of the period are represented, and generally the scale, proportion, and construction materials of the buildings are compatible. Typical of a once-thriving river port, the structures on one side of the street back up either on the Kennebec River or its tributary, Cobbosseecontee Stream.

Within one mile of its confluence from the west with the Kennebec River, Cobbossee Stream descends 126 feet to the high-tide level of the Kennebec River. This stretch includes eight natural waterfalls. This topographical accident exerted an enormous influence on the development of the city of Gardiner.

Gardiner Historic District

*1876 Commercial Block,
Gardiner Historic District*

Originally part of the town of Pittston and known as Cobbossee Plantation, virtually all of the land forming present-day Gardiner was early acquired by Dr. Sylvester Gardiner, a wealthy minister and land speculator from Boston.

Robert Hallowell Gardiner, his grandson, who built the great stone Tudor Revival mansion, "Oaklands," devoted his not inconsiderable talents to the development of the town, and, aided by its natural endowments, it grew rapidly and prospered. In 1850, Gardiner was chartered as a city and was on its way to becoming the most important river port on the Kennebec.

Varney's *Gazetteer of the State of Maine* cites Gardiner as having a population of 4,440 in 1880 and describes the industrial development along the Cobbossee Stream. There were then six large stone dams that provided power for at least twenty-one industries whose total annual production was estimated at over $2 million. By the turn of the century, a large shoe-manufacturing industry had also developed.

It is against this thriving, burgeoning economic background that Gardiner's business district along Water Street developed. In its heyday, ships and barges in large numbers were tied up to the docks and piers at the rear of Water Street warehouses and shops on the stream and river side. The railroad put through along the river in the 1860s added further stimulus to the city's economy.

Although Gardiner no longer ranks as an important industrial center and commerce on the river has ended, Water Street stands, largely intact, as a remnant of the city when it was queen of the river. Buildings representing virtually every stage of development stand as chronological signposts along the community's remarkable historical road.

Laura Richards House, 3 Dennis Street — ca. 1810

This fine Federal house is noted as the home of Laura Richards, noted author of poems, short stories, and books for children, during the last 65 years of her life. The daughter of Samuel Gridley and Julia Ward Howe, she is perhaps best known for her short novel, *Captain January* (1890), which has been filmed twice.

Christ Episcopal Church, 1 Dresden Avenue — 1829

This small Gothic Revival–style church faces the common in Gardiner. The granite building was constructed between 1819 and 1820 from plans by the Reverend Samuel Forman Jarvis of Bloomingdale, New York.

The style of church had no precedent in Maine or even the country when it was built. The style should perhaps be termed "Gothic," for it comes from eighteenth-century English architectural forms of that name, which were presented in a work by Betty Langley. The Reverend Jarvis recognized that "Gothic" could play a role in the religious experience of the Episcopal church at a time when it was trying to recover from the Revolution and was seeking a new identity.

The design of Christ Church was an important step in introducing a new style to America and in paving the way for a more academic Gothic Revival, which was to dominate America's church architecture for decades.

Christ Episcopal Church, Gardiner

"Oaklands" — 1835–36

This granite Tudor Revival mansion was designed by noted architect Richard Upjohn. The 2-story main house and 2½-story ell are built on bedrock and faced with granite ashlar. This was an early commission for Upjohn, and the Tudor Revival design is highly unusual for Maine. Built for Richard Hallowell Gardiner, "Oaklands" is still owned by the Gardiner family.

Edwin Arlington Robinson House,
67 Lincoln Avenue — ca. 1855 (NHL)

Edwin Arlington Robinson was born in 1869 at Headtide, Maine, and the next year moved with his family to Gardiner. Their new home, built in around 1855 for S.W. Bates, was the poet's residence from 1870 to 1891 and from 1893 to 1896. The house has been altered somewhat through the years, but it has retained its essential integrity and is evocative of the poet.

Robinson attended Gardiner's public schools, began to write verse, and fell under the tutelage of a local poet, A.T. Schumann. By 1899, he entered Harvard University, which he attended for two years as a special student. Robinson then returned to Gardiner and wrote verse. His first two volumes of poetry, *The Torrent and the Night Before* (1896) and *The Children of the Night* (1897), were composed during this three-year stay in Gardiner.

Robinson's poetry won wide popularity as well as critical acclaim and, during his later years, he received many honors, including three Pulitzer prizes.

The remainder of the poet's years were spent between New York, Boston, the MacDowell Colony in Peterborough, New Hampshire, and Gardiner, the model for his fictional "Tilbury Town."

HALLOWELL

Hallowell Historic District

Originally called "The Hook," Hallowell, as incorporated in 1771, included Augusta, Chelsea, and part of Manchester. It was named for Benjamin Hallowell, who was a large proprietor in the Kennebec patent.

During the nineteenth century the town grew rapidly, spurred on particularly by Benjamin and Samuel Vaughan, who had settled in the community at the end of the previous

W.C. Johnson House, Hallowell Historic District

(Above) Artemus Leonard House
(Below) Captain Henry Hooper House, Hallowell Historic District

century. By the time of its incorporation as a city in 1852, it was a thriving and prosperous river port, whose granite quarries were widely known for their quality. Several mills, including a large cotton textile factory, operated within the community and bulging warehouses along the river attested to the shipping activity. During much of the century, Hallowell was, in fact, busier and more prosperous than its neighbor Augusta, the capital of the state.

It is from this period that the bulk of the historic district dates — from the great houses in all the principal nineteenth-century styles that dot the hillside to the unusually well-preserved commercial section, which parallels the river. In many ways, the Hallowell Historic District is a virtual time capsule that preserves for our eyes a vision of the last century.

Vaughan Homestead, off Litchfield Road — 1797

The names of Benjamin Vaughan, M.D., LL.D., and Charles Vaughan, Esq., are pre-eminent on the list of the founders of the city of Hallowell. Charles came to Hallowell in 1791, Benjamin in 1797, and the two brothers settled on a large tract of land, which they had inherited through their mother, Sarah Hallowell Vaughan. They came to Hallowell to make permanent homes, and they devoted all their energies and resources to the material, social, intellectual, and religious upbuilding of the place.

Benjamin Vaughan was the oldest son of Samuel Vaughan, a London merchant with interests in the Colonies. Samuel married Sarah Hallowell, daughter of Benjamin Hallowell, one of the proprietors of the Kennebec Purchase, for whom the town of Hallowell was named. Vaughan, a physician, preferred business and political life to medical work. He was instrumental in settling the terms of the Treaty of Paris, through which the American Colonies gained their independence. As a member of Parliament from 1783 to 1794, Vaughan became an unwelcome opponent to the Pitt administration and decided to move to the United States.

Charles Vaughan, already in Hallowell, built the great home on the bluff overlooking the river in anticipation of Dr. Vaughan's arrival in 1797. Together, the brothers became activists in the public life and development of Hallowell.

Today, the mansion house is still owned and occupied by

Vaughan descendants and, with its numerous additions and enlargements, remains a landmark in the community and region.

Elm Hill Farm, Litchfield Road — 1799

This large and finely appointed Cape was built by John Merrick, whom Benjamin Vaughan brought with him from England as a tutor for his children. Merrick became a leading citizen and justice of the peace in Hallowell and married one of Samuel Vaughan's daughters, for whom he built the house in 1799. In addition to his local prominence, he became an overseer of Bowdoin College.

Although later sold to other parties, the house was reacquired by the Vaughan family, in whose ownership it has remained.

The Row House, 106–114 Second Street — ca. 1840

Isaac Gage's Row House was built in about 1840 and was first occupied by Italian stone carvers, who helped to make Hallowell granite nationally known. Maine's last wooden row house of the period, the building is filled with early machine-produced woodwork, nails, and hardware and is constructed and ornamented in a simple Federal and early Greek Revival manner, making it a rare example of labor housing in the 1840s. Sociologically and architecturally fascinating, the Row House has been recently restored.

LEWISTON

Holland-Drew House, 377 Main Street — 1854

This impressive, 2-story, Italianate house with remarkable stained-glass portrait windows was originally owned by Captain Daniel Holland, an early leader in the promotion of industrial development in Lewiston. A later owner was Judge Franklin M. Drew, a prominent political figure in the state and leading banker in the city.

Hathorn Hall, Bates College — 1852–57

Built for the Maine State Seminary, this red brick, granite-quoined building housed recitation halls, the library, the chapel, and administrative offices. The interior has been altered as the needs of the college (now Bates) have changed. Although the campus has increased in size, Hathorn Hall remains at its center, giving promise of service to future generations of students.

Continental Mill Housing, 66–82 Oxford Street — 1865–66

Lewiston's cotton textile mills, such as the Continental, with their combined demands for labor in the second half of the nineteenth century, drew thousands of French-Canadians to the city. "Little Canada," that richly ethnic, still largely French-speaking neighborhood, grew up literally in the shadow of the Continental Mill. To accommodate this influx of labor, mill owners built special tenements called mill blocks, each supervised by a director. The two buildings are all that is left of the many mill blocks that once lined Oxford Street. Originally fronted by elm trees and lawn between them and the canal, these substantial brick structures gave the neighborhood a dignity and character not matched by the later wooden tenements. Restoration of these buildings for modern low-income housing is anticipated and will be a strong factor in preserving the unique character of the area.

Savings Bank Block, 215 Lisbon Street — 1870

This impressive Mansard-style block at an important downtown intersection attests to the maturation of Lewiston as a significant industrial center in the later nineteenth century. Built in response to the growing need for financial institutions in the burgeoning city, it is symbolic of the aspirations of the community.

Senator William P. Frye House, 453–461 Main Street — 1874

Designed by George M. Coombs of Lewiston, the William P. Frye House is a grand example of the Second Empire style. Frye himself was one of Maine's outstanding political figures in the second half of the nineteenth century. A lawyer, he served three terms in the Maine state legislature, was mayor of Lewiston from 1866 to 1867, and became attorney general of Maine. He was elected to Congress in 1870 and served until 1881. Upon the resignation of James G. Blaine in 1881, Frye entered the United States Senate, where he remained until 1911, serving many years as president pro tempore. He was a Republican and a staunch party loyalist.

Bradford House, 54–56 Pine Street — 1876

This high-style Mansard urban residence, owned by a prominent Lewiston physician, set the tone for what was in the 1870s a fashionable neighborhood surrounding a city park.

Trinity Episcopal Church, Bates and Spruce Streets — 1879

An impressive and sophisticated example of late Gothic Revival ecclesiastical architecture, Trinity Church was designed by the C.C. Haight Company of New York City. The development of this parish has interesting ties with the growth of industry in Lewiston, since it was markedly stimulated by the influx of textile workers in the mid 1800s, largely from Lancashire, England.

Dominican Block, 141–45 Lincoln Street — 1882

Founded by the Reverend Louis Mothon, the first school for Franco-American religious and secular instruction in Lewiston-Auburn was housed in this building. The impressive Queen Anne structure was designed by the noted local architect, George M. Coombs, and became the social and political nerve center of the French Catholic population.

Grand Trunk Railroad Station, Lincoln Street—1885

By no means an important structure architecturally, this humble station holds a high symbolic value for the Franco-American community in Lewiston. It was through this terminal that many thousands of French-Canadian immigrants passed as they came to work in the rapidly growing textile industries in the last decades of the nineteenth century.

James C. Lord House (Callahan House), 497 Main Street—1885

This dramatic example of eclectic architecture, combining elements of the Italianate, Queen Anne, and High Victorian Gothic styles, is typical of a prosperous merchant's house of the period. Designed for James C. Lord, a grocer, by local architect Jefferson Lake Coburn, it symbolizes the aspirations of the rising Victorian middle class.

Oak Street (Dingley) School, Oak Street—1890

The Oak Street School of 1890 is an excellent example of the Richardsonian Romanesque style. George M. Coombs, the Maine-born architect of the building, used Richardsonian motifs to construct a well-proportioned and interesting building.

The interior of the school was divided into large classrooms, which have been adapted for use by the Lewiston

Oak Street School, Lewiston

School Department as administrative offices. Most of the original woodwork remains in excellent condition.

Lewiston City Hall, Pine Street—1892

This impressive Baroque Revival structure replaced Lewiston's old city hall, which burned in January 1890. The architectural firm of Brigham and Spofford from Boston was chosen to design the new city hall. After nearly two years of construction the building was dedicated in May of 1892.

John Calvin Spofford, a native of Maine, designed many public buildings in Maine, but when he was given this commission, much criticism was voiced. Most citizens would have preferred that Lewiston's own George M. Coombs be given the job. Nevertheless, Lewiston City Hall is of unusual distinction, bespeaking the aspirations of this thriving manufacturing city.

The interior of the City Hall has been adapted over the years to meet the needs of the city government. Only the front halls of the first two floors have retained their original grandeur.

Lewiston City Hall. Photo by Gridley Barrows.

Healy Asylum, 81 Ash Street — 1893

Designed by Jefferson Lake Coburn, this large structure is a well-preserved example of the Mansard style. Its primary significance, however, lies in its ties with the development of social and humanitarian institutions in Lewiston, particularly as a result of the efforts of Franco-American influence within the Roman Catholic church.

Lewiston Public Library, Park Street — 1902–3

An important example of the work of the Lewiston architect, George M. Coombs, the library is a dignified, granite-ashlar structure in the Romanesque Revival style. Like the city, the library has its roots in manufacturing and has grown and changed with it. Today, it serves the needs of the French-speaking population — children, researchers, and those who read for recreation.

Kora Temple, 11 Sabattus Street — 1908

Built in 1908, the Kora Temple strikes an unusual note amid the traditional architecture of Lewiston. Moorish in inspira-

Kora Temple, Lewiston

tion, the 3-story red brick structure with copper covered domes, is unique and decidedly exotic. It was designed by local architect George M. Coombs, while the interior work was done by Frank Haynes with murals painted by Harry Cochrane.

LISBON AND SABATTUS

Cushman Tavern, Route 9 — ca. 1825

In the first- and second-story center hallways and stairwell of this large, plain, Federal house are located probably the finest and best preserved examples of the mural art of Orison Wood, an outstanding follower of Rufus Porter. According to Porter's biographer, Jean Lipman, "Wood was . . . no mere assistant; his animated murals have, within the Porter formula, a distinctive gracile style of their own."

The Lisbon-Sabattus town line runs right through this historic tavern.

LISBON

The Worumbo Mill, Lisbon Falls — 1864

Named after an Anasagunticook tribal chief, the Worumbo Mill was constructed in 1864 in the utilitarian style so common in mid-nineteenth-century Maine river towns. The woolen textiles produced there won gold medals at national expositions in 1876 and in 1893. Closed and reopened in the mid 1960s, the mill still operates, using much of the same technology that it did at the time of its founding.

St. Cyril and St. Methodius Church, Maine Street — 1926

Though not an outstanding architectural work, this structure represents achievement of another kind. It stands as a testament to the aspirations and struggles of a small, Slovak immigrant population in an often hostile environment. Typical of later-nineteenth-century immigrants, the Slovaks who came to Lisbon Falls in the 1890s found that earlier ethnic arrivals treated them with ill-concealed contempt. This even included the local church. This church represents their attainment of respect and a place in the community, and it was at least in part built with their own hands.

LIVERMORE

The Norlands Historic District

The Norlands was the birthplace and lifelong family home of Israel and Martha Washburn's three daughters and seven sons, four of whom became prominent nineteenth-century Republican politicians. The four — Israel, Jr., Elihu, Cadwallader, and William Drew — served as U.S. congressmen from as many states, and, between 1855 and 1861, the first three were representatives together. Subsequently, Israel, Jr., and Cadwallader became the governors of Maine and

Norlands Historic District, Livermore

Norlands Historic District, Livermore

Wisconsin, respectively. The fourth brother, William Drew, served as a congressman from Minnesota between 1879 and 1895 and later rose to the Senate. Elihu was the "political sparkplug of the dynasty," however. An Illinoisan, he won nine consecutive terms in the House, knew Abraham Lincoln intimately, and promoted the military and political fortunes of his townsman Ulysses S. Grant. He served as Grant's secretary of state in 1869 and then as his ambassador to France between 1869 and 1877. Elihu's representation of the United States abroad won such high public commendation that he received a number of votes for the presidential nomination at the Republican Convention of 1880.

The other three sons — Algernon Sidney, Charles Ames, and Samuel Benjamin — were also achievers, being respectively a bank president, a newspaper editor and later minister to Paraguay, and a naval captain serving with distinction in the Civil War.

About 1869, Charles named the family home "the Norlands," after a phrase in Tennyson's "Ballad of Oriana." Today, the estate comprises the mansion that the sons rebuilt for their father in 1868, the school and church that they attended as youngsters, and the library that they erected as a memorial between 1883 and 1885. Also, the 170-acre property encompasses much of the original family farm. Although in various states there are other structures associated with individual Washburn brothers, the Norlands is the only place that commemorates all members of this unique, single-generation dynasty.

Deacon Livermore House, Billman's Ferry Road — 1793

This substantial farmhouse of 2½ stories has a granite foundation and a double-chimney arrangement; it was the earliest frame dwelling erected in the town. Elijah Livermore came to Maine to explore English land grants and became a leading citizen in the town where he settled. His house was used for church services and town meetings.

MADISON

Weston Homestead, Weston Avenue — 1817–18

This handsome Federal-style house was built by Deacon Benjamin Weston, son of Joseph Weston, one of the first settlers in the region, who arrived with his family in 1772. This substantial home, with unusually fine detail for such a remote area, provides the most significant link with the settlement of Madison and remains an important regional landmark.

Lakewood Theater, Route 201 — 1925–26

Lakewood Theater is of major importance to American theater history as the nation's first summer theater. In the last fifty years, Lakewood has brought scores of famous stars to perform in Maine.

MANCHESTER

Cobbosseecontee Dam Site — Prehistoric

The Cobbosseecontee Dam site flanks a series of falls and rapids near the outlet of Cobbosseecontee Lake, in the lakes district of central Maine. Collections and test excavations at the site show that it has been in use for at least the last seven thousand years. From the physiographic location, we strongly suspect that seasonal use of the site was focused around fishing for anadramous species, perhaps for salmon, alewife, sturgeon, or eels. The site's potential has yet to be fully developed by excavation.

MERCER

Ingalls House, off Route 2—1835–37

The Ingalls House is architecturally significant as an imposing rural dwelling that looked backward in its eighteenth-century form, was contemporary in its handsome Greek Revival trim, and reflected nineteenth-century technological advances in its early use of stoves rather than fireplaces for heating.

MONMOUTH

Cumston Hall, Main Street—1899–1900

Cumston Hall is an unusual, multi-purpose, community building. Built between 1899 and 1900, the large Romanesque edifice stands in the center of Monmouth, a gift to the town from Dr. Charles M. Cumston. Harry Hayman Cochrane designed the structure, supervised the construction, and decorated the interior.

The 2½-story wood frame building with a dramatic square tower houses a public library and public meeting room on the first floor and a theater on the second floor. Connected to the main building is a hexagonal structure that houses the town office. The exterior detail is flamboyant with much decoration. The interiors of Cumston Hall are intact. Of special note is the domed and vaulted theater, elaborately stuccoed and frescoed.

The architect, H.H. Cochrane, was an Augusta native. He was a photographer, portrait painter, composer, musician, writer, and primarily a muralist. His best-known

Cumston Hall, Monmouth

works are the murals in the Kora Temple in Lewiston, the Methodist Church in Monmouth, and Hebron Academy. Cochrane was also a historian and a politician.

NEW PORTLAND

New Portland Wire Bridge, Wire Bridge Road — 1841–42

The townspeople of New Portland appropriated $2,000 in 1840 for the construction of a bridge over the Seven Mile Brook (Carrabasset River) in order to allow settlers on the north side of the river to travel to New Portland Village more easily. Colonel F.B. Morse designed the bridge and directed the construction. Two steel support cables were made in Sheffield, England, especially for the bridge, and 204 steel connectors hold the bridge to the cables. The bridge towers are 25 feet high, but the entrances are narrow in order to discourage vehicles from attempting to cross (the load limit is four tons).

NORRIDGEWOCK

Old Point and Sebastian Rale Monument, Route 201A — 1833

One of the most important French missions in early colonial Maine was known as Narantsouak, the principle village of the Norridgewock Indians. The first Jesuit missionary to live there was Gabriel Druillettes, who periodically based himself at Old Point from 1646 to 1652.

In the late 1680s, Jacques and Vincent Bigot were often in residence, but the mission became most prominent after 1695, when Sebastian Rale became both spiritual and temporal leader of the Norridgewocks.

By the early eighteenth century, Narantsouak had become a palisaded village, 160 feet square, with four gates providing access to a church and twenty-six houses of largely European design. Although this Indian settlement was flourishing, it became the focus of the nearly continuous war between the English and the allied French and Indians. In 1724, an English force marched north and attacked the village, killing Rale and dispersing the other inhabitants.

As a memorial to this sad chapter in Maine history, a monument, in the form of a granite obelisk, was erected in 1833 to commemorate Sebastian Rale's contribution as a leader, missionary, and scholar.

Norridgewock Free Public Library, Sophie May Lane — 1841

This small, Greek Revival, temple-style structure originally served as John S. Abbott's law office. Like many such buildings in Maine, it is a fine example in miniature of an important architectural fashion. The library is of brick construction with wood and granite trim and a granite foundation. A one-story wing on the west side of the building is a later addition. It was given to the town in 1903 by Rebecca Sophia Clark, better known as "Sophie May," noted author of children's books.

Sophie May House, Sophie May Lane—1845

This fine example of Greek Revival, temple-style architecture was built by Cullen Sawtelle, a two-term congressman from Maine, who sold it in 1849 to Asa Clark. His daughter, Rebecca Sophia, except for brief intervals, spent her entire life in this home and here wrote over forty volumes of children's books under the pseudonym of Sophie May. She was the first to present child characters who were lifelike, high-spirited, and mischievous, and her works achieved great popularity.

C.F. Douglas House, Route 8—1868

The C.F. Douglas House is a rare and fine example of Italian-villa–style architecture in inland Maine. This particular style is represented by very few buildings in the state, and these are mostly located in cosmopolitan coastal areas. They are also, with few exceptions, less well-executed than this particular design.

The reason for the quality of this house becomes clear when it is understood that it was designed for himself by Charles F. Douglas, an architect of rare talents, the brevity

C.F. Douglas House, Norridgewock

of whose career may be responsible for his being less well-known than some of his less gifted contemporaries. In the early 1860s, he opened an architectural office in Skowhegan and in 1868 built his home in Norridgewock on land abutting that of his wife's parents. Examples of his work at this time, mostly domestic but including the Methodist Church in Waterville, show him to be very much in tune with the latest fashions in architecture.

His talents in design were apparently not matched by business acumen, because in 1869, after living there only a year, he lost his house in bankruptcy. The following year he established an office in Lewiston and during the next three years produced building designs remarkable in both quality and quantity.

For reasons unknown, though possibly financial, Douglas suddenly moved to Philadelphia in 1874, where he appears in city directories through the years as a dealer in building supplies but does not seem to have further pursued the architectural career that for a brief time had seemed so brilliant. He died in the first decade of this century.

OAKLAND

The Pressey House, 287 Summer Street — 1854–58

One of a relatively small number of octagon houses in Maine, the Pressey house is decorated in the Greek Revival style. This architectural form was popularized by Orson Squire Fowler in the 1850s and appears over the next three decades dressed in the detail of varying prevailing styles.

Memorial Hall, Church Street — 1870–73

Begun in 1870 but not completed until 1873, Memorial Hall was an extraordinarily ambitious Civil War monument to be undertaken by a relatively small town. Thomas Silloway, the architect of this handsome Italian-Gothic structure, designed or remodeled over 300 churches in New England and was also responsible for Vermont's state capitol in Montpelier. Of particular interest is the commercial space included in the basement of Memorial Hall.

PITTSFIELD

Founders Hall, South Main Street—1868

This impressive example of mid-nineteenth-century academic architecture was the first permanent building at Maine Central Institute, founded in 1866. Despite the addition of numerous modern structures, Founders Hall is still the dominant feature of the campus.

Pittsfield Railroad Station, Central Street—1888

Recently restored by the Athenaeum Club of Pittsfield, this station was in keeping with the prevailing trend in late-nineteenth-century railroad architecture, combining Italianate features with Stick-Style elements. Of particular interest are the stained glass windows.

PITTSTON

Major Reuben Colburn House, off Route 27—1765

In September 1775, under orders from General George Washington, Colonel Benedict Arnold led a mixed force of Continental units on a march to Quebec. The plan was to occupy this strategic strongpoint in British North America in the earliest stages of the Revolutionary War.

The operation was a disaster for several reasons. The season was advanced for a northern campaign; most of the route from the Kennebec, across the Appalachians to the St. Lawrence, was a trackless wilderness of bogs and forest, largely uncharted; supplies were ill-planned; and finally, the bateaux supplied for the invasion were constructed of green wood and constantly leaked. Those hungry and weary troops who survived the forty-five-day trek failed to take Quebec by storm, and the expedition was a tactical disaster. Strategically, however, it succeeded in delaying Britain's invasion south to New York for over a year.

Few buildings of the period survive in Maine along Arnold's route. One of these belonged to Major Reuben Colburn, the man who built most of Arnold's leaky bateaux.

Major Reuben Colburn House, Pittston

Today, the Reuben Colburn House is administered by the Maine Bureau of Parks and Recreation. This sturdy, two-story dwelling with large central chimney is open to the public and recalls a dramatic campaign in America's struggle for independence.

Pittston Congregational Church, Intersection of Routes 194 and 27—1836

A pleasing combination of Federal and Greek Revival architecture with Gothic elements, this was the first church building of the Congregational denomination in Pittston. The organization was originally formed in 1812 at the home of Major Reuben Colburn.

POLAND

Maine State Building, Poland Spring—1893, 1895

In 1892, an international exposition was opened in Chicago to celebrate the four hundredth anniversary of the discov-

Maine State Building, Poland Spring

ery of America by Christopher Columbus. Maine's response to the Columbian Exposition was an octagonal Queen Anne–type structure, the shape of which was dictated by the irregular lot assigned to it on the far eastern end of the exposition.

The architect chosen for the building was a Lewiston native, Charles Summer Frost, who had achieved a national reputation for his buildings in Chicago.

When its role as the Maine exposition building had ended, it was decided that it would be an advantage to the granite and slate industries of Maine to donate the building as a permanent fixture to the city of Chicago. The park commission subsequently informed the Maine representatives that all buildings in that section of the park were to be removed.

At this point, several parties made offers to purchase the building. The committee considered all proposals and decided to sell the building to Hiram Ricker and Sons, who were the owners of the celebrated Poland Spring summer resort at Poland Springs, Maine. The Rickers paid $30,000 for the building, and it cost them approximately $5,000 to move it to Poland Spring. A sixteen-car train was hired, and the building was loaded piece by piece. It was finally reconstructed in front of an oak grove beside the Grand Hotel at Poland Spring. On July 1, 1895, the building was dedicated as a library and arts building and thereafter advertised as a additional attraction of this famous watering place of the turn-of-the-century leisure class. The Maine State Building is a rare surviving example of a pavilion from one of the great nineteenth-century expositions.

Poland Railroad Station, Plains Road—1901

The former Maine Central Railroad Station in Poland is probably the best-preserved specimen of standard turn-of-the-century depot architecture in Maine. It is also the finest example of several Maine railroad buildings converted for residential use.

All Soul's Chapel, Poland Spring—1912

A church as part of a hotel resort is not a common thing, although several were to be found throughout the country at the beginning of the twentieth century. An edifice as substantial as All Soul's Chapel and designed in a restrained Gothic Revival style was rare indeed in such a setting.

The first impulse toward public religious observances at the huge and highly fashionable Poland Spring resort began among the employees in 1885 under the leadership of one Julius Gassauer. At first, services were held outdoors, but occasional inclement weather resulted in the inauguration of a "chapel fund" to provide a suitable shelter. Money-raising efforts continued for several years until approximately $15,000 had been raised. The Ricker family, proprietors of the inn, took great interest in the project and donated a site for the chapel on the highest point of land on the hotel property.

Ground was broken in September 1910, and contributions continued to swell the fund. G. Henri Desmond, a prominent Boston architect, was retained to design the structure. Among other Maine commissions executed by Desmond was the expansion and remodeling of the Maine State House in Augusta.

The chapel was formally opened on September 1, 1912, and the following year a peal of four bells was installed in the tower.

READFIELD

Kent's Hill School Historic District, Route 17

Before the advent of publicly supported secondary schools in Maine, this level of education was in the hands of private academies, or so-called seminaries affiliated with some Protestant denomination. Academies were far more common and were scattered widely, so that almost every community of any size boasted one. Seminaries, however, existed in very small numbers, and one of the earliest of these is now Kent's Hill School, a private, non-denominational, preparatory school.

Bierce Hall, Kent's Hill School Historic District, Readfield

Luther Sampson, the founder, inspired by the itinerant Methodist evangelist, the Reverend Jesse Lee, formed the Readfield Religious and Charitable Society in 1821. The purpose of the organization being to provide Christian education for young people, Sampson donated 140 acres of land for a school site, together with a new house, barns, sheds, cattle and sheep as well as equipment, all at a cost of over $10,000. The school, soon named Maine Wesleyan Seminary, began operation in 1824, at first admitting only boys but shortly after becoming coeducational.

SIDNEY

Powers House, Route 104 — ca. 1770

Named for Sir Philip Sidney, the Elizabethan statesman and poet, the town of Sidney was incorporated in 1792, one of the earliest in Kennebec County. One of the first settlers, Levi Powers, arrived shortly after 1760 to take up a grant obtained in Boston from unknown sources. It is presumed that the large and substantial house that he built was not erected for some time because he must have spent the early years

Powers House, Sidney

establishing himself in what was then heavily timbered virgin forest.

The remarkably preserved Colonial house is of particular importance because of its size and fineness of proportion in the context of a newly settled area. It remains little changed either externally or internally and conveys better than most an accurate impression of its time and place.

SKOWHEGAN

Skowhegan Historic District, Water and Russett Streets, and Madison Avenue

The town of Skowhegan got its start in 1771 when Peter Heywood and Joseph Weston of Concord, Massachusetts, trekked up the river with their families and a few head of cattle to homestead the land granted to them by the Kennebec Proprietors. The area was then known as Canaan Plantation. In 1836, Canaan changed its name to Skowhegan, which, with many variations of spelling, was the name that had been used to designate the falls for many years. In 1861, the towns of Bloomfield and Skowhegan were united.

The mid 1800s were a time of rapid growth and prosperity for the town. With the coming of the railroad in 1856, the telegraph in 1862, and the telephone in 1883, Skowhegan became a pivotal center for regional business and industry. It became Somerset County's shire town in 1872. The buildings constructed during this boom were, for the most part, functional brick structures in the commerical vernacular, except for a few more ornate buildings, such as the First National Bank.

The historic district includes the southernmost block of Madison Avenue and the two westernmost blocks of Water Street, comprising the principal commercial section of the town. The thirty-eight buildings in the district represent all the major styles from 1880 to 1910. In general, the buildings are well-maintained though in some cases the first-floor facades have been severely altered. As a whole, the district retains its turn-of-the-century ambiance.

Though many of Skowhegan's grand architectural structures — notably its hotels and Coburn Hall — were destroyed, the buildings that do remain stand as tributes to the historical, commercial, and cultural life of this significant settlement on the Kennebec.

Samuel Weston Homestead, Route 201—1798–1800

This beautiful house, built by an early pioneer and community leader, is an interesting example of transitional architecture that shows how Georgian features were retained in remote areas long after the style had given way to the Federal in more cosmopolitan regions.

Bloomfield Academy, Main Street—1840

First chartered by the Massachusetts legislature in 1807 in the early years of settlement, Bloomfield Academy erected this building in 1840 in the typical Greek Revival style used for such structures. The school was originally called Canaan Academy, but when the town changed its name in 1819, the school followed suit. When the academy needed more space, the town turned to local brickmaker and master builder Asa Dyer to erect this building. Although Bloomfield became part of Skowhegan in 1861, the academy kept its name. Today the two-story brick structure is part of the local school district. This handsome landmark is a reminder of the importance early settlers place on education.

Governor Abner Coburn House, Main Street 1849

The Abner Coburn House, built in 1849 by the master builder Joseph Bigelow, presents an impressive example of the Greek Revival temple style at the zenith of its development in Maine. It was the home of one of Maine's leading citizens, governor and lumber magnate Abner Coburn, and his brother, Philander, also a leading businessman.

The firm of A. and P. Coburn was so well known for its integrity that notes signed "A. and P. Coburn" were used as currency around the state. The brothers were always generous to deserving causes but were never wasteful. Abner, publicly active and politically involved, was considered the richest man in Maine in 1882, being worth $6 million to $7 million. His honesty would not allow him to succumb to political pressures while in office as governor and, as a result, after only one term in 1863, he was not renominated.

Both Philander and Abner and their two sisters, who served them as housekeepers, died in the fine Skowhegan residence.

Governor Abner Coburn House, Skowhegan

Samuel Gould House, 31 Elm Street — 1887

One of the finest examples of Queen Anne residential architecture in Maine, this handsome house was built by Samuel Gould, a prominent local attorney. Gould served one term in the U.S. House of Representatives and was an unsuccessful Democratic candidate for governor of Maine. He also ran the Oxford Hotel for twenty years. This well-preserved home is of 2½-story brick and frame construction, with a gabled roof, three ornate internal brick chimneys, a corner tower, and shingle siding.

SOLON

Evergreens Site — Prehistoric

The Evergreens site occupies 400 meters of riverbank on a flat, shady terrace at the bend in the Kennebec River 110 kilometers upstream from the head-of-tide at Augusta. An extensive collection from the site has been made by the landowner and by test excavations run by the Maine State Museum. The site seems to have been occupied for at least the last four thousand years; however, there are many stone-point styles in the collection that do not have recognizable counterparts in New England. Many of the stone raw materials used at the site are also exotic to the state of Maine.

The large area of the site and the frequent preservation of hearths and other subsurface features offer excellent opportunities to recover those rare point styles in association with other artifacts and radiocarbon dates. Many of the stone raw materials that do not occur in Maine probably originate in the St. Lawrence drainage, so the site contains evidence of cultural contact and canoe travel between the lower Kennebec River and the Bas Saint-Laurent via the classic Rivière Chaudière route.

South Solon Meeting House, U.S. Route 201 — 1842

This remarkably well-preserved church is an extremely early structure for its location and retains virtually all its original external and internal features. The interior is distinguished by frescoes done between 1952 and 1957 by nationally known artists attached to the prestigious Skowhegan School of Painting and Sculpture.

TURNER

Turner Town House, Route 117, Turner Center — 1831

One of the older town houses in Maine, having been in continuous use since its construction until very recently, this building is also of unusual interior design and has a history of strange and amusing political strife. Inside the structure, benches in tiers descend from either end to a large cast iron stove. The only known structure with a similar arrangement is the Wayne Town House, but there the seats descend from either side. When the Turner Town House was built, there was an acrimonious debate between the Center and the newer part of the town, called the Village, as to its location. In spite of the final decision taken by vote, members of the two factions alternately and surreptitiously disassembled it (it was fastened with pegs) and moved it to a preferred location *three* times before it came to its final resting place and was spiked together!

VASSALBORO

The River Meeting House, Route 201 — 1786, 1895

The frame of the main part of this structure is the original meeting house built in 1786 by a group of Quakers known as the River Meeting. They founded the Oak Grove School, and in 1895 the old building was completely remodeled in the Shingle Style, including the addition of a tower and porch. It is now the chapel for the Oak Grove–Coburn School.

East Vassalboro Grist and Saw Mill, Route 32 — 1798, ca. 1805

Still used as a sawmill, this complex may well be the oldest mill site in Maine continuously operating in its original buildings. The sawmill was built by John Getchell about three hundred feet from its present location. In 1805 the building was moved across from a gristmill that Jabez Dow has just erected. Herman Masse bought the sawmill in 1929. In 1948 the gristmill housed the pumping facilities of the East Vassalboro Water System, which Masse also owned. Mr. Masse and his son continue to operate the sawmill, which now has modern equipment but still relies entirely on water as a source of power.

VIENNA

Klir Beck House, off Route 41 — 1927

Set in an area of woodland and lakes, this unique example of early-twentieth-century eclectic architecture was designed by its owner Klir Beck, a man of broad artistic talent and skilled in a variety of crafts. Beck, although reticent and retiring by nature, was esteemed highly within his professional circle as both an artist and naturalist. Perhaps best-known among his works are the dioramas depicting Maine's flora and fauna in the old state museum.

WATERVILLE

Redington House, 64 Silver Street — 1814

Asa Redington, a soldier in the Revolution and corporal in the Commander-in-Chief's Guard, was a pioneer settler in Waterville in 1792. He became a prosperous merchant and built this rural Federal house for his son, Silas. It is now a museum and headquarters of the Waterville Historical Society.

First Baptist Church, Park and Elm Streets — 1826

The original dimensions of this impressive structure were retained, but external and internal details were dramatically altered in 1875 by the distinguished Portland architect, Francis H. Fassett. As a result, the present structure represents a combination of styles ranging from the neo-Classical to the High Victorian. Despite this mélange, the present building achieves a remarkable textural unity and rational design.

Universalist-Unitarian Church,
Silver and Elm Streets — 1832

This is an interesting example of a late Federal-style meeting house of excellent proportions with early elements of the Gothic Revival incorporated in the design. Universalism was introduced in Maine in 1802 by Thomas Barnes, a traveling minister from New Hampshire. By 1826, a congregation was organized in Waterville and five years later this handsome and well-sited church was built.

Waterville Opera House, Castonguay Square — 1897–1902

The Waterville Opera House is an unusually well preserved Colonial Revival theater, which continues its original function as a facility for theatrical productions by both visiting and local companies, as well as for other civic events. It remains as a rare holdover from the pre-motion-picture era when nearly every community of any significant size maintained a theater, or "opera house," for live entertainment. Of further interest is the fact that it was built as part of a municipal "complex" housing the city offices in the same structure, a typical late-nineteenth-century trend.

Touring companies, individual artists, and local performers have appeared in the auditorium. Although it was used largely for movies between World War II and 1960, it has since reverted to its original use.

A.O. Lombard House, 65 Elm Street — 1908

One of Maine's nearly forgotten geniuses, A.O. Lombard was a prolific inventor best remembered for the caterpillar tread that he incorporated in the Lombard Steam Log Hauler, a revolutionary development in lumber harvesting. Born in 1856, Alvin began inventing things as a child. This bent later dovetailed with his career in lumbering. He designed his own sawmill, created the first turbine water wheel control, invented a bark stripper, a knot separator, a pulp crusher, and a steam-driven automobile. His Elm Street house, built at the peak of his success, is a large and impressive Shingle–Style residence in central Waterville.

Waterville Post Office, Main and Elm Streets — 1911

Designed in the latter-day tradition of Greek Revival public architecture by the Treasury Department architect, James Knox Taylor, this structure is cleverly arranged to fit its location at the intersection of two streets at an acute angle. The building was clearly inspired by William Strickland's Philadelphia Exchange of between 1832 and 1834.

Professional Building, 177 and 179 Main Street — 1923

This distinctive commercial structure, designed by Miller and Mayo of Portland, is a rare example of a very early Art Deco impulse in architecture. The four-story block is built of concrete and steel. Entrances on both facades are surmounted by low arches with elaborate low reliefs and shields. At the time of construction it was the largest structure in Waterville. Described in the press as "the finest of Waterville office buildings," it remains an outstanding landmark in the city's downtown area.

WATERVILLE-WINSLOW

Two Cent Bridge, Temple Street — 1903

This small, steel suspension-type bridge was built in 1903 and is the last private toll footbridge in the United States. A structural rarity, the 700-foot-long bridge has also proved a godsend in times when other bridges were washed out and it was the only link between Winslow and the food and health services in Waterville.

WAYNE

Wayne Town House, Route 133 — 1840

This structure, one of few in original condition, is a representative example of a public building type popular in rural Maine during the first half of the nineteenth century. The interior features rows of benches facing each other on sloping floor originally to segregate the men from the women (who could not vote).

WINSLOW

Fort Halifax Blockhouse, U.S. Route 201 — 1759 (NHL)

A National Historic Landmark, the Fort Halifax blockhouse, built in 1754, is the oldest surviving such structure in the United States. It was constructed by Isaac Isley of Portland and Gershom Flagg of Boston under orders from Royal Governor William Shirley and the General Court of Massachusetts.

Designed to block a major French and Indian interior artery at the junction of the Kennebec and Sebastacook Rivers, Fort Halifax was originally designed as a large, four-pointed-star fort of wood, containing four small barrack-blocks and a central blockhouse. This design, however, was seen as requiring far too large a garrison for defense, so a different arrangement was built.

The final design was typical of eighteenth-century Kennebec Valley forts. A square palisade contained two diagonally opposed, 2-story blockhouses, as well as a long narrow barrack-block and a rectangular officers' quarters.

Like Fort Western, Fort Halifax was an important point of rendezvous for the various military units commanded by

Fort Halifax Blockhouse, Winslow

Benedict Arnold in his invasion of Quebec in 1775. Today, only the blockhouse adjacent to the river bank survives from this most northerly of Anglo-American Kennebec forts. This historic structure is administered for the public as a memorial by the Maine Bureau of Parks and Recreation.

The Brick School, Cushman Road — ca. 1810

This humble but well-preserved structure is important as a survival of early educational institutions in the Kennebec Valley. Its sturdy construction reflects the determination in the region to provide public education on a permanent basis.

Shurtleff House, U.S. Route 201 — 1850–53

This is an excellent example of an American Gothic Revival cottage of the mid-nineteenth century; it was probably the creation of a rural builder who made his own interpretation of the published sources of the period. The interior of the house was executed in the simplest Greek Revival manner; the exterior, while Gothic for the most part, does include many Greek Revival features. The result of this combination of styles is as engaging as the more traditionally designed cottages found in urban areas.

Shrewsbury Round Barn, 109 Benton Avenue — 1913

The Round Barn of Winslow is a remarkable structure. Its footings, ground floor, and silo are of concrete, while the walls and roof are of frame construction with intricate wooden trusswork. The most distinctive element of the design is the central position of the silo, which facilitates transport of the sileage to all parts of the barn.

The building was the brainchild of James N.Dean. It was finally constructed in 1913 after extensive experimentation. The barn is unique in Maine agricultural architecture, and received much public attention at the time of its construction.

WINTHROP

John Lund Site — Prehistoric

The John Lund site is located on an island in the middle of Cobbosseecontee Lake. It is very small, clinging to a flat, silty terrace just above the present water's edge. This site is the first in Maine to contain exclusively Middle Archaic–age material, dating between eight thousand and six thousand years ago. Thus, this is the only site where we can study the full range of stone tool manufacture of the period without interference from the detritus of later peoples.

Moreover, the site preserves foodbone fragments, which give us the first glimpse of how Middle Archaic people made their living. Apparently, the site was used only during the warm season of the year, and subsistence activities were highly diversified: trapping or hunting beaver, muskrat, and other furbearers was very important. Deer and bear hunting occurred, and there was some effort to hunt waterfowl, such as loons.

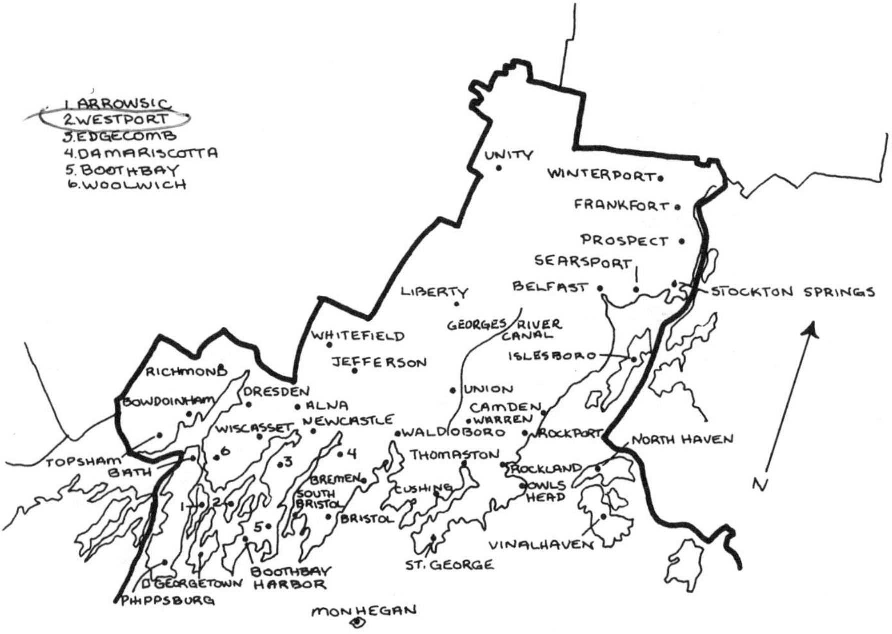
1. ARROWSIC
2. WESTPORT
3. EDGECOMB
4. DAMARISCOTTA
5. BOOTHBAY
6. WOOLWICH
UNITY
WINTERPORT
FRANKFORT
PROSPECT
SEARSPORT
BELFAST
STOCKTON SPRINGS
LIBERTY
GEORGES RIVER CANAL
WHITEFIELD
JEFFERSON
ISLESBORO
RICHMOND
DRESDEN
UNION
BOWDOINHAM
ALNA
CAMDEN
WARREN
WISCASSET
NEWCASTLE
WALDOBORO
ROCKPORT
NORTH HAVEN
TOPSHAM
BATH
THOMASTON
ROCKLAND
BREMEN
CUSHING
OWLS HEAD
SOUTH BRISTOL
BRISTOL
VINALHAVEN
ST. GEORGE
GEORGETOWN
BOOTHBAY HARBOR
PHIPPSBURG
MONHEGAN
N

Mid-Coastal Region

ALNA

Head Tide Historic District

The village of Head Tide began to develop as a mill community in the mid eighteenth century because of its excellent location on the Sheepscot River. From before the Revolution through the first half of the twentieth century, the river's water power was harnessed for sawmills, gristmills, a stave mill, a shingle mill, a planing mill, a carding mill, and a fulling mill.

By the early nineteenth century, the village of Head Tide held the major concentration of mills in Alna.

Head Tide's growing influence in Alna became apparent in the 1830s, when three-fourths of the town's church services were transferred to the new Head Tide Church completed in 1838. After 1868, most of the town's services were held there.

Head Tide Historic District, Alna

Head Tide Church, Alna

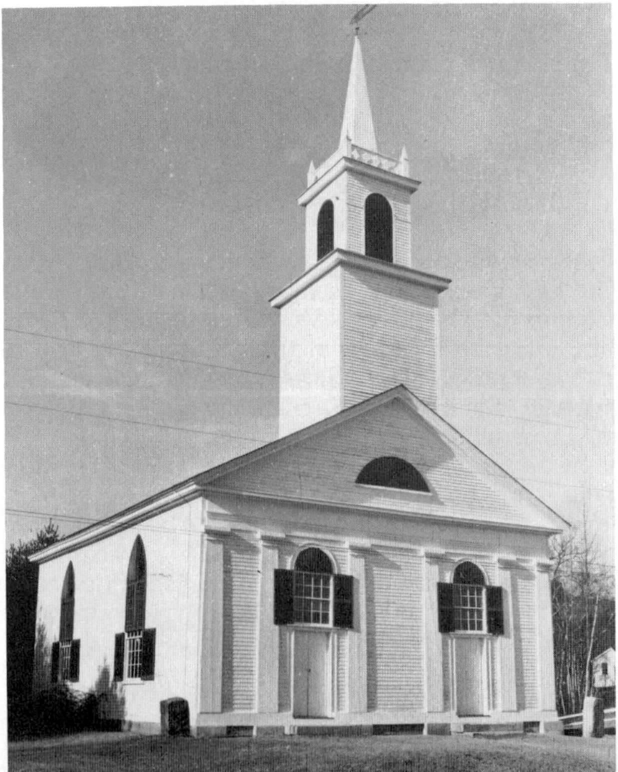

By the late nineteenth century, however, the rural economy that had supported Head Tide for almost a century and a half began to change. When a freshet in 1896 destroyed the mills on the north side of the river, they were not rebuilt. In 1924, a fire leveled the mills on the river's south bank. Of these, only one gristmill was replaced, and this was destroyed by fire twenty-five years later.

Today the tangible remains of Head Tide's more than two centuries of history are its fourteen fine eighteenth- and nineteenth-century homes and buildings as well as its beautiful natural setting. Among these dwellings is the birthplace of the celebrated poet, Edward Arlington Robinson. The structures are characteristic of rural Maine architecture in the forthright simplicity of their design. With the exception of the now-vanished mills, these buildings are representative of the basic elements of an old Maine village: dwellings ranging from a humble Cape to the parsonage, a store, a stable, a school, and a church. The current residents fully appreciate the manmade and natural assets of Head Tide, and they have worked individually and collectively to maintain the special character of their community. The result has been the preservation of one of the most authentic village settings to survive from Maine's past.

Alna Meeting House, Route 218 — 1789

Built in 1789, this building, a splendid example of Colonial architecture, was used only until 1876. Since then other churches have replaced this Congregational meeting house. The interior of the building is as austere as its exterior, with wooden seated box pews, an adjustable high pulpit (to make any pastor a perfect fit), and the infamous "Deacon's bench."

Alna Schoolhouse, Route 218 — 1795

The Alna School is a small square building with a low hipped roof topped by a delicate Federal-style octagonal cupola. This cupola, which is of a slightly later date than the rest of the building, is the school's most distinctive feature. It adds an architectural quality to the small building and is well scaled to the school's simple proportions.

This small frame structure, built in 1795, is the second oldest surviving one-room schoolhouse in Maine, the only earlier one being in York.

Alna Schoolhouse. Photo by Ivan Flye.

ARROWSIC

Clarke and Lake Company, Archaeological Site — ca. 1650–76

In 1654, two prosperous Boston merchants, Thomas Clarke and Thomas Lake, established a remarkable commercial enterprise on Arrowsic Island, across the Kennebec River from today's city of Bath. The company quickly constructed and controlled a fortified headquarters/trading post, foundry, shipyard, mills, and outlying farms.

For a generation this complex thrived, until in August 1676 it was attacked by Indians and burned to the ground, with thirty people killed or captured.

To this day, the Clarke and Lake Company is a series of cellar holes and depressions representing prosperity and tragedy. Archaeological excavations in the charred remains have yielded a wide range of artifacts of high quality, indicating a high standard of living for successful merchants and tradesmen in early colonial Maine.

BATH

Bath Historic District

Historically, the residential area of the City of Bath was divided into the North End and the South End, with the compact business district in the center. The South End is the older section and contains an abundance of dignified representatives of early-nineteenth-century architecture. It was in the North End, however, that Bath's prosperous shipbuilders chose to build their new homes. This area abounds in significant architecture encompassing the whole nineteenth century. Together with a part of the commercial district that retains its nineteenth-century flavor, this North End makes up the Bath Historic District.

Bath, named for Bath, England, began as an offshoot from the earlier settlements on Georgetown and Arrowsic islands. The area, called Long Reach, came under the jurisdiction of several companies of proprietors, but during the Indian Wars was protected by none. Finally, in 1753, it was designated the Second Parish of Georgetown; then, in 1781, it was incorporated as Bath in the District of Maine.

In 1800, when William King, later Maine's first governor, established his shipyard, wharf, and store in Bath, there were already shipyards both north and south on the river bank. A lively trade with the West Indies and the East

Bath Historic District

Swedenborgian Church, Bath Historic District

Coast, and a cotton-carrying trade with New Orleans and Europe grew up, and, even with the Embargo of 1807 and the War of 1812, Bath's shipyards continued to prosper. They lined the waterfront from one end of town to the other and turned out ships that sailed throughout the world. When other yards began to decline in the 1890s, Bath Iron Works took the lead in local production. With its almost 400-year history of shipbuilding (the first vessel was launched by the Popham colonists in 1607), Bath can fairly be called the oldest continuously active shipbuilding center in America.

The peak of Bath's prosperity came between the 1820s and the 1890s, when shipbuilding and industries allied to it flourished. Many of the lovely homes and churches were built during this period, and the business district developed an urban flavor. Greek Revival, Gothic Revival, and Italianate houses were constructed in the 1840s and 1850s, while one Shingle-Style residence, erected in 1898, rose at the end of the period. Greek and Gothic Revival churches and business blocks, along with the Italianate U.S. Custom House and the County Courthouse, are all representatives of Bath's mid-nineteenth-century economic success.

Governor William King House, Whiskeag Road — ca. 1812

This remarkable stone farmhouse was built by Maine's first governor between 1809 and 1812 on Whiskeag Road, about two miles north of the center of Bath. It is the earliest known example of Gothic Revival architecture in Maine and one of the earliest in New England. It was part of a working farm, including an orchard of 500 trees, the produce from which was shipped in the several vessels owned by Governor King, who lived in a large home in Bath proper.

Winter Street Church, Washington Street — 1843

The Winter Street Church is a striking Gothic Revival edifice that dominates Bath's city park. Erected in 1843, it is the work of Anthony C. Raymond, a local master builder active in the community from about 1835 to 1875. Congregationalists built this church, which is ranked as one of the major interpretations of American Gothic Revival architecture surviving in New England.

Winter Street Church, Bath

Anthony C. Raymond, a native of Brunswick, learned carpentry and joinery early in life and worked on some of the first structures at Bowdoin College. He became a master builder in Bath, and by 1861 he was referred to as a "house architect." Raymond continued his career until, at age 77, he was partially paralyzed by a fall from a building in 1875.

The Winter Street Church, dedicated on February 1, 1844, became the religious home for many shipbuilders, owners, captains, and their families. The church proved so popular that in 1848 its seating capacity had to be enlarged. The interior, especially the altar area, was remodeled in 1890 under the supervision of John Calvin Stevens of Portland.

W.D. Crooker House, 71 South Street — ca. 1850

Designed and built by Isaac D. Cole, noted housewright and mentor of Francis H. Fassett, this handsome residence is a dignified and architecturally rare example of the Greek Revival style. Whereas most temple-style dwellings in Maine feature a colonnaded portico across the gable end, the Crooker House portico runs parallel to the roof ridge and carries an ornate second-story cast-iron porch in the central bay between the columns. The house, as the residence of William Donnell Crooker, a highly successful merchant-shipbuilder, reflects the burgeoning prosperity of mid-nineteenth-century Bath.

U.S. Custom House and Post Office, Front Street — 1858

The United States Custom House and Post Office in Bath was designed by Ammi Burnham Young, who was supervising architect of the Treasury Department from 1852 to 1861. Stylistically a prime example of the Italianate Renaissance Revival, the structure was completed and occupied in 1858. It represents Young's work at its best.

The first custom house in Bath owned by the United States was secured in 1834, but the property was sold in 1858. Until 1975, the present building fulfilled its original function. After being declared surplus property in 1975, the Custom House was purchased by the city of Bath and was restored to nearly original condition. Law offices, shops, and a district court now occupy the building.

U.S. Custom House and Post Office, Bath

Tugboat *Seguin,* Percy and Small Shipyard — 1884

The steam tug *Seguin,* a familiar sight during the heyday of shipping on the Kennebec in the late 1880s and early 1900s,

Tugboat Seguin, *Bath*

will be seen sailing up and down the river again when its restoration is completed. Launched in 1884 at the B.W. and H.F. Morse shipyard, the *Seguin* is now the oldest steam vessel under U.S. registry. She is being restored at the Percy and Small shipyard, which belongs to the Maine Maritime Museum.

While active, the *Seguin* towed hundreds of ice-laden schooners, sometimes four or five at a time, from the dozens of icehouses stretching from Richmond to Gardiner. The vessels were taken out past Seguin Island at the river's mouth to begin their voyages under sail. Another major chore for the *Seguin* was towing coal barges bringing fuel to industries and homes along the upper tidal sections of the river. The *Seguin* also towed cargoes as far south as Norfolk, Virginia, as well as tending oil tankers and destroyers.

The vessel, now being accurately restored, will eventually serve as a floating museum cruising the coastal waters where so much of her working life was spent.

Percy and Small Shipyard, 451 Washington Street — 1894

The city of Bath has long been associated with the shipbuilding industry. As early as 1607, the Popham colonists built the 30-ton *Virginia*, the first English vessel built in America. In 1762, Bath's first commercial shipyard was opened. After the Revolutionary period, local maritime activities expanded rapidly, making Bath fifth in the nation in the shipping industry. By 1857, over five hundred ships were operating out of the Bath customs district. After the Civil War, with the decline in world trade, the schooner came into its own because of its ability to maneuver along the coast.

The Percy and Small Shipyard was involved in building forty-four vessels between 1894 and 1920, forty-two of which were schooners. The yard earned a reputation as one of the finest producers of wooden sailing craft. The owners, Captain Samuel R. Percy and Frank A. Small, specialized in the construction of large schooners for the coastal trade. The most famous of these was the 329-foot *Wyoming*, built in 1909, the largest American wooden vessel ever built.

The Bath shipbuilding tradition has been carried over to the present time by the Bath Iron Works shipyard. Percy and Small, now owned and operated by the Maine Maritime Museum, is possibly the only wood shipbuilding yard that built large merchant vessels still existing in this country.

Percy and Small Shipyard, Bath, 1909

Hyde Mansion, 616 High Street — 1913

Built in 1913 from designs by John Calvin Stevens, Maine's most prominent turn-of-the-century architect, the Hyde Mansion (or "Elmhurst," as its first owner called it) is a dramatic example of Colonial Revival architecture. John Sedgewick Hyde, son of the founder of the famous Bath Iron Works shipbuilding facility, had the ambitious country house built on the site of an earlier "Elmhurst" erected by his grandfather Zina Hyde on the 160-acre estate seventy years earlier. The interior of the mansion is in keeping with its neo-Georgian exterior, with rich detail everywhere.

John S. Hyde purchased Bath Iron Works in 1905 and restored the struggling company to its former position of esteem in the shipbuilding world. B.I.W.'s success continued after Hyde's death in 1917. During both world wars numerous naval vessels were constructed, and in the 1920s private yachts, including J.P. Morgan's *Corsair*, were built. In the Depression years, B.I.W. constructed fishing vessels, Coast

Guard patrol boats, and, most notably, the *Ranger*, the 1937 America's Cup Defender.

"Elmhurst," now the home of the Hyde School, a secondary preparatory institution, stands as a monument to the success of its builder, John S. Hyde.

BELFAST

Belfast Commercial Historic District

The Belfast Commercial Historic District is comprised of forty-seven architecturally significant buildings, primarily commercial in nature and spanning a period from 1823 to 1909. The district is a cohesive grouping covering two blocks on both sides of Belfast's Main Street as well as entering side streets. All major styles of the period are represented, as is the work of several important architects.

Masonic Temple, Belfast

With the possible exception of Portland's Waterfront Historic District, no other such uninterrupted concentration of worthy nineteenth-century commercial structures exists in Maine. This rare grouping, with the exception of some modern veneer, appears essentially as it did at the end of the last century. The middle to late nineteenth century saw Belfast's heyday as a bustling seaport with a thriving shipping and shipbuilding industry.

Although two major fires ravaged the city in 1865 and 1873, the commercial area was in both cases only partially destroyed, leaving buildings from all earlier periods.

The prosperity of nineteenth-century Belfast, as reflected by the architecture of the commercial area, is also attested to by the distinguished list of architects whose designs are represented in the district. Buildings by the best-known among these include the Waldo County Court House, 1853, and the City Block, 1850, by Benjamin S. Dean; the Post Office and Custom House, 1855–56, by treasury architect Ammi B. Young; the Masonic Temple, 1877–78, and the Belfast National Bank, 1878–79, by George M. Harding; the Odd Fellows Block, 1888, by Wilfred E. Mansur; and Memorial Hall, 1889, by John C. Spofford.

The bustling energy of the port of Belfast in the later nineteenth century still finds expression in this handsome grouping of commerical structures.

Church Street Historic District

Church Street Historic District is a remarkably unchanged residential section reflecting the economic prosperity which the city of Belfast experienced during the first three quarters of the nineteenth century. With almost all the buildings built in one of three successive styles — Federal, Greek Revival and Italianate — the district achieves an architectural unity and scale expressive of the period, as well as an ambiance of comfortable security.

The First Church of Belfast, a beautiful Federal structure located at the north end of the district, recalls the emergence of Belfast as a thriving seaport in the years following the end of the War of 1812.

Throughout the district are homes built by sea captains, shipbuilders, industrialists, and businessmen, all of whom rode the wave of Belfast's nineteenth-century prosperity. Standing at the extreme southern end of the district is the

William H. Burrell House, Church Street Historic District, Belfast. Photo by Arvin Robinson

Joseph P. Williamson House, Church Street Historic District, Belfast

1840 James P. White House, a magnificent and highly sophisticated Greek Revival interpretation by architect Calvin Ryder.

Little changed since the 1870s, the Church Street Historic District conveys today a remarkable picture of affluence and security in an atmosphere of nineteenth-century grace and dignity.

Primrose Hill Historic District

The development of that area of Belfast known as Primrose Hill began shortly after High Street was laid out and named in 1805. Primrose Hill was the site selected by the leading men of Belfast for their houses. This development reflected the growing economic prosperity of Belfast as it emerged as a bustling seaport in the first quarter of the nineteenth century. A stopping place for people and goods from several directions, Belfast felt the tread of immigrants from the Maritimes, lumber dealers from Bangor, and merchants from Boston as she sent her own vessels out to capture a part of the coasting trade.

Like Broadway in Bangor or Washington Street in Bath, Primrose Hill was a spot where the upper crust looked out over its domain after weighing, measuring and directing it during business hours.

Taken as a unit, the buildings visually define the meaning of an historic district in giving the viewer a sense of time and

Primrose Hill Historic District, Belfast

place. The architecture of Primrose Hill in its natural surroundings reveals not only the architectural tastes of weathy Maine citizens in the first half of the nineteenth century but also their commercial and psychological connection with the sea.

Black Horse Tavern, U.S. Route 1—ca. 1795

This sturdy Cape, built by Jerome Stephenson for his wife and fourteen children, served also as the first tavern on the east side of the Passagassawakeag River in Belfast. In 1800 Stephenson converted part of his home into a public house. After the death of the original proprietor the business was carried on by his son and grandson until about 1852.

The interior is in a remarkable state of preservation and the original tavern sign survives. In the left front room the wainscoting consists of single knotless pine boards measuring 25 inches wide. Both front rooms have original fireplaces, mantels, and paneling. Partitions in the rear of the building consist simply of vertical boards, adze-finished.

The First Church of Belfast, Church Street—1818

Belfast was founded originally by Scotch-Irish Presbyterians who came in 1770 from Londonderry, New Hampshire, and settled on a tract of land purchased from the heirs of General Samuel Waldo. The settlers, however, soon suffered unusual hardships as a result of the American Revolution. Their homes and crops were burned and laid waste, and they themselves were obliged to flee for safety. At the conclusion of the war, resettlement took place and a large number of new people arrived, mostly of the Congregationalist denomination. In 1796, a church council, comprised of ministers from the neighboring towns of Bristol, Warren, Penobscot, and Hallowell, was called for the purpose of organizing a church for the town. On December 29, The First Church of Belfast, Maine, was formally organized, consisting of seven members.

After some initial dissension, the parish began to thrive and by 1818 had decided to erect a larger building. Started on June 13, the frame building was ready for use, though still unfinished, in five months. The dedication took place on November 15, 1818.

First Church of Belfast. Photo by Arvin Robinson.

Since its completion the church has remained virtually unchanged externally, except for the installation of the clock that was placed in the belfry in 1836. The present organ, a Stevens tracker instrument, was bought in 1848 and is considered to be a fine example of organ-building of its time.

The First Church of Belfast is a distinguished Federal-style church closely linked with the city during most of its history.

James P. White House, 1 Church Street—1840

The James P. White House is recognized by architectural historians as one of the most sophisticated examples of the

James P. White House, Belfast. Photo by Richard Cheek.

Greek Revival style in New England. Designed by Calvin A. Ryder in 1840, this home of one of Belfast's leading businessmen is an impressive and unique building. Ryder did not use the typical temple style in planning the James P. White House; instead, he developed Greek Revival details and created a variation on the Greek theme that is unsurpassed in Maine.

Ryder, born in Orrington, Maine, designed many great homes in Belfast, Bangor, and the surrounding communities before moving to Boston in the mid nineteenth century. When all of his work has been documented, Ryder will rank as one of nineteenth-century Maine's leading architects, possibly the best interpreter in Maine of the Greek Revival style.

Hayford Block, 47 Church Street — 1866, 1869

The Hayford Block of 1866, with its addition of 1869, was constructed on the heels of the disastrous fire of 1865. A handsome transitional Greek Revival–Italianate structure including within it a large opera house, this building clearly shows the determination of Belfast to build a new and better city out of the ashes of the old.

Masonic Temple, High Street — 1878

In 1875, the Belfast Masonic Hall burned, but by 1878 construction of the new temple was under way. The large, elaborately decorated, 3½-story, brick building was designed in the High Victorian Gothic style by George M. Harding. Israel Parker was the builder and Charles Bray, the master of brickwork.

Belfast National Bank, Main Street — 1878–79

The Belfast National Bank is one of the finest and most elaborately decorated commercial buildings surviving in the state of Maine. Roughly triangular in shape, this unusual structure was erected between 1878 and 1879 from designs by George M. Harding. Israel Wood Parker was the

Belfast National Bank

master builder. Parker and Harding had collaborated earlier to erect Belfast's Masonic Hall between 1877 and 1878.

This superb piece of High Victorian Gothic commercial architecture is located in the midst of many other early- and late-nineteenth-century commercial buildings in Belfast. This grouping represents the economic growth of a city that grew up as a seaport in the heyday of Maine's commercial power and importance.

BOOTHBAY

Knight-Corey House, Corey Lane — 1784

The Knight-Corey house was erected by Nicholas Knight in 1784 on the site of an inn built by John Murray, a very prominent early resident of the region. This lovely example of an eighteenth-century house is in an excellent state of preservation and features among other things gunstock posts, five working fireplaces (including the original kitchen fireplace with its 12-foot hearth), and a unique and beautiful enclosed circular stairway. This early Federal house is an out-

Knight-Corey House, Boothbay

standing feature of the Bristol peninsula on the central Maine coast.

The entire house, ell, and large attached barn are occupied by the Boothbay Theatre Museum, which, at the time of this writing, is the only museum in the country devoted solely to the exhibition and preservation of theatrical memorabilia. Its holdings from the late Middle Ages to the present include stage jewelry, costumes, portraits, photographs, sculpture, playbills, figurines, holograph material, set models, and toy theaters. The extent and importance of the museum holdings are nationally recognized.

BOOTHBAY HARBOR

Damariscove Island Archaeological Site, Boothbay Harbor — 1620–77

In 1614, Captain John Smith of Jamestown identified anchorages and harbors along the Maine coast that would be suitable as locations for permanent fishing stations: "Monahigan [Monhegan] is a round high isle; and close by it, Monanis [Manana], betwixt which is a small harbor where we ride. In Damerils isles is such another [harbor]."

The name "Damerils Isles" may have derived from Humphrey Damerell, a shadowy fisherman and fur trader who was engaged in seasonal business at that time. Not long after Smith's voyage in 1614, Damariscove Island was certainly being used as a spring fishing station. In May of 1622, agents from the Plymouth Colony desperately sought food for their starving settlement from these very fishermen, and the Damariscovers gladly supplied provisions from their ships.

That same summer saw the establishment of the first successful permanent settlement on the Maine coast. Thirteen men, sponsored by Sir Ferdinando Gorges (the father of English colonial Maine), "fortified themselves with a strong palisado of spruce trees of some 10 foote high, haveing besides their small shott, one peece of ordinance and some 10 good dogs." A permanent fishing station had been founded that would flourish through the seventeenth century.

Damariscove's harbor, some sixteen hundred feet long and two hundred to three hundred feet wide, provided a safe haven during the early Indian Wars (1676–1700). Although all but abandoned in the eighteenth century, in the nineteenth and early twentieth centuries the island had a strong agricultural economy. Today Damariscove Island is owned by the Nature Conservancy as a preserve for wildlife and history. Recent archaeological excavations have uncovered artifacts from the earliest period of occupation, which represents the beginning of successful European colonization in Maine.

Burnt Island Light Station, Boothbay Harbor — 1821

This relatively early navigational beacon is an important guide for mariners entering Boothbay Harbor from the west or east. The light tower and all the major adjunct structures date from the original construction as ordered by President Monroe.

Boothbay Harbor Memorial Library, Oak Street — 1842

Originally designed as a private home, this beautifully proportioned, Greek Revival, temple-style structure was built by Cyrus McKown, an important mid-century local figure whose interests were largely in shipping and shipbuilding. The town acquired the building in 1923 from the heirs of Chapman Reed, who had purchased the house from McKown.

BOWDOINHAM

Cornish House, Main Street — 1885

There is probably no more ornate example of "gingerbread" decorative detail on any other Italianate house in Maine. George Curtis of Bowdoin was the designer of this delightful flight of fancy.

BREMEN

Daniel Weston Homestead, Route 32 — ca. 1806

Built by the son of pioneer settler Arunah Weston, this handsome and generous vernacular Federal house reflects in its construction the techniques of the shipwright, the craft of its builder. Its ties with the early history of Bremen make it an important local landmark.

BRISTOL

The Nahanada Village Site — Prehistoric–1650 (?)

The Nahanada site is a coastal Indian encampment near Pemaquid, but it is unusual in that it is not a shell midden. The campsite has been used sporadically for about the last two thousand years, but the major occupation at the site is from the period of European exploration.

More than ninety-five percent of the cultural material at the site and all of the foodbone debris date from about A.D. 1600. Even by that time, the Indians of Maine's coast were heavily involved in trade with Europeans.

Cultural material at the site includes European nails, glass trade beads, European tobacco pipes dating before 1625, and pig and cattle bones probably representing trade in foodstuffs. Stone material flaked into tools with an aboriginal technology is also common in the historic component, although the Indians had already begun to adopt much European technology, as shown by some native Maine felsite flaked into gunflints, as well as the flaking of European flint ship's ballast.

The site appears to have been occupied seasonally during the warm months of the year, with subsistence based upon deerhunting and fishing for species including striped bass.

It is very probable that the site is the location of Nahanada's village, visited by the Popham colonists in 1607.

Colonial Pemaquid Archaeological District, Pemaquid — 1625

Pemaquid, as a name, was first recorded by the Popham colonists of 1607, when the place was inhabited by Indians who eagerly traded with the English newcomers. So was it in 1614 when John Smith explored the area and in 1623 when Christopher Levett was sailing in the mid-coastal region.

Archaeological excavations at Colonial Pemaquid (Bristol)

Although during those years occasional fishermen may have made seasonal use of Pemaquid Harbor and New Harbor, the first permanent settlement was founded much later than many have thought: "Westward from Penobscot . . . fourteen Leagues of[f] is Pemaquid, in which River Alderman Alworth of Bristole (England) setled a Company of People in the year 1625, which Plantation hath continued and many Families are now settled there." This according to Samuel Maverick, writing in 1660.

The first years of settlement at Pemaquid must have been grim. A bitter episode occured in 1632, when an English pirate raided the village for its valuables. And three years later, the Bristol merchantman *Angel Gabriel* sank in a hurricane at Pemaquid, taking with it all of the possessions of newly arrived immigrants.

During the middle decades of the seventeenth century, however, Pemaquid thrived as a village and port, with a custom house, tavern, and many dwellings. Beginning in

1676, though, wars with the Indians and their French allies devastated the community repeatedly (1676, 1689, 1696). Fort after fort was built on the mouth of Pemaquid Harbor in a vain effort to defend England's northeasternmost colonial outpost.

Archaeological excavations since 1965 have uncovered the fragile and burnt traces of this early and very important English settlement, the history of which reflects the ebb and flow of European wars and their effect upon colonies far from their mother countries.

Fort William Henry (replica), Pemaquid — 1692–96 (1908)

In 1676, the important English village at Pemaquid, lacking any fortification, had to be quickly evacuated and was destroyed in the first of nearly a century of Indian Wars. A year later a wooden fort, Fort Charles, arose as the settlement was reoccupied. However, a surprise attack in 1689 once again destroyed Pemaquid.

Fort William Henry, Pemaquid (Bristol)

Three years later one of the first stone forts in New England was built at Pemaquid and named Fort William Henry. Sir William Phipps, the first royal governor of Massachusetts, was the chief proponent of the construction, which cost the huge sum of £20,000. Sir William wrote that "the fort is strong enough to resist all the Indians in America." How wrong he was! In 1696, the French and Indians accepted its surrender and razed it.

In 1729, yet another stone fort, Fort Frederick, was built on the same site, part of a scheme to resettle Pemaquid in the waning years of the Indian Wars. This fortification was leveled by local residents in 1775 to deprive the British of its use against them in the Revolution.

Since 1974 archaeological excavations have been conducted on the site of Forts William Henry and Frederick, uncovering the officers' quarters of two periods. The site, administered by the Maine Bureau of Parks and Recreation, is open to the public as a memorial to the struggles of the early colonial period.

Harrington Meeting House, Old Harrington Road — 1775

The frame of this building was constructed in 1772, then taken down, and reassembled in 1775. It was moved and remodeled in the 1840s. In the 1960s it was restored to the appearance of the eighteenth-century meeting house with box pews. The balcony was left empty so that the building could be used as a museum.

CAMDEN

The Conway House, Conway Road — ca. 1770

This late-eighteenth-century, Cape Cod–style farmhouse is one of the oldest in the region. Of simple rural construction, the house contains many original features, such as a bake oven built with small bricks, cellar beams still with their bark covering, hand-split laths, hand-hewn beams and sills, and the four light transoms over the front door. Also on the property are a late-eighteenth-century barn filled with carriages and farm tools and a fully equipped blacksmith shop.

Curtis Island Light, Camden Harbor — 1836, rebuilt 1896

Constructed in 1836 and rebuilt in 1896, Negro Island Light was renamed in honor of philanthropist Cyrus Curtis in 1934. The island serves as a natural breakwater for Camden Harbor and as a signal station and picnic spot for boaters. The light tower and power station were built of brick, while the keeper's house and toolshed are of wood. The light is automated at this time.

"Norumbega," High Street — 1886–87

"Norumbega" is one of the great late-nineteenth-century villas of the Maine coast. Erected by Joseph B. Stearns, it was built between 1886 and 1887 from plans by Arthur Bates Jennings, a New York architect. It was designed in the popular Queen Anne style of the 1880s, carried out in rubble stone and wood, with its emphasis on picturesque effect and varied surface treatments. Both the exterior and interior of "Norumbega" have survived in an excellent state of preservation, the elegance for which the grand coastal "cottages" of the late nineteenth century strove.

The life story of Joseph B. Stearns, the original owner,

"Norumbega," Camden

reads like a Horatio Alger story. Born in the small town of Weld, Maine, Stearns was deeply in debt from business failures by the time he was nineteen. He entered the telegraph business in 1850, and after eighteen and one-half years became a millionaire. It was not through careful saving that he accumulated his wealth, but rather through the invention of the duplex system of telegraphy — allowing two messages to be sent over one wire at the same time — which revolutionized the telegraph industry. Mr. Stearns received royalties for his invention from all over the world.

By 1885, when he was only fifty-four, Stearns was ready to retire. He ended his active career and settled in Camden, where he built his great stone house. Stearns had left Maine to make his fortune, but returned to enjoy its benefits in a baronial estate on the coast. By the mid 1880s, Bar Harbor with its grand vistas and Camden with its fine harbor and yacht basin were becoming the frontier "Newports" for the leisure class. The Camden of today retains this same flavor as one of Maine's leading summer resorts. "Norumbega," with its fine architecture and beautiful location, remains one of Maine's outstanding examples of the great "cottages" that dotted the Maine coast in the heyday of late Victorian wealth and ostentation.

Norumbega Carriage House, High Street — 1886

This delightful piece of architectural frivolity was executed by architect Arthur B. Jennings and reflects the spirit of ostentatious recreational building common to the early resort era. The Queen Anne style Carriage House complements the main house, "Norumbega," which is itself entered on the National Register. Both structures are on the former estate of telegraph magnate and inventor Joseph B. Stearns.

American Boathouse, Atlantic Avenue — 1904

This remarkable structure, built to house Chauncy B. Borland's steam yacht *Maunaloa,* may be the oldest surviving example of its type in the country. The one-story frame structure has a gable roof and shingle siding. At the north end is a single-story, hipped-roof office of a later date. Now used for commercial purposes, it calls up images of Maine as a playground for the very rich in an era of extravagance and opulence.

Camden Yacht Club, Bayview Street — 1912

Founded in 1906 largely through the efforts of George B. Phelps, the Camden Yacht Club, with Chauncey B. Borland as Commodore, initially leased a storefront property and cottage for a wharf and clubhouse. In 1912, Cyrus H.K. Curtis — founder of the *Ladies Home Journal*, publisher of the *Saturday Evening Post*, and an avid Camden yachtsman — erected a very attractive and fully appointed clubhouse at one of the finest locations in the harbor. Curtis retained John Calvin Stevens, Maine's most noted architect, to design the building in the Shingle Style. Sumptuously furnished and built with the finest materials, the structure cost $60,000, a very large sum for the period. Retaining ownership, Curtis generously offered the building to the Yacht Club at a very nominal rent. At the time of his death, it was left to the town with the provision that its use by the Yacht Club continue.

Schooner *Bowdoin*, Camden — 1921

The significance of the *Bowdoin* is inextricably entwined with the life of Donald Baxter MacMillan (1874–1970), who

The schooner Bowdoin, *Camden*

made twenty-nine trips to the Arctic during his life, twenty-six of them with the *Bowdoin* between 1921 and 1954. MacMillan was a combination of educator, geographer, anthropologist, philanthropist, and aviator, and because his life spanned two world wars, a planner of Arctic military defenses.

MacMillan sailed the *Bowdoin* with crews of "amateur" seamen — college students and scientists with their own investigations to perform. All the voyages were accomplished without fatality.

To the literate world, *Bowdoin* is a lasting symbol of a strong tradition of cultural and scientific ties between Maine and the eastern Arctic. To the older Innuit of Labrador and Greenland, *Bowdoin* brought the best of men and the best of wishes from the south.

CAMDEN AND ROCKLAND

Maine Commercial Schooners — 1871–1926

This thematic group includes a variety of examples of the two-masted schooner, once the principal carrier in the coasting trade and the heart of the dory fishing industry. Now preserved as "dude" schooners in the Maine windjammer fleet, these sturdy vessels are important survivors from the great era of sail.

CUSHING

King Inscription — 1605

In the summer of 1605, George Waymouth in his ship, the *Archangel*, sailed out of Plymouth, England, on one of the last voyages of exploration on the eve of settlement. Waymouth concentrated his efforts on the St. George estuary and the islands south of what is now Thomaston. Few of the expeditional personnel are known to us by name, but one crew member was Thomas King, boatswain. Carved in bedrock ledge on the shore of the Meduncook River, just west of the St. George, is a weathered but mostly legible inscription that reads, below a small cross: "1605 Abr [Abraham?] King." The carver may have been a relative of the boatswain. This seems to be the oldest dated inscription in the Thirteen Colonies and Canada, and it is a rare artifact from the elusive age of exploration.

Benjamin Burton Garrison Site — 1753*

A large assemblage of mid-eighteenth-century artifacts found by plowers led to the discovery of this garrison house site. The complex consisted of a stone house, with palisade and outbuildings, constructed in 1753, attacked by Indians in 1756, subsequently abandoned, and dismantled around 1815. Although somewhat disturbed by the plow, the site seems largely intact, the first of its kind identified in Maine.

DAMARISCOTTA

Main Street Historic District

Damariscotta was originally part of two towns, Bristol and Nobleboro. Before its incorporation as a town in 1847, it was called Walpole. Located on the eastern shore of the Damariscotta River, at the head of navigable waters, it is within the bounds of the first deed given in the state territory by Samoset to John Brown in 1625. The first dwelling in the future Damariscotta was built in 1754. Other dwellings followed, and the settlement grew as shipbuilding prospered.

A fire in 1845 destroyed all earlier buildings in the present district but three: the Cottrill, Austin and Fly houses. The main street was rebuilt quickly, materials coming from the brickyards along the river. By 1875, all the buildings in the district as we know it today had been constructed, with the exception of three modern structures and three buildings of the late nineteenth century.

Fortunately the buildings in the district have been little altered. Their original character remains. The commercial purposes for which they were built remain the same, with some variation.

During the middle of the nineteenth century when most of the buildings were erected, Damariscotta, although too far from the ocean to be an important seaport, was ideally

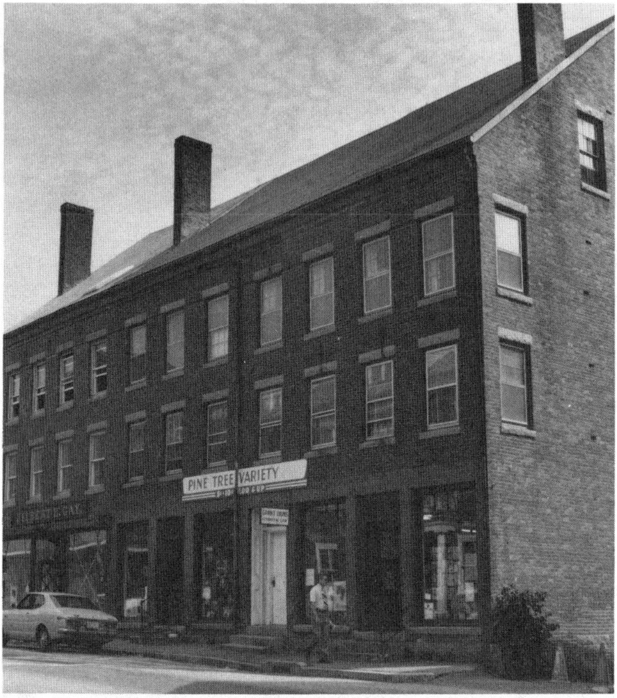

Main Street Historic District, Damariscotta

located for shipbuilding, an industry that developed on a large scale. The post-fire commercial renewal of Main Street was largely based on the economic prosperity that shipbuilding brought.

Architecturally, Main Street faithfully retains its mid-century stylistic ambiance. Later structures have, for the most part, been compatibly designed and preserve the dominant scale.

Damariscotta Oyster Shellheaps,
Damariscotta River — Pre-Columbian

The Whaleback Shellheap on Salt Bay in Damariscotta is a remnant of one of the largest shellheaps, or shell middens, on the coast of North America. It is composed primarily of shells from oysters that lived in Salt Bay, rather than the more common clamshell middens of the Maine coast. Several other oyster-shell middens remain in the vicinity.

From a few radiocarbon dates and associated artifacts, we suspect that these sites were occupied from about 1,000 B.C. on, and that the oysters growing in Great Salt Bay began to attract seasonal gatherings of Indians to the area after that date. The main component of the middens is decomposing oyster shell, and there are relatively few artifacts in them. However, none of these oyster middens have been excavated by a modern archaeologist, and all conclusions must therefore be considered temporary.

Chapman-Hall House, Main Street—1754

The first permanent settler in Damariscotta was Anthony Chapman of Ipswich, Massachusetts. His half-brother, Nathaniel Chapman, was later persuaded to settle in Damariscotta to build homes for the handful of settlers who had set up crude dwellings. A talented housewright, Nathaniel constructed his own home in 1754. He owned nearly all of what is now Main Street and is referred to as "the father of Main Street."

The Cape Cod–style house, restored by the Chapman-

Chapman-Hall House, Damariscotta

Hall Preservation Society, is Damariscotta's oldest surviving building. The fine dwelling is interesting for its sturdy construction, including ceiling beams that extend the full width of the building, central chimney with four fireplaces, double-thickness vertical planking, and original floors, plaster and paneling. Nathaniel Chapman was obviously a skilled master builder, and his home has survived to demonstrate that fact in the twentieth century.

Matthew Cottrill House, Main Street — 1801

This fine example of Federal architecture is in excellent condition. The house was designed by Nicholas Codd, an Irish immigrant who also drew plans for St. Patrick's Catholic Church, the Moses Carlton House, and the Governor Kavanaugh House. Cottrill, also an Irishman, had his home built onto a smaller 1760s house in 1801. He and his partner, James Kavanaugh, had chosen Damariscotta as a promising place for mercantile business; together they made great economic contributions to the area.

DRESDEN

Pownalborough Courthouse, Cedar Grove Road — 1760–61

Built by Boston housewright Gershom Flagg for the Kennebec Proprietors in 1761, Pownalborough Courthouse served Lincoln County when that political division included all of Maine east of the Kennebec River.

The courthouse, which overlooks one of the eighteenth century's major "highways," the Kennebec River, is a large, 3-story, hipped-roof building of post and beam construction, with two large chimneys servicing twelve fireplaces.

In the 1770s, John Adams, later to become the second president of the United States, practiced law here. The building also served as a tavern and inn for travelers.

Today Pownalborough Courthouse, Maine's oldest surviving judicial building, is seasonally open to the public as a museum.

Pownalborough Courthouse, Dresden

Bowman-Carney House, Route 128—ca. 1762

This Colonial mansion was built for Jacob Bowman, a "Son of Liberty" and judge of probate for the District of Maine, around 1762. James Carney, a blacksmith-turned-shipbuilder, bought the house in 1804. The mansion was used as an office building during the boom of the ice industry, but the present owners have restored the house using as much original material as possible. About ninety-nine percent of the house dates from its construction.

St. John's Anglican Church and Parsonage, The Common Road—1770–79

Though not of great age by normal archaeological standards, this site is important for several reasons. The remains of the cellars of a church and parsonage, as well as formal gardens and other features, are well preserved and identified. The site's destruction in 1779 was a result of the tragic Tory-Rebel struggle, an important yet often unknown chapter in American Revolutionary history.

EDGECOMB

John Moore House, Cross Point Road — ca. 1740, 1765, 1850

One of the earliest houses in the Edgecomb-Wiscasset area, this finely preserved structure was built by John Moore on land granted to him in 1736. Notable for its age, it is also remarkable structurally as a Cape whose roof of which was raised up in around 1765, not a full story, as in a number of other examples, but only about five feet, to provide a heightened ceiling for the second floor and small windows on the front for added light. Spectacularly sited on the crest of a hill overlooking the tidal estuary of the Sheepscot River, this remarkable house with its attached barn (1850) is an important landmark recalling the period of earliest settlement in the region.

Fort Edgecomb, Davis Island — 1808–12

Fort Edgecomb, built in 1808, overlooks the Sheepscot River and was designed to protect one of Maine's busiest seaports of the period, Wiscasset.

The fort consists of a series of stone bastions and earth-

Fort Edgecomb

works, with sections of reconstructed palisade, dominated by a remarkable and well preserved octagonal wooden blockhouse 27 feet in diameter at ground level and 34 feet high, with an overhanging second story.

Fort Edgecomb succeeded in protecting Wiscasset during the War of 1812 because it was never attacked by the Royal Navy. The only times its guns were fired were on March 4, 1809, when they saluted President Madison's inauguration, and on February 14, 1815, when they signaled news of peace with Britain.

Today the fort is administered for the public by the Maine Bureau of Parks and Recreation as a historic memorial. Fort Edgecomb is the best-preserved fortification of its period in Maine.

FRANKFORT

Mount Waldo Granite Works, U.S. Route 1A — 1851 or 1852

This 125-acre site in Frankfort was once an active, prosperous, nationally known granite-quarrying and cutting area. Between 1851 and World War II, Maine was a leading granite supplier. New building materials and increased transportation costs, however, led to a decline in the demand for granite. Now the Maine industry is limited to special contracts and monuments.

GEORGETOWN

Seguin Island Light Station — 1790

Seguin Island Light Station is the second oldest on the Maine coast. Construction started in 1790, five years after the completion of Portland Head Light. The original wooden tower was completed in 1797 but was replaced by a stone tower in 1820. In 1857, the present granite structure was erected. As many as 2,734 hours of fog in one year probably necessitated the replacement of the first two towers.

For many years local folklore maintained that pirate treasure was buried on Seguin Island. In 1936, Archie Lane of

Northeast Harbor was granted a license to dig for the treasure, but he was unsuccessful in his quest.

Seguin Island Light Station continues to exemplify America's commitment to the safety of life and property at sea as an integral element of its social and commercial policies.

Stone Schoolhouse, District 3, Bay Point Road — ca. 1820

A small, primitive, rough-laid stone structure, the Stone Schoolhouse represents an early response to the impulse toward public education. It was built by Irish stonemasons under the direction of General Joseph Berry, a prominent ship owner and builder in Georgetown.

JEFFERSON

Dr. F.W. Jackson House, Route 32 — 1903–5

This large and splendid Colonial Revival house, an architectural landmark in Jefferson, was built by a native son who returned after a successful medical career and a prosperous and happy marriage.

LIBERTY

Old Post Office, Main Street — ca. 1870

Of the relatively few octagon buildings in the country, there is only one octagon post office, and it is in Liberty, Maine. Constructed around 1870 by a harness maker, it was used as his shop until 1878, when part of the building was taken over as a post office. It continued in that dual existence for many years. When the building was closed in 1960, it was a post office only. The Old Post Office has been restored, with all the original equipment returned to the building.

MONHEGAN PLANTATION

Monhegan Lighthouse and Quarters — 1824

Probably familiar to Basque, Breton, Spanish, and Portuguese fishermen in the late fifteenth century, Monhegan

Monhegan Lighthouse

Island was recorded by John Cabot in 1498. One early visitor aptly described this lonely outpost as "a great island that was backed like a whale." The colorful and imaginative Captain John Smith landed on Monhegan in 1614, and his account of the attractions of the island and its anchorage eventually led to settlement as early as 1625. Since 1674, the island has been continuously inhabited, with its economy based largely on fishing.

Today, Monhegan supports a year-round population of about one hundred, which climbs to over 300 in the summer with the arrival of cottage-owning summer residents. The rich and unusual flora has been carefully guarded by controlling wild areas of the island, so that natural beauty has remained largely unspoiled.

By act of Congress in 1822, $3,000 was appropriated to establish a lighthouse and keeper's dwelling on Monhegan Island. The first keeper, Thomas B. Seavey, and his family occupied the quarters and lit the light July 2, 1824. The light was supervised by the Lighthouse Service until that organization was consolidated with the Coast Guard beginning in July 1939. In 1959, the light was automated and the buildings were declared surplus.

By sealed-bid public auction held on June 1, 1962, the buildings were acquired by Monhegan Associates, Inc., an organization formed in 1954 "to preserve for posterity the natural wild beauty, biotic communities, and desirable natural, artificial, and historic features of the so-called 'wildlands' portions of Monhegan Island, Maine, and its environs, as well as the simple, friendly way of life that has existed on Monhegan as a whole."

In the summer of 1966, after extensive repairs, a few museum exhibits were opened to the public in the keeper's quarters. Since 1968, the buildings have been open on a daily basis during the summer, with a constantly expanding group of exhibits designed to exemplify the historical, natural and economic features of Monhegan Island.

The rugged stone column of the light tower and the simple white wooden structures standing atop a bare exposed hill overlooking the sea in all directions epitomize the wild beauty and rugged life that is Monhegan Island.

NEWCASTLE

Governor Kavanaugh House, Route 213 (Damariscotta Mills) — 1803

Designed by Nicholas Codd and built for James Kavanaugh in 1803, this beautiful Federal-style mansion was the home of the Irish lumber baron and shipowner for about twenty years. His son, Edward, was its most remembered resident. A member of the legislature, a congressman, chargé d'affaires to Portugal, and governor of Maine in 1843, Edward Kavanaugh was the first Catholic to hold any public office in New England.

St. Patrick's Catholic Church, Academy Road — 1807

St. Patrick's Catholic Church at Damariscotta Mills is not only the oldest Catholic church in Maine, but also the oldest surviving Catholic church in New England. The parish was founded in 1796, mainly through the efforts of James Kavanaugh and Matthew Cottrill, two Irish merchants who settled at Damariscotta in the late eighteenth century.

The architect of St. Patrick's was Nicholas Codd, who was brought from Ireland to design the church and the homes of Kavanaugh and Cottrill. The church was designed and

St. Patrick's Catholic Church, Newcastle

built for solidity and permanence. The walls are 1½-foot-thick solid brick. The bricks were made on the opposite shore of Damariscotta Lake and hauled across by oxen during the winter of 1807. The mortar was made from limestone imported from Ireland; apparently Maine's vast limestone beds were unknown to these early settlers.

The original altar, floors, two of the pews, stair railings, and inner doors are intact and in use. The doors are decorated with the harp of Ireland and a sprig of leaves. A Paul Revere bell, donated by Cottrill in 1818, still calls St. Patrick's congregation to worship. St. Patrick's is the only Catholic church in New England to possess a Revere bell.

Glidden-Austin Block, Main Street and River Road — 1845

The Greek Revival–style Glidden-Austin Block is a good example of the mid-nineteenth-century coastal Maine commercial building. The brick and granite structure, built in 1845, was used as a chandlery and tenement originally; since then it has housed a garment factory, an undertaking parlor, and an antique shop, all of which had apartments on the upper floors. Glidden and Austin were shipbuilders and shipping magnates; Glidden was also a sea captain.

Second Congregational Church, River Road—1848

A prominent landmark at the head of the harbor, this building is the most outstanding and largest example of vernacular Gothic Revival ecclesiastical architecture executed in brick to be found in the entire mid-coastal region of Maine.

St. Andrew's Church, Glidden Street—1883

St. Andrew's Church, called the most beautiful little church in America, was the first American church to be designed by the English Gothicist, Henry Vaughan. Built of half-timbered construction in 1883, St. Andrew's was Vaughan's first Maine commission. During the next twenty years, he designed other churches in the state, as well as the Searles Science Building and the Hubbard Library at Bowdoin College. In the early twentieth century, Vaughan began his most famous design, that of Sts. Peter and Paul Cathedral in Washington, D.C.

The interior of St. Andrew's, decorated with hand-carved oak, includes the finest Hutchings organ in existence. Both interior and exterior are in excellent condition.

NEWCASTLE AND ALNA

Sheepscot Historic District (includes Davis-Tobie Site)

The Sheepscot Historic District contains important historic resources of virtually all periods, from the prehistoric era through the nineteenth century.

The prehistoric Davis-Tobie site has been excavated in Sheepscot, yielding evidence of four different Indian occupations beginning as early as 3,000 B.C. An English village was established in Sheepscot in the mid seventeenth cen-

Sheepscot Historic District, Newcastle / Alna

tury, known as Sheepscott Farms, which was destroyed in 1676. The site of this village lies largely undisturbed since that time, as later Anglo-American settlers selected a different focus for their community.

The modern village of Sheepscot, split between the towns of Newcastle and Alna, straddles the scenic Sheepscot River. The community was established in the 1730s, when the mid-coastal region was resettled in the closing years of the Indian Wars. Fine houses of the Federal period survive, as well as examples of the later-nineteenth-century styles, all set in an unspoiled environment.

NORTH HAVEN

Prehistoric Sites in North Haven

Analysis of the faunal material at these sites has for the first time provided substantive data on prehistoric northern New England subsistence and settlement patterns and their changes over time in a limited geographic area.

Turner Farm Site — Prehistoric

The Turner Farm site is one of the largest clam-shell middens on the coast of Maine. It is without doubt the most

Prehistoric stone tools from the Turner Farm Site, North Haven. Courtesy of Maine State Museum.

important coastal shell midden for Maine prehistory at present, because it contains the longest known sequence of occupation and has received the most extensive archaeological attention. Occupation at the site began at least seven thousand years ago. Intact deposits, still stratified within the layer-cake of the shellheap, date back at least 5,200 years. Importantly, the shells' calcium carbonate has preserved animal foodbone debris at the site, which has allowed reconstruction of environmental change in Penobscot Bay and the Indians' way of life over that five-thousand-year span.

The first occupations were by the Small-Stemmed Point complex around 5,200 years ago, and the Moorehead Phase between approximately 4,500 and 4,000 years ago. Those groups lived at a time when Gulf of Maine waters were warmer than they are now; swordfish hunting was a major activity of both groups. The total seasonal round of use of the site by the Moorehead Phase people is now known and includes summer swordfishing, a major fall codfishery, major fall and winter hunting seasons for whitetailed deer (especially), bear, seamink, and other furbearers, and spring subsistence based primarily on raiding great auk and other seabird nesting areas for birds and probably eggs. Seal and other sea-mammal hunting played a very minor part in these peoples' lives.

The succeeding Susquehanna occupation, dating around 3,600 years ago, was the most land-oriented occupation at the site. The seasonal round included some fishing for flounder and sturgeon and some seal hunting, but was primarily based upon hunting whitetailed deer, bear, some moose, other furbearers and waterfowl.

The site was occupied by Ceramic (pottery-using) Indians from about 2,500 years ago to about A.D. 1500. During this time, certain aspects of the basic Susquehanna-style subsistence pattern were intensified — fishing for sturgeon and flounder (especially); seal hunting during the spring, summer, and fall, and moose hunting during the winter. At the end of the Ceramic period, moose and seal became the prime subsistence basis at the site. Trapping and hunting for furbearers such as seamink, otter, beaver, fisher, and fox were also important. The later Ceramic-period occupants at the site may be the ancestors of some of Maine's modern Indians.

The site is important too for the study of patterns of trade in raw materials, such as stone and copper, and the investigation of ceremonial behavior, particularly burials.

Several house floors and associated fireplaces were identified in the Susquehanna level. The houses seem to have been oval in outline, from three to five meters long, and large enough for one or two families each.

The Turner Farm provides the key to the prehistoric occupation of lower Penobscot Bay, while the prehistoric sites in North Haven provide a background and perspective to the settlement patterns reconstructed at the Turner Farm, as well as preserving some occupations that are not recorded at the Turner Farm. All these sites are private property and are inaccessible without the owner's permission.

OWLS HEAD

Owls Head Light Station, Owls Head — 1826

Picturesquely located on a high, wave-swept promontory at the entrance to Rockland Harbor, Owls Head Light Tower is visible to all who sail the western reaches of Penobscot Bay. Established by President John Quincy Adams, the light is now automated.

PHIPPSBURG

Popham Colony–Fort St. George, ½-mile west of Fort Popham — 1607

Under the leadership of George Popham and Ralegh Gilbert, a party of about 100 Englishmen attempted to establish England's first permanent colony in the Northeast. This venture was named the "Northern Virginia Colony" to complement a simultaneous effort called the "Southern Virginia Colony." The latter, better known as Jamestown, has become forever famous because it was England's first successful colony in North America. The former, known as the Popham Colony, has been all but forgotten because of its failure.

The Popham colonists selected a sheltered neck of land overlooking Atkins Bay in what is now the town of Phippsburg, on the west side of the mouth of the Kennebec River (then known on its southern reaches as the Sagadahoc). It was August 18, 1607. On the following day, work commenced on the construction of Fort St. George, designed to protect the settlement from potentially hostile Indians. By October, the settlers had "fully finished the fort, trencht, and fortefied it with twelve pieces of ordinaunce." Of the buildings, a food storehouse was the first to be erected, followed by more than a dozen primitive dwellings — all within the fort's walls. A London shipwright by the name of Digby supervised construction of the pinnace, *Virginia*, the first European vessel built in America.

On October 8, 1607, one John Hunt drew a detailed plan of the Popham Colony and its fort that surely cannot be accepted as literal. Yet, generally the drawing may be useful in giving us a picture of what was built. Archaeological excavations on Sabino Head in the 1960s yielded early artifacts but failed to locate the fort, and further fieldwork is needed to provide data on the colony.

George Popham died at Fort St. George in the winter of 1607–08, and the following spring Gilbert returned to England to claim an inheritance. Leaderless and disillusioned, the colonists all returned home in the summer of 1608.

McCobb-Hill-Minott House, Parker Head Road — 1744

This exceptionally fine, foursquare, Georgian frame house was built by James McCobb, an early settler in the area who prospered in lumber and commerce. It was later occupied by Mark Langdon Hill, shipbuilder and congressman from 1819 to 1823 (during Maine's admission as a state). A subsequent owner was Charles V. Minott, one of the most successful shipbuilders in the region between 1853 and 1904.

Fort Popham, Popham Beach — 1861

The strategic mouth of the Kennebec River has been fortified repeatedly throughout the historic period, from the beginning of European settlement (the Popham Colony of 1607) through World Wars I and II (Fort Baldwin).

In 1862, during the Civil War, Fort Popham, named in honor of George Popham's 1607 settlement, was begun when fears of European intervention on the side of the Confederacy revealed how vulnerable Bath's strategic shipyards and the state capital in Augusta were.

Although the war ended before Fort Popham could be completed, a massive granite fortification with a circumference of 500 feet was built. Facing the river, two tiers of vaulted gun emplacements for thirty-six cannon were fitted into walls over thirty feet high. Fort Popham is a historic

Fort Popham, Phippsburg

memorial, open to the public and administered by the Maine Bureau of Parks and Recreation.

Fort Baldwin, Sabino Hill — 1905–12

One of the last major defences built on the Maine coast, Fort Baldwin today consists of three massive concrete batteries near the summit of Sabino Hill, overlooking the mouth of the strategic Kennebec River. During the Great War, two companies of artillerists were stationed here, and a tall fire-control tower of concrete was built on the site during World War II. Fort Baldwin, however, never fired a shot in anger. As a well-preserved example of early-twentieth-century fortification design, this state-owned site complements the Colonial and nineteenth-century forts being preserved and interpreted for the public benefit.

PROSPECT

Fort Knox, Route 174 — 1844–64 (NHL)

When Maine very nearly went to war against the British Empire in 1839 over its disputed northern boundary with Canada, it was quickly recognized that the important lumber capital of Bangor — and indeed the whole Penobscot Valley — was completely defenseless against attack by enemy naval vessels.

Therefore, in 1844, Maine's largest and most impressive fortification began to be built on nearly 125 acres of land facing the town of Bucksport and Verona Island. This work, named Fort Knox after General Henry Knox, Washington's commander of artillery during the Revolution and America's first secretary of war, was still not quite finished twenty years and one million dollars later.

The fort is enormous, measuring 350 by 250 feet (not including additional gun emplacements to the north and south), with granite walls twenty feet high and forty feet thick, built to mount 137 guns. Although it never fired a shot in anger, Fort Knox is a National Historic Landmark by virtue of its engineering alone and is administered as an historic memorial for the public by the Maine Bureau of Parks and Recreation. Nothing like it will ever be built again.

Fort Knox parade ground, Prospect

RICHMOND

Richmond Historic District

The significance of the Richmond Historic District lies within its nineteenth-century history. It was in this century that Richmond reached the peak of its prosperity, and its architecture reflects this success both in quality and variety of styles.

Richmond's history begins in 1649 with the purchase of a tract of land from the Indians by Christopher Lawson. Fort Richmond was constructed in 1719 to protect the few settlers. In 1823, with a population of 850, Richmond was incorporated as a town. Until the 1890s, Richmond enjoyed increasing prosperity as a result of the shipbuilding industry that produced some 236 vessels. Combined with the short-lived ice industry of the late nineteenth century, Richmond's shipbuilding led to notoriety and success for the river town.

Thomas Jefferson Southard was Richmond's most successful businessman. His ornate Italianate-style home, his mill, and his Mansard-style commercial block are all part of

Richmond Historic District

this district. Nothing remains of any of the shipyards, but the surviving Greek Revival, Italianate, and Mansard architecture reflects the mid-century prosperity of the town.

Southard Block, 25 Front Street — 1882

The Southard Block, a 3-story, Mansard-style commercial building, was completed in 1883 for use as a bank and several apartments. The banker, Thomas Jefferson Southard, was a shipbuilder, the village postmaster, and the owner of a drygoods store, a drugstore, a planing mill, a gristmill, as well as several other commercial buildings. The Southard Block is a reminder of Richmond's days as an important shipping port and of T.J. Southard, the man who helped make it so.

ROCKLAND

Main Street Historic District

That section of Main Street in Rockland included in the historic district is of double significance: first, it contains a remarkably well preserved collection of commercial buildings that exhibit a rare chronological and architectural uniformity, and second, it demonstrates the amazing resilience and vitality of this thriving mid-nineteenth-century city in the wake of a major disaster.

Originally a part of Thomaston, where settlement took place along the St. George River by the mid seventeenth century, the area on the shore of Penobscot Bay now encompassed by the city of Rockland was not occupied until the late eighteenth century. Lime-burning, an industry later to become a mainstay of nineteenth-century Rockland's economy, was begun in the region during the 1730s, but it was not until 1785 that George Ulmer established the first such enterprise on the bay shore.

In the nineteenth century, Rockland harbor, although somewhat exposed, became the focal point of three major industries: shipbuilding, lime burning in the great kilns that lined the shore, and salt manufacture (the latter died out by mid century).

In 1853, a series of fires broke out in the Rockland busi-

Main Street Historic District, Rockland

ness district on Main Street. These occurred on January 1, February 28, March 28, and May 22. The last of these was particularly disastrous, beginning at the site of the present Pillsbury Block, and destroying all the buildings on the west side of Main Street between Spring (now Museum) Street and Limerock Street and most of those immediately opposite. There was, of course, speculation that these conflagrations were the work of an "incendiary," but no definite proof was ever produced.

Rebuilding was begun immediately, and such was the economic climate in Rockland that, in spite of capital losses, a business boom resulted. It is interesting to note that two of the first three blocks erected, the Kimball Block and the first Berry Block, were designed in the Greek Revival style, which had dominated the earlier streetscape. All the subsequent buildings, however, beginning the following year, displayed the new movement in architecture and were either Italianate or Mansard in design.

As further evidence of the resiliency of the community,

it was incorporated as a city in 1854, the eighth in the state. By 1860, its population had grown to 7,317.

Rankin Block, 600–610 Main Street — 1853

Symbolic of Rockland's remarkable recovery from the holocaust of 1853, this well-designed Greek Revival commercial structure was built by Samuel Rankin, a descendant of Constant Rankin, one of the earliest settlers in the region. The building has recently been rehabilitated and, with additions in the rear, serves as a housing center for the elderly.

The Farnsworth Homestead, 21 Elm Street — 1854

The Farnsworth Homestead is a fine mid-nineteenth-century town house of Greek Revival design. Built in 1854 by the W.H. Glover Lumber Company, this was the home of Rockland's well-known Farnsworth family.

William A. Farnsworth of Rockland was a prominent and prosperous businessman who acquired his wealth from ownership of limerock property and the Rockland Water Company, which he founded and ran as president. William had six children, but two of the boys died very young, leaving James, Fanny, Josephine, and Lucy. By 1907, all were dead but Lucy and her mother, from whom the former subsequently inherited the estate in 1910. When her mother died, Lucy pulled down all the window shades and lived as a recluse.

In October 1935, Miss Farnsworth's death was discovered by a milkman when seven full bottles accumulated on her side doorstep. The house was a shambles literally stuffed with money and bonds; the ninety-six-year-old woman, serving as her own broker, had accumulated an estate worth $1,300,000. Her will, which was found in a cupboard, stipulated that all her money was to go to the city of Rockland. An art museum dedicated to her father was sketched in the will, and the house was to be preserved exactly as a middle-class home of the Victorian era.

Lucy C. Farnsworth, who had spurned Rockland for ninety-six years, made the memory of her family the pride of Rockland. The art museum, which owns America's largest collection of Andrew Wyeth paintings, and the house, a time capsule of the Victorian lifestyle, are monuments to this eccentric benefactor.

Knox County Courthouse, 62 Union Street—1874

This impressive brick and granite Italianate structure contains not only the Knox County courts, but also county offices, fireproof storage areas, and jail facilities.

Before 1860, what is now Knox County was divided between Lincoln and Waldo counties. Unhappy over the distance to the county seats of Wiscasset and Belfast, the people of the mid-coast area succeeded in establishing a new county named in honor of General Henry Knox. The city of Rockland was chosen as the county seat, and county offices were scattered throughout already existing commercial buildings. In 1875, a new courthouse was officially opened.

Gridley F. Bryant and Lewis P. Rogers designed the massive Italianate building, which captures an unusual spirit of gravity and authority.

Rockland Breakwater Lighthouse—1902

The construction of this important navigational beacon at the end of the 4,300-foot Rockland Breakwater completed the development of Rockland Harbor and marked its establishment as a major coastal port.

Rockland Public Library, Union Street—1903

During the fifty-year period from 1880 to 1930, the public library in Maine underwent its greatest development as an educational resource and as a distinctive building type. As a result of this activity, there appeared across the state architect-designed, special-function buildings in a great variety of styles, often regionally unique. The Rockland Public Library, one of some twenty in Maine funded by Andrew Carnegie, is a prime example of this architectural and cultural development. Designed by Clough and Wardner of Boston in a rare combination of Romanesque Revival and Beaux Arts Classicism, it is unique in the city and a landmark for the area.

Security Trust Building, Elm and Main Streets—1912

This very high quality example of an early-twentieth-century, small-town bank was designed by R. Clipstone Sturgis of Boston. Basically in the Colonial Revival tradition, the building is in keeping with present-day bank architecture, which strives for modernity while retaining an air of soundness and solidity. The building is currently in service as a fashionable restaurant.

Rockland Railroad Station, Union Street — 1917

This very late example of a relatively ornate railroad-station facility marks the last years of high-quality luxury passenger service, which never fully recovered after the government takeover of the railroads in 1918. Now the Rockland City Hall, this structure is a fine example of successful adaptive re-use.

ROCKPORT

Rockport Historic District

First discovered by the explorer George Waymouth in 1605, the Camden area, of which the present Rockport was a part, was not permanently settled until the early 1770s. A survey

Rockport Historic District

was conducted in 1768 by David Fales, and settlement began three or four years later.

That part now known as Rockport was originally called Goose Creek but was renamed in 1852 because the residents wanted a more euphonious and appropriate name. In 1891, after a long and acrimonious debate, Rockport, against the wishes of most of its residents, was set off as a separate town by the Maine legislature.

By this time, Rockport, because of its excellent small harbor, had become an important seafaring community, where shipbuilding and the manufacture of capstans and windlasses, bricks, tinware, boots and shoes was carried on. There was also a considerable ice shipping trade and, most important, the manufacture and shipping of lime produced in kilns still in existence on the waterfront.

After 1900, most of Rockport's commercial enterprises began to decline as Rockland, with its much larger harbor, became the center of such activity and changes in methods of lime manufacture destroyed the industry locally. Fortunately, in these same years, its extremely beautiful location and surroundings began to attract an increasing number of summer residents and tourists, and its harbor became a yachting center of great popularity. Rockport also became an important summer musical center through the efforts of Mrs. Efrem Zimbalist, Mme. Lea Luboshutz, her brother and his wife, the famed duo-pianists, Luboshutz and Nemenoff, and the Walter Wolfs and their sons, Thomas and Andrew, who initiated the Bay Chamber Concerts.

Beyond its architectural beauty, Rockport still possesses many reminders, in its commercial buildings and its waterfront, of its heyday as a thriving nineteenth-century Maine seaport.

The Spite House, Deadman's Point — 1806

This house, built in 1806 at Phippsburg in the Federal style, was constructed by Thomas McCobb to spite his stepmother who had cheated him out of his father's mansion (the McCobb-Hill-Minott House). The beautifully proportioned wood frame house is two stories high and has an octagonal cupola on it slow hipped roof.

In 1925, the Spite House was moved by barge eighty-five miles to Rockport. A 1796 house from South Harpswell went along, too, and was used for the wing of the house on its present site. The building is an excellent example of the Federal style, since it has not been greatly altered and its lovely balustrade and unusual panels with swags give it an air of particular sophistication.

Rockport Historic Kiln Area, Rockport Waterfront — 1817

For over a century, Maine lime, produced for use as mortar and finishing plaster, dominated the East Coast market. Almost all of it was produced in the Knox County towns of Thomaston, Rockland, Rockport, and Camden. Aside from water-filled quarries, the physical evidence of this once-flourishing industry has all but disappeared. Fortunately, several relatively well preserved kilns on the shore of Rockport Harbor still exist.

A map of Rockport published in 1875 shows the location of eight lime kilns. In 1889, there were fourteen kilns in operation. During the 1880s and 1890s, Knox County kilns produced over two million casks of lime annually. The bulk of the total was manufactured in Rockland, but some of the most efficient kilns were in Rockport.

With increasing competition from other lime-producing states and the introduction of new building materials in the twentieth century, the Knox County kilns closed down. Seven kilns remain on this site in Rockport. Later iron kilns were removed (sold for scrap), but the old fieldstone and brick kilns remain.

ST. GEORGE

Mosquito Island House, Mosquito Island — ca. 1780

This rare, early, stone Cape Cod house was built of granite from quarries on this island located one-half mile off Mosquito Head. The method of cutting the granite, using a tonguing iron and soft wooden wedges, was not commonly used after 1750.

The Sail Loft, Tenants Harbor — 1860

This sturdy structure is all that remains of the great shipbuilding heritage of the town of St. George and of Tenants

Harbor in particular. Housing at one time a ship chandlery on the first floor, a sail loft on the second and a moulding shop on the third, it was built and owned by the Long family, who also engaged in shipbuilding on the land in front. Volumes of papers concerning the various Long businesses were found in the building and are now on loan to the Maine Maritime Museum.

SEARSPORT

Penobscot Marine Museum Historic District

Mid-coast Maine, stretching from Wiscasset to Frenchman Bay, was of great importance in the heyday of New England shipping. Its rich history tells of the rise and fall of Maine shipbuilding and of innumerable men who left seacoast towns to sail vessels into ports throughout the world. The scope of activity in the area can be measured by the nineteenth-century town of Searsport, which alone produced 250 sailing vessels of substantial size and 286 sea captains, more than any other small town in the United States. This is a remarkable feat when one considers that the population of Searsport never went over five thousand.

The Penobscot Marine Museum is a state-chartered, nonprofit institution that opened to the public in 1936. Eight buildings make up the complex that forms the nineteenth-century village museum. The Searsport Town Hall, the

Penobscot Marine Museum Historic District, Searsport. Courtesy of Penobscot Marine Museum.

Searsport Historic District

homes of four sea captains, and three other exhibit buildings create a reminder of Searsport's period of prosperity. Exhibits on navigation and shipbuilding, on the Oriental trade, of ships' models and Chinese port paintings are of splendid quality and quantity. Amid this cluster of buildings on Church Street, just off busy Route 1, the past seems uncontrived and immediate.

Searsport Historic District

Located in an area once part of the Muscongus Patent (1630) and later Franklin Plantation (1756), Searsport was first settled in the 1750s by members of the garrison at Fort Pownal in Stockton Springs. As early as 1791, shipbuilding took place in the community, reaching its peak between 1845 and 1866, when six yards operated full time and twice that number operated on a seasonal or sporadic basis. The prosperity created through these operations is reflected by most of the buildings here during this period.

Nowhere outside of Portland are there finer examples of the heavy, granite, post-and-lintel façade than in the buildings which line Main Street in Searsport. The sturdy brick

Searsport Historic District

Methodist church clearly expresses the economic confidence of mid-century Searsport.

Although the meeting house was originally Presbyterian, because of the preponderance of settlers of Scottish origin sion. In 1885, one tenth of all full-rigged ships sailing under the American flag were commanded by men from this small community. The unusually sophisticated architecture of the Merrill Trust Bank building may be attributed in part to the cultivated tastes acquired by these cosmopolitan seafarers.

The buildings are not only well maintained, but they are also so little altered from their original state that they retain the flavor of the mid-nineteenth-century seaport.

SOUTH BRISTOL

Sproul Homestead, Route 129—1749, 1815

The fine Federal house and the Colonial Cape, which now serves it as an ell, were both built by members of the Sproul family, a numerous clan in the region. All are descendants of James Sproul, born in Ireland, who came to Pemaquid in 1729 with Colonel Robert Dunbar, who built Fort Frederick, the last of a series of forts built on the site of the original trading post of about 1630.

Old Walpole Meeting House, South Bristol

Old Walpole Meeting House, Route 129 — 1772

Built by the town of Bristol in 1772, the Walpole Meeting House stands virtually unaltered. It is one of the oldest churches in Maine still serving as a place of worship.

Athough the meeting house was originally Presbyterian, because of the preponderance of settlers of Scottish origin in the area, its distance from Boston, where the Presbytery met, was so great that it subsequently became a Congregational church.

The original hand-shaved shingles are intact. When extensive general repairs of the church were undertaken in 1872, the shingles were found to be so far superior to the modern product that it was decided not to disturb them. The interior also retains original features, such as the handcrafted pulpit and box pews and the paneled balcony set aside for slaves and servants.

As an unspoiled and unaltered building reflecting unusually fine colonial craftsmanship, the Walpole Meeting House is a rare historic relic.

Thompson Ice House, Route 129 — 1826–99

Maine's last commercial ice house is located on a pond in South Bristol where ice has been harvested since 1826. The frame building is insulated with nine inches of sawdust between its double walls. Once the building is filled with ice, a twelve-inch layer of marsh hay is placed on top. Maine once supplied over three million tons of ice annually to the rest of the country, but now only this one ice house remains as a monument to a virtually vanished American industry.

STOCKTON SPRINGS

Fort Pownal, Fort Point — 1759

Built in 1759 during the French and Indian War to protect the northernmost boundary, Fort Pownal was disarmed and destroyed at the beginning of the Revolution. The blockhouse was burned in 1779, but the earthworks on three sides remain visible.

Privateer Brigantine *Defence* Shipwreck Site, Stockton Springs Harbor — 1779

When a Massachusetts fleet of forty-four vessels sailed to Castine in the summer of 1779 to dislodge the British from their newly constructed Fort George, one of the ships in the group was the privateer brigantine *Defence,* built that same year in Beverly, Massachusetts.

The Penobscot Expedition was the worst naval disaster in American history. Fort George withstood a haphazard siege and bombardment, and six British vessels soon arrived on the scene. Immediately the Continental forces re-embarked and the entire fleet of warships and transports fled north. Most were scuttled by their crews or captured in the river between today's Bangor and Brewer. The *Defence* scurried into Stockton Springs Harbor to hide but was followed by the British and blown up by her crew.

In 1972, the site of the *Defence* was relocated, and, since then, underwater archaeological excavations have been conducted to investigate the body of the vessel and to recover hundreds of well-preserved artifacts. The site is one of the most important of its period in America.

THOMASTON

Thomaston Historic District

The town of Thomaston, on the banks of the St. George and Mill rivers, is a showpiece of nineteenth-century architectural styles, from the Federal to the Greek Revival, Gothic Revival, Italianate, and French Second Empire. The town today remains much as it was a century ago.

The site of modern Thomaston was first seen by white men in June of 1605, when Captain George Waymouth sailed up the river that now bears his name.

Settlement began in 1630 when a truckhouse was erected. It was used for trading between Plymouth Plantation and the Indians until 1675. Between 1719 and 1720 two blockhouses were erected and garrisoned. Ownership of the surrounding land was claimed by General Samuel Waldo, who engaged twenty-seven people to settle there. The town of Thomaston was incorporated in 1777.

The first major industry, which prepared the way for the rest to follow, was lime burning. Naturally, all the plaster produced from this process could not be used in one small town, so shipping and shipbuilding industries grew up,

Thomaston Historic District

Thomaston Historic District

with their attendant rigging and sailmaking shops. The plaster was shipped in casks, which were made locally, giving birth to a flourishing cooperage trade.

Whether because of its greater importance or greater romantic appeal, it is for the seafaring days that Thomaston is best remembered. Practically every family of any importance in town was connected to the sea in some way, either through a shipbuilder, a captain, a merchant, or a rigger. Boys signed on for voyages as early as age ten, sometimes rising to become captain's at the salty old age of nineteen or twenty. Wives would frequently accompany their husbands on voyages.

Thomaston is rich in heritage from three centuries. Its houses, especially, are visible reminders of what was once a smoky village of lime kilns, and later a busy port town. Today it is a quiet, unhurried town, like others in many ways except for two-mile long Main Street, which is included in the boundaries of the district. This street, with many of Thomaston's more prominent houses, and Knox Street form an impressive field museum of the past.

"Montpelier" (replica), High Street — 1793–95 (1929–31)

The home of Major General Henry Knox and his family stood on the banks of the St. George River from 1795 to 1872, when it was razed to make way for the Knox-Lincoln Railroad. The present "Montpelier" is a reproduction constructed between 1919 and 1931 through the combined efforts of the local Knox Memorial Association and Cyrus H.K. Curtis. Now furnished with many of the original Knox possessions, "Montpelier" is operated by the state of Maine as an historic house museum.

Henry Knox began his career at the age of nine as an apprentice in a bookshop in Boston. When he was twenty-one he acquired his own shop. An ardent patriot, Knox was a self-taught military historian and tactician who became the commander of the American artillery under General Washington during the Revolution. In the winter of 1775–76, he led an epic expedition, which transported fifty-seven cannon from Fort Ticonderoga in upper New York State to Dorchester Heights outside of Boston. During the war, Knox was one of Washington's most trusted officers. In 1783, he became secretary of war, a post he held until 1793.

Through his marriage to Lucy Flucker, Knox became the

"Montpelier," Thomaston

owner of much of the Waldo Patent in Maine and decided to build a summer house in Thomaston from which he could oversee the property. Financial setbacks, however, made Thomaston the Knoxes' year-round home.

Montpelier, built between 1793 and 1795 was a magnificent Federal-style home that Knox, his builder, Ebenezer Dunton, and his carpenter, Ebenezer Alden, designed and built. Much of the design is said to have come from Charles Bulfinch, but Knox specified many details, such as the completely oval front room, the semi-flying staircase, and the clerestory windows that light the hall.

After Knox's death in 1806, "Montpelier" was used by his widow and then by his daughters. When the last child died in 1854, the furnishings of the sadly neglected home were sold at auction to pay off family debts. In 1871, after being lived in by tramps and homeless sailors, "Montpelier" was torn down. One outbuilding, the brick farmhouse, was saved for use as a railroad station.

In the early twentieth century, the local D.A.R. chapter

began raising money to fund a monument, probably a statue, in Knox's memory. World War I delayed the drive, but by the late 1920s the Knox Memorial Association had raised $50,000. The famous publisher and philanthropist, Cyrus H.K. Curtis, contributed another $250,000.

Today's "Montpelier," a well-conceived and beautifully furnished reconstruction, is a fitting tribute to one of Thomaston's, and Maine's, most famous residents. Administered by the State Bureau of Parks and Recreation, "Montpelier" may be visited seven days a week during the summer months.

TOPSHAM

Topsham Historic District

Originally settled as part of the Pejepscot Purchase of 1714, Topsham was incorporated in 1764 but did not achieve economic prosperity until the full development of the water power potential of the Androscoggin River.

The first sawmills in Topsham were erected before 1772, and subsequent years saw the addition of at least five more mills. The manufacturing of lumber during the first part of

Topsham Historic District

Topsham Historic District

the nineteenth century made Topsham the most active commercial center for the entire area west of Bath. Other industries, such as paper and box manufacturing and feldspar mining, were later established, and a whole range of professions and services came into being.

With subsistence farming no longer the dominant occupation, the way was clear for the construction of a residential community where men could be close to their work in the village. Such was the beginning of the Topsham Historic District, just east of the present town center.

The Topsham Historic District preserves within its boundaries an area of development drawn from two American lifestyles — that of the pioneer settler and that of the working-class landowner. The district is unique not only because it appears today much as it did during its heyday in the nineteenth century, but also because local builders, such as the prominent Samuel Melcher, were able to imbue over a century of architectural styles with a consistently appropriate manner of construction and physical appearance.

Pejepscot Paper Company, Brunswick Falls — 1868

The Pejepscot Paper Mill at Topsham is the earliest surviving example of Maine's nineteenth-century, wood-pulp

Pejepscot Paper Company, Topsham

mills. Constructed in 1868, this mill was the first in Maine to produce paper from wood pulp. The mill itself was owned by three separate companies in the nineteenth century; the third, the Pejepscot Paper Company, still owns and operates the mill.

Architecturally, the mill building is an unusual example of the Italianate style, having a gambrel roof. The formal dignity of the brick mill is an interesting contrast to the vernacular forms of its adjacent wooden structures. The Pejepscot Paper Mill is one of the finest and best-preserved industrial sites in Maine. It belongs to a period of industrialization when the exterior design and appearance of buildings were matters of pride. The mill is of major importance to the nineteenth-century architectural heritage of the state.

UNION

Ebenezer Alden House, Union — 1797

The Ebenezer Alden House looks both backward and forward: it is Colonial in form, but Federal in its beautiful detail. It is a notable example of provincial architecture, rely-

Ebenezer Alden House, Union

ing for decorative example on such planbooks as William Pain's *Practical House Carpenter*, published in London in 1794. Its construction date, 1797, makes it a most remarkable and advanced structure in a town that was still largely wilderness.

The builder was a sixth-generation descendant of John and Priscilla Alden of Plymouth Colony. He came to nearby Thomaston in 1792 and spent two years there as a woodcarver completing some of the interior decorations at Montpelier, the home of General Henry Knox. In 1795, Alden moved to Union where he built himself a small house and store and became involved in a dozen or so business ventures.

Alden was a bachelor when he built his spacious home, but in 1799 he returned to Massachusetts, where he married Patience Gilmore. They returned to Maine and produced twelve children.

The house itself is largely a product of Alden's own hand. On the site, he constructed a brickyard to make bricks for the chimneys and walls. Alden personally carved all the finish detail in wood with the tools he had used at Montpelier.

Local history maintains that Alden became a personal friend of General Knox during his employment at the general's estate and that Knox was an occasional visitor in the Alden home. Tradition holds that it was here at a banquet in the late summer of 1806 that Knox swallowed a chicken bone, which pierced his intestine and caused peritonitis to set in. Knox died from the effects in October of the same year.

UNITY

Hezekiah Chase House, Route 202 — 1826

This solid, well-designed, brick Federal-style house was built by Hezekiah Chase, son of Stephen Chase, a Quaker from Durham, Maine, who came to Unity in 1782. George Colby Chase, grandson of Hezekiah, was born and raised in this house. A graduate of the second class at Bates College, he later served on the faculty and became president in 1894. During his tenure in this office, which lasted until 1917, he promoted the attendance of women, established a significant endowment, and conducted an extensive building program.

VINALHAVEN

Star of Hope Lodge, Maine Street — 1885

Dating from the era when Vinalhaven was the center of the Maine granite-quarrying industry, this impressive Mansard structure, is one of the few buildings remaining from this great period. The three-story frame building features a central facade tower, clapboard siding, and cast iron cfesting. It was built for the International Order of Odd Fellows. It is now owned and being faithfully restored by Robert Indiana, the internationally renowned pop artist who designed the famous "LOVE" postage stamp.

The Vinalhaven Galamander, East Maine Street — 1880s to 1914

Although this machine is a restoration of an old galamander, not one that was ever used, it is still a worthy tribute to the Maine granite industry. The handmade oak and iron wagons, equipped with hand-operated derricks, were pulled by eight-horse teams. Blocks of granite were carried between the nine-foot rear wheels of such galamanders (the origin of the name is unknown) between 1880 and 1914.

WALDOBORO

Old German Church and Cemetery, Route 32 — 1772

German Lutheran immigrants built this austere, frame building in 1772. Their descendants moved it in 1794 across the ice of the Medomak River, filled it with box pews, and added a hanging pulpit. The church was abandoned in the first half of the nineteenth century because of the older members' insistence that the sermons be preached in German. The third generation lost interest in the unintelligible services, and membership declined. The church and cemetery today are a well-preserved memorial to the early German settlers.

Godfrey Ludwig House, Route 32 — 1800

Because of its ties with Jacob Ludwig, leader of the German community in Broad Bay, and its interesting and unusual folding walls dating from its use as an early Methodist circuit meeting house, this building is important locally.

Waldoborough Town Pound, Route 235 — 1819

On May 15, 1819, it is recorded that the citizens of Waldoboro voted to rebuild the town's old wooden pound, which had apparently been built in 1785. The replacement, a stone enclosure, survives today as a tourist attraction and educational tool. The pound's six-foot-high walls were constructed of dry-laid, rough stones capped by flattened slabs held in place by forged staples. The opening under a huge lintel stone originally had a swinging wooden gate. The pound's state of preservation is remarkable.

Town pounds became common in the early nineteenth century, as Maine communities began to assume a more settled appearance. The regulation of the increasing number of livestock was necessary; the town pound was used to confine wandering animals until they were redeemed by their owners for a small fine.

U.S. Custom House and Post Office, Main Street — 1855–57

When the district of Waldoboro was created in 1799, a customs house was built. In 1854, this wooden building burned, and, to replace it, Ammi B. Young, supervising architect of the U.S. Treasury, designed the present Italianate, 2-story brick building. Situated in the heart of Waldoboro village, the Custom House was at one time the hub of all commercial activity. Since 1963 the building has housed the town library.

Hutchins House, 77 Main Street — ca. 1879

This important example of the comparatively rare Stick Style was built by the widow of the builder of the famous Palmer fleet of five-masted schooners. The house is 2½ stories with a 3½-story tower. Now adaptively reused as a funeral home, the Hutchins House is one of the most architecturally distinguished residences in the state.

WARREN, UNION, APPLETON, SEARSMONT

Georges River Canal Historic District

Canals for navigation on the Georges River (St. George River) had an important influence on the development of the valley. Without roads, the river served to connect the seaports with the upcountry sources for local industry. The Georges River was early used for access to the rich forest in its watershed, and mills were built at its lower falls.

In 1793, Charles Barrett of Hope constructed a canal from Warren to Union to enable him to move lumber. Major General Henry Knox purchased Barrett's locks and constructed three mills and two houses near the canal. Between 1806 and 1820, the locks decayed, but during the "Canal Era" after the War of 1812, popular enthusiasm led to the repair of the canal. It reopened in 1847. Unfortunately, maintenance of the wooden locks and earthen embankments consumed the earnings from tolls, and the canal closed in 1850.

The canal's water power continued to be used until the mid twentieth century when modern power sources made this source of energy obsolete. Nonetheless, the 28-mile canal route, including parts of the Georges River and the ponds through which it flows, is a visible reminder of the beginning of industrialism in the Georges River valley.

WESTPORT

Josiah Parsons Homestead, Greenleaf Cove Road — 1792, 1815

A veteran of Bunker Hill, Josiah Parsons established a residence of restrained Federal charm. His store (the only one on the island for many years) is still well preserved. It was built over the water with a boathouse below. The tidal gristmill is now gone. This beautiful and important complex later became the site of pathfinding experiments on dolphin behavior and communication by Dr. John C. Lilly and his wife, the present owner.

WHITEFIELD

St. Denis Catholic Church, Route 128 — 1833

This simple transitional Greek Revival church building was erected around an earlier frame structure of 1818. Organized to serve a large Irish immigrant population in the area, this is the second oldest Catholic parish in Maine and the third oldest in New England. Its young Irish pastor, Father Dennis Ryan, was the first priest ordained in New England.

WINTERPORT

Winterport Historic District

Winterport on the Penobscot River has survived as a prime example of a nineteenth-century Maine river town. Located thirteen miles below Bangor, Winterport was, as its name implies, the ice-free winter port for that lumber boom city.

While much of the evidence of Winterport's once thriving waterfront commercial and industrial activity no longer exists, the community's mid-nineteenth-century success remains apparent in the many substantial homes and buildings that comprise the historic district along Main, Elm, Cushing, Commercial, Dean, and Water streets, and Leba-

Winterport Historic District

Winterport Historic District

non Road. Although styles range from the post-Colonial period into the twentieth century, the predominant architectural theme is the Greek Revival, with more than half of the structures in the district (86 of 150) in this style.

Originally part of the town of Frankfort, Winterport was incorporated on March 12, 1860. By this time, Winterport had become a manufacturing center for sugar, hogsheads, butter and cheese, harnesses, and clothing. Shipbuilding and lumber production also ranked as important industries. A steam sawmill annually produced about eleven million feet of lumber and about two hundred thousand sugar-box shooks.

The key to the town's prosperity was the ice-free winter port for the lumber capital of Bangor. Large quantities of flour, grain, and other commodities were unloaded at Winterport from ships during the winter. The cargo was then hauled thirteen miles to Bangor, providing employment for many local farmers and their teams.

The depression of 1857 damaged Winterport's extensive shipbuilding. This, coupled with the disrupting effects of the Civil War and the establishment of improved railroad lines to Bangor, brought an end to the town's prosperity. There was no further large-scale growth, so that Winterport still preserves its mid-nineteenth-century appearance.

Winterport Congregational Church, Alternate Route 1 — 1831

In 1820, the Methodists, Episcopalians, Congregationalists, Unitarians and Universalists of Winterport formed a society in order to build a church. The Gothic Revival–style church was built in 1831 and soon became solely Congregational after interdenominational squabbles. Designed by local architect Calvin Ryder, the church, with its beautiful simple lines, is an important part of Maine's architectural heritage.

WISCASSET

Wiscasset Historic District

Wiscasset's name comes from a Warwenock word translated as "the place where three waters meet." The area was long used by the Indians before the English and French explored the harbor in the seventeenth century. The initial development of Wiscasset Point was undertaken by George Davie in the 1670s. By the end of the century, English settlements were dotted all along the Sheepscot River valley. Several

Silas Lee House, Wiscasset Historic District

Lincoln County Courthouse, Wiscasset Historic District

times, the joint efforts of the French and Indians drove off the settlers, but after 1763 the area became safe and the local economy began to stabilize.

Immediately after the Revolution, an extensive trade developed between foreign ports and Wiscasset, which was also a trading center for the local region. Most of Wiscasset's inhabitants were interested in the shipping industry, but the Embargo of 1807 and the War of 1812 ended the village's chances of becoming a major port. Wiscasset did achieve relative prosperity but never regained its importance as a port.

The boundaries of the Wiscasset Historic District encompass the village and its waterfront and contain both private homes and public buildings as well as a cemetery. Pre-Revolutionary Capes, Federal-style mansions, such as the famous Nickels-Sortwell House, and even a rare octagon house, built by Captain George Scott, are to be found in the Wiscasset district. These architectural specimens reflect Wiscasset's early years as a pioneer settlement and its later years as a thriving seaport.

Wiscasset's public and commercial buildings are also noteworthy, especially the Customs House, the Lincoln County Courthouse, and the old jail. Even in its exposed location on Route 1, Wiscasset remains a beautiful and carefully preserved village of quiet charm and outstanding architectural merit.

Red Brick School, Warren Street — 1807

This schoolhouse was built of handmade "mud bricks" in 1807 by Wiscasset townspeople (the Wiscasset Academical Association) who were anxious for an academy-level education facility. The building was used as a school until 1923. Since then, it has served as an American Legion post, a polling place, and an art gallery. The interior has been remodeled, but the exterior, with its charming Federal cupola, is the same as it was in 1807, except for the addition of a wooden fire escape.

Nickels-Sortwell House, U.S. Route 1 — 1807–12 (NHL)

Captain William Nickels, a shipmaster, erected this 3-story residence between 1807 and 1812. It is a splendid example of a large and elaborate frame town house designed in the

Nickels-Sortwell House, Wiscasset

Adamesque Federal style. Nickels died shortly after construction was completed, and the house passed through many hands. From 1820 until 1900, it was used as a hotel. The property was acquired in 1900 by Alvin F. Sortwell, who restored it between 1917 and 1918. In 1958, the mansion was deeded to the Society for the Preservation of New England Antiquities, which maintains it as a furnished historic house museum.

The Nickels-Sortwell House is of fine but provincial design. So much decoration was attempted on the façade that it may seem a bit overwrought. The beautiful detail on the interior, however, more than compensates for the overwhelming effect of the exterior. Few Maine houses of the period rival the Nickels-Sortwell House in the elaboration of their design.

Wiscasset Jail and Museum, Route 218 — 1809

Lincoln County had built two jails since its formation in 1760, but neither had been designed to hold prisoners for long terms of confinement. Meanwhile, by the early nineteenth century, the population had increased, the port towns were crowded with shipping, and a great lumber industry had developed. The influx of seamen and woodsmen from other parts introduced an element of disorder that was new to the area, and the small wooden jail was no longer adequate.

A new jail, begun in 1809, was finished two years later. It consisted of two floors of cells in a rectangular granite building with walls up to forty-one inches thick. A third floor contained dormitories for debtors, women, and the insane.

In 1837, a brick jailer's house was built onto one end of the jail to replace an earlier house, which had burned. Both buildings are open seasonally to the public as museums.

Captain George Scott House, Federal Street — 1855

This 2½-story brick home, with sandstone and granite lintels and sills, is an Italianate, bracketed, octagonal structure following plans by Orson Squire Fowler. One of the few octagonal houses in the state, it was built in 1855 for the famous shipmaster, George Scott, and his bride. The house remains in its original condition and is a reminder of Wiscasset's bygone era of maritime prosperity.

Captain George Scott House, Wiscasset. Photo by Arvin Robinson.

Old Customs House and Post Office, Water Street—1870

This 2-story, brick and granite Italianate building has remained structurally unaltered since it was built. Originally used as a customs house and post office, with administrative offices, the building continued to serve one or more of these purposes until the early 1960s. Today, it is a private residence with a gift shop on the first floor.

WOOLWICH

Days Ferry Historic District

The portion of the town of Woolwich known as Days Ferry was included in a tract of land purchased by James Smith in 1648 from the Plymouth Proprietors, the Indian Sachem Robin Hood, and Mahatiwormet, Chief of Nequat, Native Lord of Sagadahoc.

The ferry, operating across the Kennebec between Bath and the old stage road to Wiscasset, was well known as early as 1750. After bearing the names of various operators,

Days Ferry Historic District, Woolwich

both ferry and village were permanently named Days Ferry in 1788 for the Day family then in charge of the crossing.

When the threat of Indian uprisings eased at the close of the French and Indian War in 1763, steady growth characterized the progress of Days Ferry. Many industries developed, including an export ice business that thrived until the 1890s. Fishing and shipbuilding were also important activities, and at least seven sea captains built their homes with bricks from local yards.

Days Ferry throughout most of its history was a self-contained community boasting a tannery, blacksmith shop, shoemaker's shop, post office, and general store. As they have for over a century, the church, the school, and the house of the village doctor still stand side by side in this lovely community at the crossing of the Kennebec.

Robert Reed Homestead, Chop Point Road — ca. 1765

This is a splendid and beautifully restored example of a rural Colonial homestead, made more interesting by the addition of a Cape of the same vintage moved onto the property soon after the construction of the main house. It is also notable as the residence of poet and author Robert P. Tristram Coffin, beginning in the early 1930s, when he was a professor at Bowdoin College.

Lieutenant Hathorn House, Route 127 — 1784

Probably the best preserved example of an early Federal farmhouse in the central coastal region, this structure retains its five fireplaces and unusually fine interior woodwork.

Old Woolwich Town House, Old Stage Road — 1837

This relatively unchanged, simple structure is a good example of a rural public building common to the early-nineteenth-century Maine landscape. Of particular interest is the fact that it was built with funds distributed by the state as a result of the "deposit" of the federal surplus among the states voted by Congress in 1836.

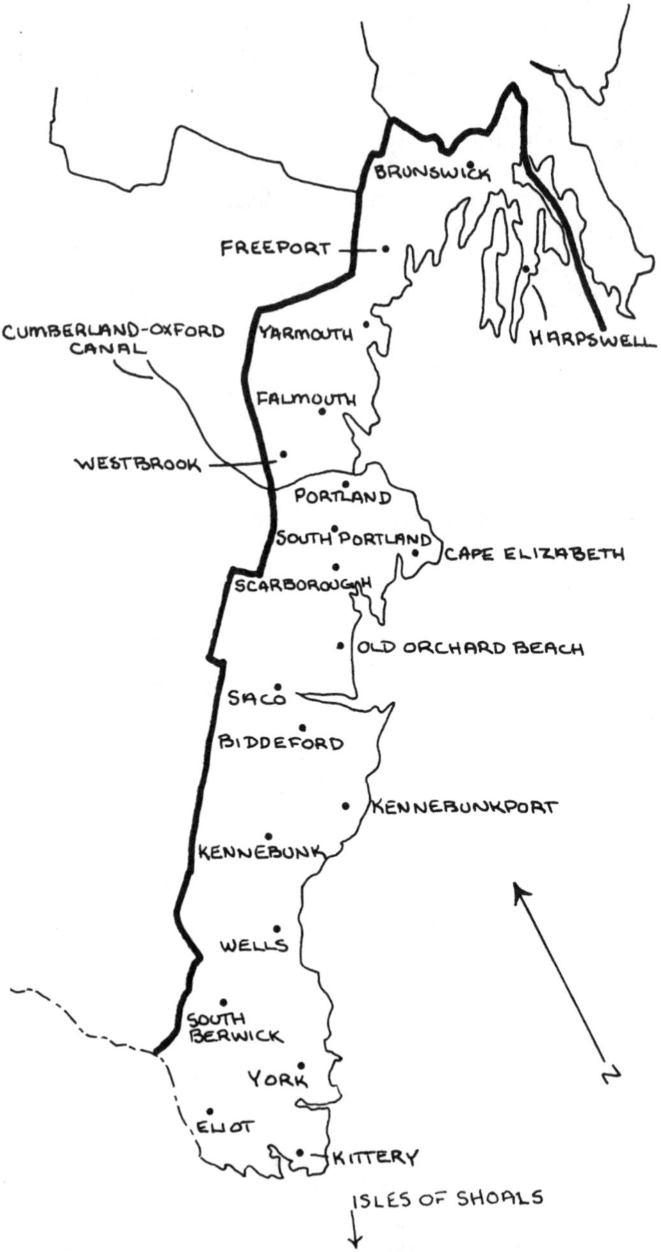
BRUNSWICK
FREEPORT
HARPSWELL
CUMBERLAND-OXFORD
CANAL
YARMOUTH
FALMOUTH
WESTBROOK
PORTLAND
SOUTH PORTLAND
CAPE ELIZABETH
SCARBOROUGH
OLD ORCHARD BEACH
SACO
BIDDEFORD
KENNEBUNKPORT
KENNEBUNK
N
WELLS
SOUTH
BERWICK
YORK
ELIOT
KITTERY
ISLES OF SHOALS

West Coastal Region

BIDDEFORD

John Tarr House, 29 Ferry Lane — ca. 1730

Among the state's earliest surviving dwellings, this Cape Cod–style house is of particular interest because of the fully panelled (walls *and* ceiling) kitchen of hand-planed panel and stile boarding. This rare feature is known to exist in only one or two other New England houses.

First Parish Meeting House, Pool Road — 1758

Nathaniel Perkins, master builder, constructed this meeting house in 1758 for the townspeople of Biddeford. Although the interior was remodeled in 1840, the framework (hand-hewn beams with wooden pins) of this Colonial building was not altered. All town meetings were held here during the Revolutionary period (sometimes the great patriot James Sullivan served as moderator), and the congregation pledged full support to the Revolutionary cause. In 1797, the congregation split and this building became known as the First Parish Church.

Fletcher's Neck Lifesaving Station, Ocean Avenue — 1874

One of the first five lifesaving stations in Maine and New Hampshire, activated on December 1, 1874, the Fletcher's Neck station is a 1½-story, Stick Style, frame building. Combining a necessary function with a picturesque design, the station housed a keeper and six men and the thousand-pound lifeboat on wheels. Now technologically obsolete, the Fletcher's Neck station stands as a monument to a century of noble service, heroism, and self-sacrifice.

Biddeford City Hall, 205 Main Street — 1895

Noted Maine architect John Calvin Stevens designed this 3½-story brick building faced with granite. The tower of the hall, with its clock, belfry, and dome, is an important feature of the Biddeford skyline. Also contained within this building is a handsomely decorated theatre.

James Montgomery Flagg House, St. Martin's Lane — 1910

This white bungalow/studio was for many years the summer home of the distinguished illustrator James Montgomery Flagg. Best known for his "I Want You" Uncle Sam recruiting poster of the First World War, Flagg was a colorful Bohemian figure, a respected portrait painter, and a successful and popular magazine illustrator.

United States Post Office, 35 Washington Street — 1914

A classic example of period architecture, this Federal building is made of brick, with granolithic quoins, lintels, and arches. The design and structure served as a blueprint for post offices built during the 1920s and 1930s; the plans were made by James Knox Taylor, supervising architect of the Treasury Department.

BRUNSWICK

Federal Street Historic District

The Pejepscot Purchase of 1714 by a group of wealthy Boston-based gentlemen marks the beginning of permanent settlement in Brunswick, since the sparse earlier settlements had been destroyed twice in the Indian wars of 1675 and 1690. During Lovewell's War in 1722, Indian raids once again nearly depopulated the area. By 1727, under the watchful eye of the Proprietors, a permanent, stable settlement was achieved. The town was incorporated in 1737 and, according to the census of 1790, boasted a population of 1,387.

The falls of the Androscoggin at Brunswick provided ample power for the variety of mills that sprang up during the eighteenth century. The town grew rapidly and experienced reasonable economic success. Easy access to the sea,

Bowdoin College Chapel, Federal Street Historic District, Brunswick

Federal Street Historic District, Brunswick

facilitating the transport of all kinds of goods, also contributed to Brunswick's prosperity. The decade beginning in 1798 proved to be Brunswick's finest. The windfall profits of the early Napoleonic war years and the founding of Bowdoin College combined to create and set the tone for the Federal Street neighborhood and profoundly affected what until that time had been primarily an agricultural, mill, and shipping community.

The original homeowners of the neighborhood established requirements for a uniform setback of twenty feet and a minimum of two stories for every house. This in itself is an interesting example of early urban planning, reflecting a conscious effort to maintain high standards. Care was also taken to establish well-proportioned lots.

Proximity to the college meant that members of the faculty chose the area for their residences. Certainly the presence of such intellectual lights also helped to establish the tone of the neighborhood.

Homes on Federal Street sprang up with considerable rapidity after its laying out. A writer in 1820 stated that there were then "about twenty houses . . . already erected with great exactness and symmetry."

The Federal Street Historic District preserves within its boundaries, which include the Campus and Park Row, not only a wealth of representative architectural styles, but also a neighborhood born out of a surge of prosperity and profoundly affected by the development of Maine's first college.

Lincoln Street Historic District, Brunswick

Lincoln Street Historic District

Lincoln Street, as a district, possesses unusual architectural homogeneity. The majority of the houses were built within a year or two of each other, the land having been owned by Dr. Isaac Lincoln, who divided it into lots, which sold out within a few months in 1843 and 1844.

Always known for his interest in orderly community growth, Dr. Lincoln, having decided to sell, set off evenly shaped lots with four rods of street frontage, the only exception being the corner lots on Union Street, which were six rods, twenty links in width. All the lots were disposed of between June 9, 1843, and September 10, 1844. Since the majority of the houses presently on Lincoln Street appear on an 1846 street map of Brunswick, it is clear that they were built within a span of two years. It is interesting that, in most of the deeds he granted, setbacks of sixteen links from the street were required. Lincoln Street still retains its uniformity and represents an interesting mid-nineteenth-century phenomenon in urban growth.

John Dunlap House, 4 Oak Street—1798–1800

Built by Dunlap, a prominent citizen and chairman of the Massachusetts Hall building committee for Bowdoin College, this house was designed by Aaron and Samuel Melcher III. It was the finest residence constructed up to that time and set the tone for the later Federal-style development in the town.

Massachusetts Hall,
Bowdoin College Campus — 1798–1802

Massachusetts Hall, built from designs by Samuel and Aaron Melcher, was the first building erected on the Bowdoin College campus. Construction began in 1798, but after the walls of brick brought from Portland were raised, a temporary roof was put on and the windows boarded up. Work had to be suspended until sufficient funds could be raised to finish construction. In 1801, after the sale of two of Bowdoin's five north-central Maine townships, work on the new hall resumed, and the building was completed in 1802, with Captain John Dunlap in charge of construction.

The hall was dedicated on September 2, 1802, remodeled between 1872 and 1873 by A.C. Martin, and restored and altered in 1936 by Felix A. Burton. Although the interior has undergone many alterations, the exterior has changed little from its original Federal appearance. Massachusetts Hall is used today as a dormitory facility.

Massachusetts Hall, Bowdoin College, Brunswick

Harriet Beecher Stowe House, Brunswick

Harriet Beecher Stowe House,
63 Federal Street — 1804 (NHL)

The Stowe House was built in 1804 and was intended for use as an inn. The building has long been closely associated with students and faculty members of Bowdoin College. It derives its historic name, however, from Harriet Beecher Stowe, who occupied it from 1850 until about 1870, while her husband, Calvin Stowe, was the Collins Professor of Natural and Revealed Religions at Bowdoin College.

Harriet Beecher Stowe was born in 1811, the daughter of the famous clergyman, Lyman Beecher, and the sister of five other ministers, including Henry Ward Beecher. While living with her family in Cincinnati, Harriet met and married Calvin Stowe, a teacher at Lane Seminary. The Stowes moved to Brunswick in 1850, and, in 1851, Mrs. Stowe began to write *Uncle Tom's Cabin*. Few books in American history have had a more profound effect on public opinion:

St. Paul's Episcopal Church, Brunswick

President Lincoln referred to Mrs. Stowe as "the little lady who made the book that started this great war."

Although the old inn has been enlarged to include a motor inn and restaurant, the rooms associated with Mrs. Stowe and her work have been preserved and are intact.

St. Paul's Episcopal Church, 27 Pleasant Street — 1845

Designed in 1845 from plans by the famous architect, Richard Upjohn, St. Paul's Episcopal Church of Brunswick is an early Gothic Revival, board and batten chapel form, which Upjohn popularized throughout the United States.

The simple but dignified one-story structure has no tower and no aisles in the nave. Cost considerations, however, did not diminish the quaintness and charm of this well-executed Gothic Revival design.

First Parish Church, 223 Maine Street — 1845

Renowned architect Richard Upjohn designed this Gothic Revival church in 1845, and members of the congregation started construction in the same year. Bowdoin College gave the parish financial assistance and in return received special rights to the use of the building. Harriet Beecher Stowe attended the First Parish Church. Henry W. Longfellow, President Taft, John Masefield, Eleanor Roosevelt, and Martin Luther King, Jr., have all spoken from its pulpit.

Henry Boody House, 256 Maine Street — 1849

The Henry Boody House of 1849 is a distinguished Gothic Revival cottage, which is considered a forerunner of the Stick Style. Designed in 1848, the cottage is the work of Gervase Wheeler, an English architect who came to America in the 1840s. Wheeler's use of exterior detail to reflect internal construction expressed an emerging aesthetic of realism in architecture. The year after its construction, the design received national attention when published in Andrew

Henry Boody House, Brunswick

Jackson Downing's *The Architecture of Country Houses* as "A Plain Timber Cottage Villa."

Boody was a Bowdoin graduate of 1842, and he served as professor of rhetoric and oratory from 1845 to 1854. The house is now the residence of the dean of the college.

Captain George McManus House, 11 Lincoln Street — 1857

The Captain George McManus, or Richardson, House of 1857 is a fine example of transitional Greek Revival–Italianate architecture. Elements of both styles are found on the interior and the exterior. Great attention was given to proportion and detail, with no significant inconsistency. Regrettably, the architect remains unknown.

The house was built as the result of the successful maritime career of Captain George McManus, a prominent Brunswick master mariner. McManus lived in the house until his death in about 1864. Subsequent owners were the Lufkin and Richardson families and St. Paul's Episcopal Church, which used the house as a rectory. The Pejepscot Historical Society, one of Maine's oldest historical organizations, now owns the home and operates a museum of Brunswick area history.

CAPE ELIZABETH

Richmond's Island Archaeological Site — 1628, 1632

One of the earliest and best-documented of Maine's seventeenth-century archaeological sites lies on Richmond's Island. Here, in 1627 or 1628, one Walter Bagnall established a trading post, where he made easy money from the Indians, until his disgruntled customers burned his house down around him in 1731. Probably buried by Bagnall, a hoard of fifty-two gold and silver coins, dating from 1564 to 1625, was found by a farmer plowing on the island in 1855. In 1632, John Winter arrived on the island and established a prosperous year-round fishing station. Most of Winter's correspondence has survived, giving the historical archaeologist remarkably detailed data on the settlement's personnel, buildings, and economy.

Portland Head Light, Cape Elizabeth. Courtesy of U.S. Coast Guard.

Portland Head Light, Portland Head — 1790

Portland Head Light is one of four lighthouses that have never been rebuilt since their construction was first authorized by President Washington. The main section of the tower, built on rubblestone, remains the same as it was in 1790. It was first lighted on January 10, 1791.

Local masons John Nichols and Jonathan Bryant built the tower. The first keeper's cottage was constructed in 1816; the present quarters, in 1891. Also within the complex of buildings are the whistle house, paint locker, and garage.

Portland Head Light has been and continues to be an important part of Maine and her history. It has stood for nearly two centuries as a beacon for the mariners of the United States and other nations. It is perhaps the best known and most photographed lighthouse on the northeast coast.

Spurwink Congregational Church — 1802, 1830

In 1733, the Second Parish in Falmouth was established and a meeting house built for the area south of the Fore River. In 1802, the Spurwink Church was built to house an enlarging congregation. It was rebuilt in 1830. A century later, it became an independent church, after having been associated with the First Congregational Church of South Portland, and disbanded only twenty-two years later. The building itself, constructed in typical early-nineteenth-century meeting-house style, is now used only by sightseers and occasionally for special religious events.

Beckett's Castle, Cape Cottage — 1871–74

This unusual gothic cottage was designed and built by Samuel Beckett, Portland lawyer, artist, poet, literateur, and ornithologist, for his summer residence, one of the first in the area. The stone building, with its 3-story tower, was a retreat for Beckett and members of his intellectual circle.

Two Lights — 1874

The two cast-iron lighthouses are 300 feet apart and were identical until World War II, when the west light became an observation post. The west light was extinguished in 1924, and the east light was electrified in 1925, but the towers stand as a reminder of an era when even the most functional structures were endowed with grace and dignity.

C.A. Brown Cottage, 9 Delano Park — 1886–87

The C.A. Brown cottage is a well-developed work in the Shingle Style, designed by John Calvin Stevens, Maine's most prominent architect at the turn of the century.

Stevens was an early advocate of what may be called organic architecture — matching the building to its surroundings. Because of this environmental and aesthetic concern, his seaside cottages are well adapted to their locations through the use of local materials and color schemes in keeping with the natural features of the landscape. Thus, the foundation and lower part of the Brown House are of "weathered fieldstone the very color of the ledges out of which the building grows," to quote Stevens himself.

ELIOT

Frost Garrisons and House,
Frost's Hill — 1733, ca. 1738, ca. 1778

Erected by a single family for defense against Indian attack, the Frost Garrisons and House date from 1733, circa 1738, and circa 1778, respectively. The earlier garrison was built of hand-hewn timbers and has portholes for firing; it was used mainly as a powder house. The second of the garrisons was built for neighborhood use; it has 12-inch outside corner dovetails of pine logs, hand-hewn into squared timbers. The first floor served for the protection of livestock, and the second for settlers. The Frost House is a 2½-story wooden frame building, which has been restored to its original condition. At one time the buildings were connected by underground tunnels.

FALMOUTH

Thomas Skelton House, 124 U.S. Route 1 — ca. 1798

This Portland house has been added to, moved, renovated, and added to again, but still retains its original flavor. Originally constructed by housewright Thomas Skelton around 1798 and enlarged by cordwainer Benjamin Deake around 1810, the building was about to be sacrificed for a parking lot when it was moved by a concerned preservation organization. The house now stands in Falmouth, an impressive example of preservation at work.

Hall's Tavern, 377 Gray Road — ca. 1800

Built by Nicholas Hall, this graceful and ample Federal house was converted by his son, Osni, into an inn or tavern. Of particular note is the taproom, preserved in nearly original condition, with a wicket through which beverages were dispensed from the bar. Two of the upper rooms retain wall stenciling in good condition.

The Falmouth House, 340 Gray Road — ca. 1820

Built in the early nineteenth century, but retaining traditional eighteenth-century forms, the Falmouth House served for nearly a century as a well-known and popular hostelry on the road from Portland to the newly emerging industrial complex at Lewiston-Auburn. The fine Federal detail of the interior survives, as well as interesting wall stenciling.

FREEPORT

Freeport Main Street Historic District

The area represented in part by the Freeport Main Street Historic District is particularly interesting in that it demonstrates a recurring phenomenon in the evolution of some older New England towns. There is mounting evidence to indicate that the present centers of such communities were often not the areas first settled, or, if they were, only sparsely so. Most early coastal communities in Maine depended largely on water transport for communication between each another and such roads as existed in the early eighteenth century were primitive at best and more often mere footpaths. Furthermore, the early settlements were mainly agricultural or oriented toward maritime activities.

Such was the case in Freeport, whose earliest settlement emerged primarily along the shore, where the convoluted coastline offered abundant opportunities for saltwater farms, fishing, and shipbuilding. The present center, based on Main Street and first called Freeport Corner, began to emerge only after a stage route developed on the road from Yarmouth to Bath and Brunswick in the later eighteenth century. Even then, what industry existed — and this was mostly shipbuilding, continued to be carried on in the coastal strip. It was not until the 1880s that shoe manufacturing, introduced by Freeport's great benefactor, E.B. Mallet, changed Freeport Center into an industrial area.

Freeport Main Street Historic District

As the community matured by the end of the eighteenth century, the Main Street section, largely because of improved transportation, began to draw to it business and professional men, as evidenced by some of the houses in the Freeport Main Street Historic District. These substantial houses reflect this trend and the real beginning of the modern town.

Thus, from a dusty country crossroads in the late eighteenth century, the modern center of Freeport evolved over the span of a century. The visual evidence of the beginning of this development lies in the nine buildings between number 30 and number 49 Main Street.

Harraseeket Historic District

The Harraseeket Historic District comprises three villages on the shores of the Harraseeket River — South Freeport, Porter's Landing, and Mast Landing. The manmade heritage from the eighteenth and nineteenth centuries remains largely unchanged and stands amidst the beautiful natural setting of the Harraseeket River. Encompassed within the boundaries of the district are approximately six thousand acres stretching from Stockbridge Point on the west side of the mouth of the river, along the western shore to the head of the Harraseeket, and all the way down Wolf Neck on the eastern shore.

South Freeport is the largest of the district's three vil-

Harrasseeket Historic District, Freeport

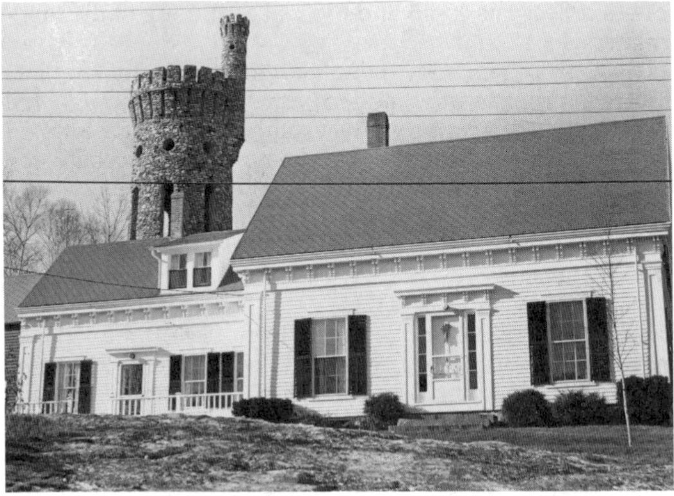

lages. Its greatest period of development occurred during its shipbuilding boom of the 1850s; this prosperous period is reflected in the many spacious Greek Revival–style homes there. Earlier and later styles are also represented. Shipbuilding held the most prominent economic position until World War I.

Porter's Landing developed between the late eighteenth and mid nineteenth century. Many of the homes in this community are of large scale and have Federal or Greek Revival detail. Porter's Landing is best known for the armed privateer *Dash*, built there in 1813.

Mast Landing is located at the head of the river. Most of the homes in the small community date from 1800 to 1850. The predominant architectural form is the 1½-story, central chimneyed Cape with Federal or Greek Revival doorways. Mast Landing was the location to which masts for the British navy were delivered from the surrounding forests. In the late eighteenth century, a village developed at the site. Of special interest in the area are the Pote House and the Pettengill House, which are also on the National Register.

The remaining houses, mill and dam ruins, and the surroundings give a strong sense of time and place in Maine history.

Pote House, Wolf Neck Road — ca. 1750

This Colonial saltbox house is undoubtedly the oldest on Wolf's Neck, because it was moved there by Captain Greenfield Pote in about 1765. The house was constructed in Falmouth but was moved thirteen miles on a flat boat after a dispute with local officials. Some shingles and windows have been replaced, but the frame, timbers, boarding, and chimney are original.

Pettengill House and Farm, near Mast Landing — ca. 1800

Few lean-to or saltbox houses were built in Maine, and not many have survived to the present day. Because the Pettengill House has never been modernized or structurally altered, it is an excellent example of this architectural type.

The serviceable farmhouse gains dignity from its simple, straightforward detailing. Most of the original woodwork and hardware are intact. In one room, there are still plaster etchings depicting the shipping activity carried on in front of the house on the Harraseeket River.

The house has recently been restored by the Freeport Historical Society using funds provided by the Maine Historic Preservation Commission.

The Pettengill Farm is an unblemished saltwater farm, once common to the Maine coast.

E.B. Mallet Office Building, Mill Street — 1888

This unpretentious but well-proportioned Italianate office building was designed by Francis H. Fassett, Maine's leading mid-nineteenth-century architect. Its major significance, however, stems from the fact that it was the headquarters of Edmund Buston Mallett, Jr., who, almost singlehanded, turned Freeport from a small rural community into a thriving industrial center. He built two shoe factories, a sawmill, a gristmill, coal yard, lumber yard, granite quarry, and water system. For Mallet's new office building, the granite came from his own quarry, the lumber from his mill, and the brick from his yard.

HARPSWELL

Harpswell Meeting House, Harpswell Center — 1757–59 (NHL)

This frame, clapboarded meeting house was built between 1757 and 1759 and is the oldest remaining meeting house in Maine. Elisha Eaton, a housewright and the son of the first pastor, probably was in charge of construction. The church had been established in 1753 and overseen by the Reverend Richard Pateshall. The Reverend Elisha Eaton, Sr., was followed by his son, Samuel, who served the parish until his death in 1822.

Although the Harpswell Meeting House is smaller than the typical Maine meeting house, its overall structure and interior design are the same. Since 1844, when use of the building as a church was discontinued, most of the pews have been removed, and the structure serves as a place for town meetings and a town office.

Harpswell Meeting House

Merriconegan Farm, Route 123 — ca. 1830–97

The primary significance of Merriconegan Farm lies in the fact that it is the most impressive example of extended, or continuous, architecture remaining, and perhaps ever to have existed, in Maine and possibly New England. In an excellent state of preservation, it comprises two complete houses with residential ells, sheds, and two large barns, one at either end. The entire complex was gradually assembled between the early 1830s and 1897. Magnificently located on a rise overlooking Harpswell Bay and approached directly from the front by a long straight entrance road that joins an oval drive passing the length of the structure, Merriconegan Farm, although a working agricultural entity, also reveals the economic and cultural background of its builders.

Thomas Skolfield, son of an Irish landowner, came to America as a young man in 1757 with the Orr family, later proprietors of Orr's Island on the neighboring peninsula east of Harpswell. Skolfield, a graduate of Oxford University, taught for a time at both Boston Latin School and Harvard College. After coming to Maine with the Orrs, he acquired a large tract of land in the area of the present farm

Merriconegan Farm, Harpswell

but, at his death in 1796, had had little time to develop it. Of his five sons, Clement, a Harvard graduate, remained on the land, built a house (now standing in Brunswick a few hundred yards north), and worked the farm. George (later always referred to as "Master George"), the eldest of Clement's seven sons, began a shipbuilding business on Harpswell Bay across the road from the farm. He became highly successful, constructing a series of large sailing vessels, many of which were captained by his younger brother.

It was Master George who, with his father, built the first in the present complex and later the older of the two barns. His son, George Roger, and grandson, Daniel T., built the remaining parts of the present structure and carried on the shipyard until the early years of this century. The property is still owned by the Skolfield family, and the desire to preserve it continues.

Elijah Kellogg Church, Harpswell Center — 1834

This very fine rural example of a transitional Greek Revival–Gothic Revival church is of particular importance as the first, and also the last, pulpit filled by Elijah Kellogg, noted author of some thirty very popular books for children written in the 1860s and 1870s.

Elijah Kellogg House, Route 123 — 1849

This simple but distinctively designed, 2½-story Greek Revival dwelling was built in 1849 with his own hands by

Elijah Kellogg, noted minister and author. Seventy-five of his parishioners from the Harpswell Congregational Church assisted in raising the frame on the granite foundation. The exterior and interior are being restored after two decades of neglect and vandalism.

A well-loved pastor in Harpswell, Boston, and other locations, Kellogg was best known in his own day as the extremely popular author of more than thirty books for children.

Eagle Island — 1904

The Indian-named island of Sawungun was purchased by Robert E. Peary, discoverer of the North Pole, in 1880. After renaming it Eagle Island (probably in honor of the *Eagle* on which he first sailed to the Arctic), Admiral Peary used the island both as a vacation home and as a headquarters for the writing and research work of his later years. Peary began building on the island in 1904 and lived in the cottage while planning his 1909 expedition to the Pole. The island was given to the state of Maine as an historic site by Marie Peary Kuhne, the Admiral's daughter, in 1966.

Bailey Island Cobwork Bridge, Route 24 — 1928

The famous cobwork bridge of 1928, connecting Orr's and Bailey islands, represents a unique solution to a difficult engineering problem and is probably the only sturcture of its kind in the world. The swiftness of the tides in Will's Gut, which it spans, and the consequent battering of floating ice in extreme weather created unusual challenges in determining its design.

On a natural reef, granite blocks are laid in open construction, first lengthwise, then crosswise in a crib manner. No mortar or cement is used. Due to the uneven shapes of the rough-cut stones, pine wedges are driven in the cracks between them at certain places to prevent rocking and shifting. At the center over the deep channel, a single steel span of 52 feet rests on solid concrete pillars lined with granite stonework. The roadway across the bridge is of reinforced concrete.

The granite slabs quarried in Yarmouth are heavy enough

Bailey Island Cobwork Bridge, Harpswell

to withstand the buffeting of waves and ice floes, and the open cribbing construction permits the tidal currents to flow freely. Beyond the occasional replacement of the wooden wedges used to stabilize the slabs, the bridge requires almost no maintenance, except for the road surface and short central span.

KENNEBUNK

Kennebunk Historic District

The early history of Kennebunk is to be found within the town of Wells, incorporated in 1653, which encompassed the present town of Kennebunk. Separation did not occur until 1820, the same year Maine separated from Massachusetts. The area now known as the town of Kennebunk lies mainly between the Mousam and Kennebunk rivers. The district extends from the middle of the commercial center easterly along Summer Street to Kennebunk Landing.

Up to 1700, little progress was made in the settlement of Kennebunk. Between 1700 and 1750, however, the lands and privileges between the two rivers were in great demand. On March 22, 1736, one hundred acres of land were

Kennebunk Historic District

Colonel William L. Thompson House, Kennebunk Historic District

surveyed for Nathaniel and Richard Kimball. This survey inaugurated the permanent settlement of the village area. Up to that time, no dwelling had been erected within its limits. There had been a few temporary structures, but by 1736 they no longer existed.

From the mid eighteenth century on, the area between the Mousam and Kennebunk rivers grew into a large town with a history significant to Maine and the nation. Local businesses prospered in the village and along the Kennebunk River. The most successful of these commercial ventures were, of course, those related to shipbuilding.

The significance of this historic district lies in its architecture, for nothing remains of the great shipyards. The homes of the shipbuilders, shipowners, and sea captains survive, however, leaving a largely unchanged picture of life in a sea-oriented village of earlier times. Within the small area is a great spectrum of architecture ranging from mid-eighteenth-century Colonial to late-nineteenth-century Queen Anne. All but one of these great houses were built of wood, the most readily available building material. The one brick house is the famous "Wedding Cake House." Almost all designed and built by local men, these homes are a great tribute to the talent of the Maine craftsmen and house joiners.

James Smith Homestead, Route 35 — 1753

This superb example of a Georgian farmhouse is an important survival from the period of prosperity that began in southern Maine in the mid eighteenth century.

Lord Mansion, 20 Summer Street — 1760, 1801

This building is both a fine Colonial house and a superb Federal mansion. The original owner built the Colonial section in 1760, and, when the house was sold in 1801, the second owner added a Federal mansion to the front, making of the first house an ell. The mansion is basically unaltered and is in excellent condition.

Bourne Mansion, 8 Bourne Street — 1812

Built in 1812 by John Usher Parsons, a successful merchant and Massachusetts state senator, the Bourne Mansion is arguably the finest dwelling ever erected in Kennebunk and one of the most impressive and well-conceived examples of

Bourne Mansion, Kennebunk

Federal architecture in southern Maine. Tradition holds that the house was based on the plan of a house occupied before her marriage by Mrs. Parsons in Newburyport. This latter residence has since been destroyed by fire.

The interior of the house matches its exterior in elegance, with a wide hall passing the length of the structure front to back and joined in the center by a slightly narrower hall leading from the east entrance. Other features include an elaborately finished spiral staircase of three flights, an arch-embellished niche for a tall clock, and an arched ceiling for the side hall.

In 1815, the house was sold to Daniel Sewall, Clerk of Courts and Registrar of Deeds in York County. It was bequeathed in the latter part of the nineteenth century by Mrs. William Sewall to her nephew, Edward E. Bourne, Jr., member of an old Kennebunk family prominent over several generations as shipbuilders, historians, jurists, and legislators.

KENNEBUNKPORT

Kennebunkport Historic District

Lying along North and Maine streets, Ocean Avenue, and intersecting streets, this district provides one of the richest

Kennebunkport Historic District

Kennebunkport Historic District

samples of eighteenth-, nineteenth-, and early twentieth-century architecture to be found in Maine. In addition, the houses and other buildings are well preserved and maintained, so that the attractiveness of the streetscapes combined with the sense of historical time and place create a visual experience of richness and beauty.

Although the earliest settlement in the town centered about Cape Porpoise Harbor in the 1620s, the community center had moved to the banks of the Kennebunk River by the later eighteenth century. This resulted from the dramatic growth in maritime activity, particularly after the Revolution, and the desirability of river locations for shipyards and accompanying businesses.

The architecture of the town dates from these years, starting with post-Colonial and Federal houses of large proportions, followed in turn by Greek Revival, Italianate and Mansard residences, reflecting continuing prosperity throughout the nineteenth century. The turn of the century brought with it the influx of summer residents and vacationers, whose impact on the cummunity resulted in an economic renewal just as the shipbuilding industry was seeing its last days.

Today, Kennebunkport again thrives as a summer resort and a sought-after residential community, but it preserves in its historical architecture the spirit and vibrancy of its past.

Maine Trolley Cars,
Seashore Trolley Museum — 1893–1926

The street car is fast disappearing from the American scene. Trolleys operate in fewer than a dozen cities in the United States and Canada, and even these remnants may be gone soon.

It is difficult to realize that as recently as 1921 the electric railway business was America's fifth largest industry. The trolley, in its heyday, had a tremendous impact on the American way of life. By providing transportation that was fast, comfortable, and reasonably priced, it promoted urban development and opened up suburban living to a large segment of the population. Trolley excursions to the beach, lake, park, and countryside were a part of everyday living in the pre-automobile age. Many electric railways, in addition to carrying passengers, engaged in express and freight

Maine Trolley Cars, Seashore Trolley Museum, Kennebunkport

business and thus contributed to the growth and flow of commerce.

Beginning in the 1890s, a vast trolley network began to spread across the state of Maine, as it did elsewhere. By 1910, there were dozens of electric railway companies in the state operating over more than two thousand miles of track. In Maine, the trolley played an important role in the development of the important resort industry. It also brought about the development of numerous suburban parks built specifically to promote travel on the newly developed lines. Yet, by the late 1920s, the trolley had almost entirely disappeared, except for some urban lines. The rural and interurban routes had been put out of business by the automobile.

The ten Maine trolley cars that form part of the collection at the Seashore Trolley Museum recall the variety of trolley services in the state during this short but important period in the history of public transportation.

Perkins Tide Mill, Mill Lane—1749

The Old Gristmill is one of the last original and well-preserved examples of eighteenth-century tidewater gristmills in the country. Built in 1749 and operated until

1939, the mill was run by tidal rather than by a dammed water head. Most of the old equipment is still intact, and architectural features include a variety of exposed framing, knee braces, mill machinery and early hardware.

The mill has been in the Perkins family since its construction. Now the building houses The Olde Grist Mill Restauant, a felicitous adaptive re-use.

Captain Nathaniel Lord Mansion, Pleasant Street—1812

This Federal-style mansion was built by ship carpenters, unemployed because of the War of 1812. The rear portion of the house was added on in 1859 in the same fine style. The interior of the home, restored in recent years, retains its exceptionally fine woodwork, with some rooms even retaining original wallpaper. Captain Lord was a wealthy shipowner, shipbuilder, and community leader.

U.S. Custom House, Main Street—1813

Kennebunkport became headquarters port for the District of Kennebunk in 1800; in 1815, this Federal-style, 2-story brick building was completed and used as the U.S. Custom House and as a bank. In 1916, the building became a library; additions were built in 1921 and 1956. Throughout its long history, the building has retained its early-nineteenth-century integrity, while adapting to the varying needs of the community.

The Clock Farm, Route 9—ca. 1850

Some part of this remarkable piece of extended Greek Revival architecture is said to date from the mid-eighteenth century. Nevertheless, its importance as a local landmark rests on the unusual four-faced nineteenth-century clock mounted in the barn cupola. Thomas Emmons, a Massachusetts manufacturer, installed this architectural curiosity in the barn at his summer place. Tradition has it that the instrument kept such bad time at the Emmons Loom Harness Company that it caused serious labor-management disputes.

Abbott Graves House, Ocean Avenue — 1905

One of only two known examples of the Prairie style existing in the state, this house was designed by its first occupant, Abbott Graves, an internationally known artist, who had also received partial training in architecture at M.I.T.

Kennebunk River Club, Ocean Avenue — 1889–90

The Kennebunk River Club of 1889–90 is a handsome example of Shingle-Style architecture, which became popular for recreational buildings and summer cottages in the late nineteenth century. Although the architect remains unknown, his bold use of the all-encompassing gable roof reflects his awareness of the most advanced design of the period.

Sited directly on the Kennebunk River, the River Club is located a quarter of a mile from the ocean. Although minor alterations and additions have been made to the building, its original function as a clubhouse and the dramatic visual

Kennebunk River Club, Kennebunkport

impact of its design have remained unchanged for eighty-five years.

Since its formal opening on August 2, 1890, the Kennebunk River Club has served as the focal point for summer activity on the Kennebunk River.

KITTERY

Dennett Garrison, 100 Dennett Road — ca. 1710

This large home built by John Dennett, a Kittery pioneer, was selected in 1720 as one of several "garrisons," or "places of refuge," for the community. Still owned by the Dennett family, it is one of the best-preserved and earliest Maine houses. Its architecture clearly owes much to seventeenth-century traditions.

Portsmouth Naval Shipyard, Dennett's Island

Located at the mouth of the Piscataqua River, between Maine and New Hampshire, the Portsmouth Naval Shipyard has been in existence for 180 years and was the first navy yard established by the Navy Department. This government establishment, however, merely continues a tradition of shipbuilding and maritime activity that began within a few years of the first European contacts with the area. As early as 1650, the British government selected this port as a suitable location to build ships for the Royal Navy. The immediate availability of mast timber was, of course, a prime consideration, in addition to the obvious geographical advantages.

For a number of years, only small vessels were built, but in 1749 the sixty-gun *America* slid down the ways, the largest Royal Navy ship ever built in the New World. In December 1775, the Continental Congress authorized the construction of thirteen frigates. One of these, the thirty-two-gun *Raleigh*, was to be built at Portsmouth under the direction of John Langdon, leader of the operation against Castle William and Mary, who offered his island in the river (now Badger's Island) for the purpose.

In April 1798, Congress established a Navy Department separate from the War Department. One of the new depart-

Portsmouth Naval Shipyard Historic District, Kittery

Commandant's Quarters, Portsmouth Naval Shipyard Historic District

Officers' Quarters, Portsmouth Naval Shipyard Historic District

ment's first actions was the purchase in 1800 of Dennett's Island, adjacent to Langdon's, as the site of the first navy yard.

Little activity took place until the War of 1812. The flagship of the Mediterranean squadron, the *Washington*, was launched at the yard in 1815.

In April 1861, the yard was placed on a war footing, and the keels of two nine-gun, screw propulsion, steam sloops were laid. One of these, the *Kearsarge*, achieved lasting fame when she sank the *Alabama*, commanded by Captain Raphael Semmes, the notorious Confederate raider, off Cherbourg in 1864. In 1863 and 1864, two four-gun ironclads were constructed.

The navy yard achieved its present size in 1866 with the purchase of Seavey Island, which is about three times the size of Dennett's Island and separated from it by narrow Jenkins Gut. Part of the gut was converted into a 750-foot dry dock, which still exists, and the rest was filled in, making one large island now called Seavey Island throughout. The historic district occupies almost the entire area of Dennett's Island.

With the launching of the "L-8" in 1917, the Portsmouth Naval Yard became the first government facility to build a submarine. Since that time, it has been the only yard devoted exclusively to submarine construction and repair and, with the launching of the *Swordfish* in 1958, the first government yard to build a nuclear-powered submarine. Submarine construction at the yard ended in 1969; since then efforts have centered on the support of a continuing program of attack and fleet ballistic missile submarine overhauls.

The Portsmouth Naval Shipyard Historic District contains a remarkable and extensive collection of nineteenth-century industrial structures of unusually fine design. There is also a distinguished row of officers' quarters executed in brick in the Greek Revival tradition. The most striking building is Quarters A, residence of the senior naval officer, built probably in 1724.

Bray House, Pepperrell Road — 1662(?), ca. 1720

In 1662, John Bray of Plymouth, England, selected this magnificent site for his home in the New World. How much of the original structure is contained within the present building of around 1720 is uncertain, but it ranks nevertheless as one of the oldest houses in Maine.

First Congregational Church and Parsonage, Pepperrell Road — 1729, 1730

These are two remarkable survivals from the early eighteenth century, a period from which little remains above ground in Maine. Despite its age, this church of 1729 is the fourth such structure on this site, the Congregational parish having been founded in 1635. The Parsonage may be the oldest building built for this purpose in the state.

William Pepperrell House, Route 103 — ca. 1720

Although this house does contain beams dating from the seventeenth century, it is almost certain that construction took place no earlier than 1720. Pepperrell's Colonial mansion was remodeled by his son and great-grandson, both named William, so its appearance now is quite Georgian. The three William Pepperrells were, respectively, a great landowner and merchant; a famous soldier, baronet, and acting Massachusetts governor; and a Loyalist refugee to

England whose estate was confiscated by Revolutionary government officials.

Lady Pepperrell House, Pepperrell Road — 1760 (NHL)

The Lady Pepperrell House is a Georgian house of great architectural distinction. Called one of the most suavely sophisticated Georgian homes in America, this magnificent dwelling was constructed in 1760 by Lady Mary Pepperrell, widow of Sir William Pepperrell. The stately atmosphere in which Lady Pepperrell dwelt is well conveyed by the house, which retains many period furnishings. The Society for the Preservation of New England Antiquities owns and administers this beautiful mansion as a museum.

Sir William Pepperrell inherited a great deal of property from his father, a Welsh immigrant, and he enlarged the fortune as the leading merchant and landowner in northern New England. He dealt in ships, lumber, naval stores, fish, and miscellaneous goods brought from England. His real estate transactions greatly increased his fortune.

When war broke out between France and England in 1744, William Pepperrell commanded the land forces during the attack on the fortress of Louisburg on Cape Breton Island. Miraculously, under the command of an untrained

Lady Pepperrell House, Kittery

soldier, the siege was successful, and Louisburg was taken. Pepperrel was made a baronet.

After Pepperrell's lavish funeral in 1759, his wife constructed her elaborate residence in the modern Georgian style on a lot near her daughter's home.

Fort McClary, Kittery Point, off Route 103 — 1844–69

A height of land on Kittery Point has been occasionally fortified since the Colonial period for a variety of reasons. In 1715, a battery of six guns behind a breastwork was erected to intimidate New Hampshire tax collectors who were persecuting Massachusetts and Maine shipping. The site was further strengthened during the Revolution and the War of 1812 to protect the important naval shipyard at Kittery.

In the years following 1844, after the alarming confrontation with Great Britain over Maine's northern boundary in the Aroostook War, Maine's last blockhouse was erected on the site. This blockhouse, hexagonal in plan, was built on a fieldstone foundation, with a cut-granite first story and log second story.

During the Civil War, Fort McClary was further strengthened with a pentagonal granite perimeter wall (never completed) and equipped with additional buildings, including a barracks, cook house and mess hall, chapel, hospital, guardhouse, and powder house. Abandoned after 1869, the fort was again armed in 1898 during the brief

Fort McClary, Kittery

Spanish-American War. Seldom has a site been fortified against such diverse enemies.

Today, much of the Fort McClary complex survives as a state memorial administered by the Maine Bureau of Parks and Recreation.

William Dean Howells House, Pepperrell Road — ca. 1870

Originally built in about 1870 by Joseph D. Brannum, a wealthy businessman from Springfield, Massachusetts, this beautifully sited residence overlooking the mouth of the Piscataqua River was the summer home of William Dean Howells during the last two decades of his illustrious literary career.

The son of a printer, Howells was born in Ohio and began writing before he was twenty. One or two of his early poems were published in the *Atlantic*. His campaign biography of Lincoln led to his appointment at the age of twenty-four as consul in Venice, where he spent five years absorbing European literature and launching a serious writing career.

Revolting against the artificialities of Victorian fiction, Howells attracted increasing attention as a leader in the movement toward realism, which gathered other adherents like Stephen Crane and Frank Norris. In 1866, James T. Fields invited him to come to Boston as assistant editor of the *Atlantic*, a prize which he had longed for. Becoming chief editor in 1872, Howells emerged as the lion of the literary scene, by all odds the most popular writer of his day. His output was prolific and versatile, including novels, plays, essays, poems, reviews, and travel pieces. He achieved remarkable success in consistently expressing himself with ease, exactness, and felicity. As editor of the *Atlantic*, his influence was widespread, and he encouraged and helped such aspiring writers as Mark Twain and Henry James, whom he later numbered among his closest friends.

His realistic style had an enormous effect in his time and later on American writing, and he is perhaps best remembered for such novels as *The Rise of Silas Lapham* (1885) and *A Hazard of New Fortunes* (1890). Howells' work dealt with everyday people and a realistic translation of their experience.

Howells's biographer, Van Wyck Brooks, tells us that "with all this going and coming and moving in New York,

Howells had a fixed base on the coast of Maine at York Harbor and after 1902 in Kittery Point where he bought a house on the shore." Mrs. Howells called it the "Maine stay" because of the sense of permanence it gave their life.

Rice Public Library, 8 Wentworth Street — 1889

This handsome, ornamental, and well-proportioned Romanesque Revival building was designed by Shepherd S. Woodcock of Boston. Of its type and style it is by far the most outstanding building in the state.

OLD ORCHARD BEACH

The Temple, Temple Avenue, Ocean Park — 1881

The Temple at Ocean Park, one of only two octagonal churches in Maine, was built in the summer of 1881. The design was obtained for $27.50 from the firm of Dow and Wheeler. Erected in less than three months by Portland builder James Bickford, the Temple cost $3,500. The building was dedicated on August 2, 1861, and has seen continuous summer use since its opening.

The community of Ocean Park was created in 1880 by the Centennial Conference of Free Will Baptists as a summer resort with religious, educational, and other programs. By 1881, building had begun, and the community has thrived over the years. The public assemblies in The Temple have dealt with a variety of interesting and inspirational topics, and Sunday services are conducted there by eminent theologians and preachers of many denominations. The Temple represents an unusual but once popular architectural form and is unique among Maine churches. It also symbolizes a lasting commitment to an admirable nineteenth century ideal.

Ocean Park Historic Buildings,
Temple Avenue — 1881, 1882, 1902, 1915

Along with the Temple, Porter and Jordan halls and the Bell Tower form Temple Square, the focal point of Ocean Park, a family-style summer community with a religious background. Religious resorts were common at the turn of the century, but, of the few remaining, Ocean Park is clearly the least changed and retains the traditions of education, self-improvement, and enjoyment of simple summer pleasures.

PORTLAND

Spring Street Historic District

Portland's Spring Street Historic District lies within an area of approximately 101 acres centered around Spring Street. The district includes part of Danforth, Pine, and Congress streets as well. During the period between 1800 and the 1890s, it was in this section of Portland that many prosperous citizens made their homes. Architectural styles ranging from the Federal period to the Greek and Gothic revivals to the Italianate and later Victorian are represented in the district.

One of the area's oldest dwellings is the lovely McLellan-Sweat Mansion of 1800; several other Federal style homes were built the same year. The Charles Q. Clapp House is Spring Street's most impressive Greek Revival–style home, while the fourteen-family Park Street Row shows Portland's increasing refinement in the 1830s. Mid-nineteenth-century prosperity led to the construction of lavish homes, culminating in the Victoria Mansion (Morse-Libby House).

This residential district also includes churches and museums, reflecting the cultural awareness of the city as it developed into an important nineteenth-century urban center.

Stroudwater Historic District

The significance of the Stroudwater Historic District is not limited to the merits of individual buildings. The whole formed by these single elements stands today as a fine ex-

Stephen McLellan House, Spring Street Historic District, Portland

ample of a nineteenth-century village. The pattern of the village's growth is visible in the sequence of its architecture. Although the commercial enterprises carried on in the village are no longer in existence, their sites are clearly evident.

The current residents of Stroudwater take pride in their historic village. Their homes are well maintained; many are restored to their original exterior appearance. The George Tate House has been professionally restored and is open to the public during the summer. The sense of history that envelops Stroudwater is heightened because the buildings have been continously lived in and cared for.

Several of the residences included within the Stroudwater Historic District are outstanding examples of the architecture of their period. The George Tate House has received recognition as a National Historic Landmark. The Thomas Means House, the Francis Waldo House, the Samuel Fickett House, the Martin Hawes House and the Dr. Jeremiah Barker House are also of exceptional quality. The other homes, built by less wealthy owners, are nevertheless of high architectural quality.

Waterfront Historic District

Portland's nineteenth-century waterfront and adjacent commercial district are of major historic and architectural significance. The city is one of the oldest ports on the Atlantic seaboard, and the relics of its maritime prosperity are among the best-preserved in the nation. First settled between 1632 and 1633, the community on the Portland peninsula has survived Indian attacks, British bombardment, economic hardship, and devastating fires to become Maine's largest city and most important commercial center.

The mast trade and, after it, the West Indies trade established Portland's maritime importance. With the Embargo of 1807 and the War of 1812, new local industries helped make Portland a commercial area. By the 1820s, Portland was a thriving port with a fleet larger than any other on the Atlantic seaboard. The city became a railroad center in the mid nineteenth century.

With this expansion and prosperity, the waterfront and commercial areas of Portland were changed and extended. New wharves, warehouses, and stores were built, and, after the Civil War, the city devoted its energies to maritime and

Waterfront Historic District, Portland

Waterfront Historic District, Portland

commercial pursuits. The Great Fire of July 4, 1866, however, left ten thousand people homeless and caused $12 million worth of damage. The new waterfront was not destroyed, but Middle, Exchange, and Fore streets were devastated.

Structures from the late eighteenth through the early twentieth centuries have survived, leaving this area of Portland with a remarkable group of commercial buildings encompassing a rich variety of styles and types. The Woodman, or Warren, shop and home of the 1780s or 1790s is the district's oldest building, and the Cumberland County Courthouse of 1910 is considered the newest of historic significance.

The architectural styles in the district range from the Federal style to the Greek Revival and the Italianate periods, through the Mansard and Queen Anne to the Beaux Arts style of the early twentieth century. Many of Maine's, and the nation's, best architects are represented in this district, which has been handsomely and sympathetically rehabilitated for modern commercial needs in the last decade.

Westbrook College Historic District

At the time the only coeducational boarding school in the country, Westbrook College was established as the result of a proposal put forward at a meeting of the Kennebec Association of Universalists in 1830. It was then determined that a "classical school" be founded at Stevens Plains in Westbrook, later separated as Deering, and still later annexed as part of the city of Portland.

The charter for Westbrook Seminary, as it was called for nearly a century, was signed in 1831 by Governor Daniel E. Smith, and the first term of classes began in June 1834. The first building occupied by the seminary was the present Alumni Hall, newly built, with a tower taken from the Portland Market House, which once stood in the present Monument Square in Portland.

Among notable alumni of the seminary was Edwin Ginn, 1855, who later founded Ginn and Company, a famous publishing house.

In 1925, Westbrook Seminary became Westbrook Seminary and Junior College for women only and, in 1933, Westbrook Junior College. Since 1974, it has operated under the name of Westbrook College with a four-year extension program in certain fields and a limited number of male students.

Site No. 9-16, Great Diamond Island — Prehistoric

Site number 9-16 on Great Diamond Island in Casco Bay is a large, complex shellheap, or shell midden. Excavations at the site have shown that it has been occupied since about 1,000 B.C. It was primarily a spring and early summer camp location, where major activities included cod-fishing and the harvesting of soft-shelled clams. This site is a major key to the reconstruction of prehistoric subsistence and settlement patterns in Casco Bay.

Eastern Cemetery, Congress Street, corner of Mountfort Street

Chartered in 1688, Eastern Cemetery was the only burial place for what was then Falmouth. The first burials took place in 1670, and the cemetery remained in use until the late nineteenth century. Many of Portland's outstanding residents are buried here: religious and political leaders, business and professional men, soldiers, and even nationally known figures. The monuments themselves — of granite, marble, sandstone, and slate — are beautiful but neglected and in many cases in poor condition.

Tate House, 1270 Westbrook Street—1755 (NHL)

The Tate House was built in 1755 by George Tate, mast agent for the Royal Navy. Tate's duties were to manage the cutting, trimming, and transportation of trees selected by the King's surveyors as potential masts. Usually white pines, these trees had to be tall and straight, measuring 24 inches in diameter at 3 feet from the ground in order to qualify as King's masts. The chosen trees were incised with a broad arrow to indicate royal ownership, no matter on whose land they stood. The Stroudwater section of Portland became the principal shipping point for masts when Portsmouth, New Hampshire, began to decline because of a lack of suitable mast trees.

George Tate himself lived in his Georgian-style home between 1755 and 1794. The home is an unusual example of its style, having a clerestory in its indented gambrel roof. Other outstanding architectural features are its fine panel-

George Tate House, Portland

ing, the bolection molding, the cove ceiling in the front hall, the wide stairways, and the tall chimney breasts. The Tate House is now open as a museum.

Wadsworth Longfellow House,
487 Congress Street — 1785–86 (NHL)

The 3-story brick house, built between 1785 and 1786, which was the boyhood home of the beloved American poet, Henry Wadsworth Longfellow, is maintained by the Maine Historical Society and is open to the public. The first brick house in Portland, it contains many objects associated with the poet's early years.

Longfellow was born in 1807 and lived in Portland until 1843, except during his student days at Bowdoin and the period of his European travels. His first wife died here in 1835, and he was inspired by his sorrow to write *The Rainy*

Wadsworth Longfellow House, Portland

Day in this house. Two of his first ambitious works were novels of European travel, but Longfellow realized his greatest achievements in poetry, from sonnets to the long narratives, such as *Hiawatha, Evangeline,* and *The Courtship of Miles Standish*. He was immensely popular in Europe, and his works had been translated into twelve languages by 1900. Longfellow's fame, fluctuating with the times, endures, and he must be counted as one of the outstanding figures in American literature.

How Family Houses, Danforth and Pleasant Streets — 1799, 1817, 1818

With the Daniel How House of 1799, this district includes three houses: Daniel's, his son John's (1817), and his brother Joseph's (1818). Together, these substantial brick structures form a Federal enclave in the midst of a peripheral commercial area and reflect the appearance of Portland at the turn of the nineteenth century.

McLellan-Sweat Mansion, 111 High Street — 1800 (NHL)

The McLellan-Sweat Mansion was built in 1800 from designs by John Kimball, Sr., who was also the builder. Hugh

McLellan–Sweat Mansion, Portland.
Courtesy of Portland Museum of Art.

McLellan, a wealthy Portland merchant, is said to have paid $20,000 for the construction of his new home. The mansion is a superb and little altered example of a Federal brick town house.

The fourth resident of the mansion, Lorenzo de Medici Sweat, left it to his widow, who in turn willed it to the Portland Society of Art on condition that a suitable memorial building be erected. This structure, designed by John Calvin Stevens and known as the L.D.M. Sweat Memorial Art Museum, was built in back of the mansion and opened to the public in 1911.

The McLellan-Sweat Mansion is in excellent condition and is open to the public as a furnished historic house exhibit.

Joseph Holt Ingraham House, 51 State Street — 1801

Architect Alexander Parris designed several houses in Portland, only two of which remain: the Hunnewell-Shepley House (1805) and the Joseph Holt Ingraham House (1801). Ingraham was a successful businessman and silversmith, but he lost his money and his home during the War of 1812. Very little of Parris' interior design remains; the exterior, too, has undergone many changes. In general, however, the Ingraham House is architecturally and historically important as one of the few Federal houses left in Portland and as one of Parris' designs.

William Minott House, 45 Park Street — 1805, 1807

This house is one of only a handful of large, foursquare, wood frame Federal residences remaining in the city. Built by William Minott, a housewright, in 1805, it has additional significance because of its unique conversion two years later into a three-family dwelling. In 1807, Minott built a substantial, 2-story, hip roof addition across the back of the house to accommodate his two sons and their families. This addition was made 16 feet wider than the original building to provide an 8-foot extension at either end, where identical smaller scaled entries with fans for the two additional family apartments are located.

Hunnewell-Shepley House, 156 State Street — 1805, 1920s

In 1805, Alexander Parris designed this Federal style mansion; in 1923 John Calvin Stevens I remodeled and enlarged it. These architects alone give significance to the building, but its occupants — a high sheriff of Portland, a prominent merchant, a senator and chief justice of the Maine Supreme Court, and a brigadier general of the Grand Army of the Republic — also add to its historic quality.

Portland Observatory, 138 Congress Street — 1807

The Portland Observatory, an octagonal tower about 82 feet tall, stands on Congress Street at the top of Munjoy Hill. At 141 feet above sea level, it affords a panoramic view of Portland, Portland Harbor, and the surrounding countryside.

The observatory, built in 1807, was the idea of Captain Lemuel Moody. Originally, there was a complex of buildings, including a bowling alley, a caretaker's house, a dance and banquet hall, and stables, as well as the observatory itself. The grounds were used for military exercises and the festive occasions of local organizations.

Portland Observatory

Moody was sole owner of the property after buying back the shares he had sold to fund construction. He managed the property, and it was passed down in his family until 1937, when the tower was given to the city of Portland. It was restored and then rededicated in 1939.

Today the observatory is open to the public during the summer season.

First Parish Church, 425 Congress Street — 1825–26

The First Parish Church was the first major granite structure built east of Portsmouth, New Hampshire, and it is the oldest house of worship in Portland. Portland's First Parish was established in 1674; in 1718, the First Parish Church began to evolve.

First Parish Church, Portland

The first church was a log building, which was replaced in 1721 by a frame church. In 1740, "Old Jerusalem," a wooden meeting house, was built to house the congregation; Maine's Constitutional Convention met there in 1819 to draw up the constitution of the state of Maine. The present church, constructed between 1825 and 1826, stands on the same site.

Many of Portland's leading citizens were members of the First Parish Church. The Longfellows, Fessendens, Mellons, and Prebles were all parishioners, and Hermann Kotzschmar was the church organist for forty-seven years.

Both interior and exterior are impressively executed. Careful attention has been given to its maintenance, so the church has the same visual impact that it had originally. The mahogany pulpit, the minister's chair, the communion table, the pulpit Bibles, the lighting fixtures, and the Simon Willard clock have all been in use since the church first opened.

Charles Q. Clapp Block, Congress Square — 1826

Built in 1826 in the Federal style, the Charles Q. Clapp (H.H. Hay) Block remains as one of the oldest commercial buildings in Portland. Originally named after its architect, Charles Q. Clapp, it has become better known as the H.H.

Charles Q. Clapp Block, Portland

Hay Block. Residents of Portland in 1826 called it the "flat-iron" building.

The druggist H.H. Hay opened several successful pharmacies in Portland during the 1800s. The Byron Greenough Block (1848) on Middle and Free streets was another H.H. Hay pharmacy, similar in its unusual, almost triangular, shape, serving the Monument Square end of Congress Street.

The architect, Charles Quincy Clapp (1799–1868), was a prominent Portland building and land speculator as well as a self-taught architect. The H.H. Hay Block was one of his earliest designs, followed by his own home (1832) designed in the Greek Revival style, which is now the Portland School of Art on Spring Street.

A third level was added to the block in 1922 by John Calvin Stevens. This extra height and the addition of a large clock emphasize its architectural presence on Congress Square.

The block has recently been rehabilitated through the efforts of Greater Portland Landmarks, Incorporated, the Maine Historic Preservation Commission, and the City of Portland.

Positioned between Congress and Free streets, the block faces the busy intersection of High and Congress streets in the heart of downtown Portland. Its unique triangular shape, dictated by the site, its Federal detailing, and its location in a major thoroughfare contribute a landmark character to the area.

Mariner's Church, 368–74 Fore Street — 1828–29

Mariner's Church in Portland was modeled after Faneuil Hall in Boston and was the first Greek Revival–style building in the city. It was also for many years Portland's largest building, constructed at a total cost of $51,000. It was conceived as a place of worship and education for seamen of the port city. Portland, where molasses from the Indies was distilled into rum, was a freewheeling seaport town. The increasingly active temperance movement set its sights on the seafarers as a place to begin its reform work.

The ground floor of the building was designed to house shops for merchants, whose rent would support and maintain the entire block. The second floor was to have a large central meeting room surrounded by shops and offices. The chapel itself was on the third floor in a room with a cathedral ceiling; smaller rooms were located on either side.

The structure remains physically unchanged and, although the chapel no longer serves as a place of worship, it is used in ways compatible with its original purpose and design.

Neal Dow Memorial, 714 Congress Street — 1829 (NHL)

The Neal Dow House, built in 1829 in the late Federal style, is well preserved both on the exterior and the interior. The substantial brick home was owned by only two generations of the Dow family before being left to the Maine Women's Christian Temperance Union. The WCTU has opened the Dow home as a museum and also uses rooms for its meetings. It is fitting that the home of the man so dedicated to temperance should continue to be a symbol of that cause.

Neal Dow, born of Quaker parents in 1804, was educated in the principles of temperance, industry, and thrift as a young boy. When he became a young businessman, he saw what the lack of these principles could do to his employees. Portland, a major rum producer, had citywide rum breaks for workers at 11 A.M. and 4 P.M. daily. On holidays, tubs of liquor were placed on the sidewalks. Dow saw the open use

Neal Dow Memorial, Portland

of alcohol and connected it to the widespread poverty in Portland. At the age of twenty-three, he made his first appeal for temperance, and for sixty-seven years he was an ardent and active crusader for the legal prohibition of liquor.

As mayor of Portland, Dow authored a bill that was submitted to and passed by the legislature. What was popularly known as "the Maine Law" became nationally famous; Dow, as its author, also received recognition. During the late 1850s, Dow toured the nation. After taking time off to serve as a brigadier general in the Union Army, he resumed his crusade, this time touring Great Britain as well as the U.S. Although Dow did not live to see a constitutional amendment for prohibition (neither did he see the chaos that it caused), it was his propaganda and his political strategy that led to the idealistic attempt to end the reign of the demon rum.

Charles Q. Clapp House, 97 Spring Street — 1832

The Charles Q. Clapp House is one of the earliest and most polished Greek Revival residences in Maine. Erected in

Charles Q. Clapp House, Portland

1832, it was probably designed by its first owner, with inspiration from Edward Shaw's *Civil Architecture* and Asher Benjamin's *The Practical House Carpenter*.

Charles Quincy Clapp was the son of one of Maine's wealthiest merchants, Asa Clapp. Young Clapp received a liberal and commercial education but turned away from his father's mercantile pursuits in favor of purchasing and improving Portland real estate. Between 1821 and 1832, Clapp redesigned several Portland buildings, as well as designing a single-story Federal-style business block and his own home.

The overall plan of the residence, both exterior and interior, attests to Clapp's creativeness in working with the Greek Revival style. Some minor alterations by John Calvin Stevens in 1914 did not change the visual impact of the building. The residence has undergone interior changes in the past few years because its owner, the Portland Society of Art, has used it as an art school. The need for large, well-lit studios has led to the repositioning of many partitions, but because the society is aware of the building's value, interior details remain intact.

Park Street Block (Row), 88–112 Park Street — 1835

Park Street Row was built in 1835 as fourteen attached single-family units, running from Spring to Gray streets. The architectural details of the brick building are simple Greek Revival in character, with handsome cast-iron second-floor balconies.

The Park Street Block is the largest row house complex ever constructed in Maine. It also ranks as one of the state's most ambitious nineteenth-century real estate projects. In 1835, forty-one stockholders purchased a four-acre tract, and lots were laid out for twenty houses. During the summer and fall of 1835, the 4½-story brick row was built. Financial difficulties halted work before the interiors were finished, and the proprietors sold their houses at auction. New owners finished the interiors to suit their tastes.

The Park Street Row presented a dramatic appearance in 1835, reflecting the sophistication the city was acquiring. It continues to be a focal point of Portland's oldest and finest residential historic districts.

The Gothic House, Portland

The Gothic House, 387 Spring Street — 1845

Although Portland's Gothic House (John J. Brown House) has been moved from one end of Spring Street to the other, its exterior and interior appearance remain substantially unchanged since its completion in 1845. The structure is an outstanding example of a mid-nineteenth-century American Gothic Revival cottage of the kind made popular by the works of Andrew Jackson Downing. Built in 1845, it was one of the earliest Gothic Revival homes in Maine and remains one of the finest of its kind in the state.

In 1971, the structure faced destruction; both a highway and a Holiday Inn were scheduled for construction on the site. Fortunately, the Gothic House was moved to a vacant lot, unaltered and unharmed. It now stands in the midst of Portland's finest and most stable nineteenth-century neighborhood, the Western Promenade.

Byron Greenough Block,
Free and Middle Streets — 1848, 1919

Better known as the Lower Hay Block, this impressive flatiron structure was built at the intersection of Free and Middle streets in 1848 by Byron Greenough. Eight years later, Henry Homer Hay moved his wholesale drug business into the building, which he later bought, and there it remained until 1964. A fourth story, tastefully designed by John Calvin Stevens, was added in 1919. This Greek Revival block is an important survival, predating the Great Fire of 1866.

Marine Hospital, 331 Veranda Street — 1855–59

This 3-story, brick and granite, Italianate-style building was designed on an "H" plan by Ammi B. Young in 1855. Still intact is Young's creative cast-iron porch which is both decorative and practical. For fifty years, sailors had been cared for in their own homes or in the poorhouse; finally, funds were secured to build them a care facility. The hospital is a rare surviving example of its type and may be the only one of its kind with Young's elaborate ironwork intact.

Chestnut Street Methodist Church, 11–19 Chestnut Street — 1856

An unusual example of early Gothic Revival architecture, the Chestnut Street Church is one of only a few survivors in that style in Portland. The building was designed by Charles A. Alexander of Portland, a prominent architect of the 1850s and 1860s, who also designed the Goddard Mansion at Fort Williams and the Samuel and Andrew Spring houses on Danforth Street.

Fort Gorges, Hog Island, Portland Harbor — 1858–64

Rising majestically above the ledges of Hog Island, Fort Gorges was built in the years following 1858 to defend the principal channel approaches to Maine's most important harbor at Portland. The fort, ironically championed by the Secretary of War Jefferson Davis, was constructed of massive cut-granite blocks, typical of military architecture of the period. The fort is hexagonal in plan, and five of its six sides contain double tiers of vaulted casemates — cannon enclosures.

The Civil War ended before Fort Gorges could be completed, and by the late 1860s its design had become obsolete because of rapid advances in the design of armored naval vessels, powered by steam and armed with rifled guns.

During World Wars I and II, Fort Gorges was used as a storehouse for naval mines. Today this impressive and important fortification is owned by the city of Portland to be preserved as one of the great forts on the East Coast.

Fort Gorges, ca. 1880, Portland Harbor

Morse-Libby House — "Victoria Mansion," 109 Danforth Street, at Park Street — 1859–63 (NHL)

Although it has long outlived its royal namesake, Portland's "Victoria Mansion" continues to reflect the pride and dignity associated with the British Queen. This famous landmark is considered the finest Italian villa–style residence in the United States.

Plans for the mansion, originally intended as a summer residence, were prepared by Henry Austin, an architect in New Haven, Connecticut. Construction began in 1859, with

Morse-Libby House, Portland

Morse-Libby House, Portland. Courtesy of the Library of Congress.

Francis D. Little as builder, but because of the Civil War, the work was not completed until 1863. Ruggles Sylvester Morse, for whom the house was built, is said to have paid $400,000 for the construction and decoration of his extravagant home. Since 1863, very few changes have been made in the brick and brownstone structure.

Ruggles Sylvester Morse was born in Leeds, Maine. After working in the palace hotels of Boston and New York, he moved on to New Orleans, where he gained control of four of the best palace hotels; he also owned a plantation outside the city. Morse's Portland villa ostentatiously exhibited his ante-bellum wealth to his Maine contemporaries.

On the exterior "Victoria Mansion" is an asymmetrical arrangement of large parts, although each part is symmetrical within itself. The interior is lavishly decorated from floor to ceiling. Wall and ceiling decorations were designed by Giovanni Guidrini of New York City, who hired eleven Italian artists to paint them. Every available surface is either painted or carved, leaving no blank spaces, except on walls where portraits would have hung. Elaborate and sometimes exotic *trompe l'oeil* painting continues through the third floor and is even found at the top of the tower. Each room has its own character and style, ranging from the Renaissance to the eighteenth century.

In 1894, a successful Portland merchant, Joseph Ralph Libby, purchased the mansion from the estate of the late R.S. Morse. The Libbys and their five children occupied the villa for thirty years; all three of the Libby daughters were married there. They took tremendous pride in maintaining and protecting the mansion and its decor and furnishings. In 1940, after the mansion had been vacant for thirteen years, Mr. and Mrs. Holmes bought it to prevent its demolition for a gas station. They in turn gave it to the Victoria Society of Maine Women in 1943. Since then, with the name "Victoria Mansion," the Morse-Libby House has been open to the public as a remarkable furnished historic house museum.

Mechanic's Hall, 519 Congress Street — 1859

The Maine Charitable Mechanic Association was incorporated in 1815 by a group of Portland citizens engaged in the "mechanic arts" to give charitable and educational aid to the members of these professions. The association sponsored exhibitions and trade fairs in 1826, 1838, 1854, and 1859. Over the years, it has established an excellent library, sponsored public lectures on appropriate subjects, and run a free drawing school, all of which it continues to do. The association is one of the oldest organizations in Maine and remains an active institution today. Mechanics' Hall was its first permanent home. It has continuously served as the association's headquarters.

Thomas J. Sparrow (1805–70), the architect of Mechanics' Hall, was a member of the association, as were all the craftsmen who worked on the building.

Prominent on its corner lot, Mechanics' Hall is one of the most handsome buildings on Congress Street. The overall effect of the building is one of great solidity. It has a massiveness that is not oppressive. Its architectural detail gives warmth and richness to the façades. It remains as elegant today as when it was built.

F.O.J. Smith Tomb, Evergreen Cemetery — 1860

One of the numerous architectural styles that were revived in nineteenth-century England and America was the Egyptian style. Because of the ancient Egyptians' belief in life after death and the funerary purpose of nearly all their surviving architecture, nineteenth-century architects found the style especially appropriate for cemetery gates, tombs, and monuments. F.O.J. Smith's tomb in Portland's Evergreen Cemetery is the only sophisticated example of the style in Maine. The choice of Egyptian style reflects Smith's artistic independence as well as his appreciation of the architectural styles of his time.

Smith came to Portland as a young lawyer in 1823 and soon demonstrated a penchant for controversy that became a dominant factor in his long and stormy career. He was continuously involved in journalism and politics. As editor of the *Argus*, a national Republican paper, Smith, ever the opportunist, supported at various times the Democrats, the Whigs, the Republicans, and the Independents. He strongly supported Lincoln and the Civil War but, as a white supremacist, was horrified by the Emancipation Proclamation and became Maine's most noted and most detested Copperhead.

F.O.J. Smith Tomb, Evergreen Cemetery, Portland

Most of his business ventures were failures, but he did achieve some political success in the state legislature and as a three-term congressman. By the end of his life, Smith had became a lonely and largely discredited figure. His obituary closed with the words: "He failed in most of his endeavors, and his record serves as a warning rather than an example." Such a tomb is fitting for one of Maine's most colorful and versatile nineteenth-century figures.

Harrison B. Brown House, 400 Danforth Street — 1861

This vernacular Italianate house overlooking Portland Harbor was, during most of his productive career, the home of Harrison B. Brown, nationally recognized, nineteenth-century marine and landscape painter.

Leonard Bond Chapman House,
90 Capisic Street — 1866–68

This Mansard-style house, with its unusual concave tower, was the home of Leonard Bond Chapman, local historian, antiquarian, and document collector. A frequent contributor to the Maine Historical Society "Collections," Chapman gave his enormous body of historical documentation to the society, where it forms an important part of the holdings on Portland history.

First Baptist Church, 353 Congress Street — 1867

This impressive Romanesque Revival structure on the corner of Congress and Wilmot streets was designed by Levi Newcomb of Boston, who had established a reputation based on commissions for several churches and residences as well as dormitories for Harvard, Tufts, and Dartmouth. Lincoln Park across the street affords an unobstructed view of its façade from many angles, which is unusual for a center city church.

Thompson, Rackleff, and Woodman Blocks,
117–133 Middle Street — 1867–68

Much of Portland's business district was destroyed in the Great Fire of 1866. Reconstruction, in the late 1860s and

Woodman, Rackleff, and Thompson Blocks, Portland

1870s, gave Portland's commercial district a homogeneous architectural appearance. On Middle Street, the Woodman, Rackleff, and Thompson Blocks of 1867–68 form the most refined Victorian commercial grouping ever built in Maine. The three blocks were designed by George M. Harding in the Second Empire and Italianate styles, and, although they are similar in composition, the detail on each is developed individually.

The Woodman building, financed by the Woodman family, was the most handsomely and elaborately designed of the three blocks. It is the grandest Second Empire–style commercial building in Maine. The cast-iron pilasters and arches on the first floor were made by the Portland Company.

The Italianate design of the Rackleff building maintains the continuity of the streetscape without overpowering or detracting from its neighbors. The cast-iron arcade on the first floor is identical to the Woodman Block's, but it is a foot lower, causing the whole façade to be lower.

Across Church Street from the first two buildings is the Thompson Block. Like the Woodman building, it has a Mansard roof and a cast-iron arcade on the ground floor. Ornamented with stone oak leaves and acorns, the Thompson Block admirably completes the triad of distinguished commercial structures.

United States Custom House, 312 Fore Street — 1868–71

The United States Custom House was built to replace one that burned in the Great Fire of 1866. Alfred B. Mullett, the

United States Custom House, Portland

supervising treasury architect, was responsible for the design of the building.

The French Renaissance structure is free standing, occupying an entire block on Portland's waterfront. Acting as a gateway to Portland, the Custom House has changed little since its construction. The interior retains its elegance, with original woodwork, marble floors, fireplaces, and counters.

A.B. Butler House, 4 Walker Street — 1868

Matthew Stead designed this "Italian Villa" for A.B. Butler, a Portland merchant, in 1868. One full story high, with a Mansard roof covering the second floor, the house is much larger than it appears; it has ten rooms and a full basement. The original fresco work is intact and in excellent condition; the exterior still has its wooden decorations and slate roofing.

St. Paul's Church and Rectory,
279 Congress Street — 1868, 1869

This small but charming example of Gothic Revival architecture, with its attached rectory, was executed by George

Browne Pelham, an English-born architect who designed the west wing of the parliament buildings in Ottawa, Canada, in 1856 and later became architect for the New York City Park Department.

Thomas Brackett Reed House,
30–32 Deering Street — 1875 (NHL)

This double house was built in 1875 by Simon H. Libby, a Portland house builder. Constructed of brick, the house is exceptional in Portland as the only residence with its extensive tile decoration intact.

Thomas B. Reed lived in the house from 1888 until his death in 1902. A Portland native, Reed practiced law in California for several years before returning to Maine in 1865. Reed served two terms in the state legislature and later became Maine's attorney general. In 1876, he ran for Congress and won the seat in the House that he was to hold for twenty-three years. In 1888, Reed became Speaker of the House. "Czar" Reed was literally master of the House after he rewrote the House rules and enforced them through sheer determination. He was considered a possible candidate for the Senate and a presidential nominee, but he de-

Thomas Brackett Reed House, Portland

sired neither position. In 1898, he resigned his seat in opposition to the U.S. annexation of the Philippines. In 1902, President Roosevelt visited Thomas Reed in his Portland home. Four months later, Reed died in Washington.

**Williston-West Church and Parish House,
32 Thomas Street — 1877, 1905**

Designed by Francis H. Fassett, with later alterations and the addition of a parish house by John Calvin Stevens, this church is particularly distinguished as the birthplace of the Young People's Society of Christian Endeavor, founded by the Reverend Francis E. Clark in 1881. The Christian Endeavor, an international organization, provided the initial stimulus for the Sunday school movement, which offered religious instruction suitable for children.

Portland Stove Foundry, 57 Kennebec Street — 1880

For almost 100 years, from 1880 to 1978, this unique manufacturing operation was conducted in the same location, using virtually the same tools and methods throughout the entire period. The company remained a family business until just before it closed down. The Portland Stove Foundry is a rare example of nineteenth-century production carried over successfully into the twentieth century.

Lancaster Block, 474 Congress Street — 1881*

This handsome Romanesque Revival block was designed by Fassett and Stevens, with the later two stories added by Fassett's firm. It is a keystone building in the redevelopment and rehabilitation now extending into Monument Square.

**J.B. Brown Memorial Block,
Congress and Casco Streets — 1883–84**

The J.B. Brown Memorial Block of 1883–84 is one of the few commercial buildings in Portland designed in the Queen Anne style. The irregularity of surface textures, attention to

J.B. Brown Memorial Block, Portland

detail, asymmetrical massing, and broken roofline of this building all contribute to the picturesqueness associated with the style. The design was the work of the noted architect, John Calvin Stevens of Portland.

The block was erected as a memorial to John B. Brown, founder of the Portland Sugar Company in 1855 and builder in 1868 of the Falmouth Hotel on Middle Street, the center of Portland's social life for half a century.

John Calvin Stevens House, 52 Bowdoin Street — 1884

Designed and built in 1884 by John Calvin Stevens I, this Shingle Style house was one of the earliest residences of this style in Portland. Around 1905, an addition was built and the interior, redesigned and enlarged; most of the building's original features remain intact. Stevens also designed the C.A. Brown Cottage, the Oxford Building, the Harry Butler House, and the J.B. Brown Block, to name just a few.

During a career distinguished for its length as well as its brilliant productivity, Stevens achieved national recognition for his unusual skill in blending styles and for his contribution to the development of the Shingle Style. From

1873, when he started out as a draftsman in the office of Portland architect Francis H. Fassett, until his death in 1940, he built a far-reaching reputation. He was Maine's first architect to become a Fellow of the American Institute of Architects.

Fifth Maine Regiment Community Center, Peak's Island — 1888

This interesting Queen Anne–style building is notable both as a summer retreat and as a memorial to the men who served in this regiment during the Civil War. The structure was built on land donated by Mrs. C.B. Goodwin, with funds collected from family members of the Fifth Maine Regiment. Presently, the building is held in trust by the Fifth Maine Regiment Community Association and is available for public or private functions. As such, it remains a part of the Peak's Island community.

St. Lawrence Church, 76 Congress Street — 1897

This dramatic example of eclectic architecture with strong Queen Anne overtones was executed by Arthur B. Jennings, well-known for his similarly striking design of "Norumbega," a Camden summer residence.

Adam P. Leighton House, 261 Western Promenade — 1903

This distinguished Colonial Revival house on the Western Promenade was the residence of Adam P. Leighton, founmayor of Portland, during the height of his career. Maine architect Frederick A. Tompson designed the house.

Maine Historical Society, 458 Congress Street — 1907

Incorporated by the state legislature on February 5, 1822, the Maine Historical Society ranks second in age among state historical societies in New England and third in the nation behind Massachusetts (1791) and New York (1804). Among the forty-nine incorporators appear names prominent in Maine history: Preble, Payson, Longfellow, King, Lincoln, Vaughan, Abbott, Williamson, Sewall, Dana, and Gardiner.

From 1822 until 1880, because of its close connections with Bowdoin College, the official location of the society and its collections was at Brunswick. In 1880, the headquarters were moved to Portland, where the majority of the members lived. In 1895, Anne Longfellow Pierce, a sister of the poet, bequeathed the Wadsworth-Longfellow House to the society, and, upon her death in 1901, it was gratefully occupied, becoming the first home owned by the organization.

The present society building, a dignified and restrained example of Colonial Revival architecture, was designed by Alexander Wadsworth-Longfellow and Francis H. Fassett and constructed on the same lot as the Longfellow House. The formal dedication took place on the centennial of the birth of Henry Wadsworth Longfellow, February 27, 1907. Over the years, the society has been extremely active both as an important historical research center and also as an agent for numerous publications.

Portland City Hall, 389 Congress Street — 1909–12

Portland City Hall rose twice from its own ashes. The first city hall, completed in 1862, was destroyed in the Great Fire of 1866. It was rebuilt in 1867 from designs of Francis H. Fassett, but in 1908 it burned. The present city hall was designed by the New York architectural firm of Carrere and Hastings, assisted by two Portland architects, John Calvin Stevens I and John Howard Stevens. The impressive building was inspired by the New York City Hall, built between 1803 and 1812. The granite for construction came from North Jay.

City Hall houses not only offices for municipal officials but also an auditorium that contains the world-famous Hermann Kotzschmar organ, the second largest organ in the world in 1912. Cyrus Hermann Kotzschmar Curtis, Portland native, editor and publisher of the *Saturday Evening Post*, and philanthropist, gave this organ as a memorial to Hermann Kotzschmar, the Portland music instructor, composer, and organist.

Portland City Hall. Photo by Richard Cheek.

Masonic Temple, 415 Congress Street — 1911

A fine example of Beaux Arts classicism by Frederick A. Thompson, this notable building features a magnificent 2-story lodge hall. Standing between the First Parish Church and City Hall, it is an important element in one of the city's finest streetscapes.

United States Courthouse, 156 Federal Street — 1911, 1932

James Knox Taylor, supervising architect of the U.S. Treasury, designed this building in the Second Renaissance Revival style. Built of granite, with a slate roof, the original section of the courthouse is two stories high and has a hip roof enclosing a third story. An addition, built in 1932, was constructed of the same materials in the same style. Together, the two sections form a trapezoid around an enclosed courtyard. The interior is as well preserved as the exterior.

Green Memorial A.M.E. Zion Church,
46 Sheridan Street — 1914

Built of textured concrete blocks in 1914, this church houses the oldest established black congregation in Maine. The building itself has no architectural significance, but it stands as an important symbol for the black community in Maine.

SACO

Jacobs Houses and Store, 9–17 Elm Street — 1820–26

This group of three buildings, all dating from the same decade and built by brothers, Moses and Benjamin Jacobs, provide a late Federal streetscape of unusual historical and architectural unity.

Benjamin Jacobs's house remains a dignified, perfectly preserved residence. His brother's house was virtually identical until a later owner changed it to a double house. In 1826, about the same time that Moses built his home, Benjamin erected a fairly ambitious brick commercial block, apparently as an investment. In 1827 Moses died, and Benjamin appears to have been bankrupted. Both houses and the store passed to new owners.

Thacher-Goodale House, 121 North Street — 1827–28

In addition to being an exceptional example of the Greek Revival temple style with Federal detail, this house achieves even greater distinction as the home of Stephen Goodale and his son, George Lincoln Goodale. The former served as the first secretary of the Maine Board of Agriculture, whose seventeen annual reports from 1856 through 1872 were considered models of their kind and were widely imitated in other states. Dr. George L. Goodale became a distinguished professor of botany at Harvard University, where he greatly enlarged and established an endowment for the Botanic Garden. His is perhaps best remembered for arranging for the acquisition of the famous "glass flowers," now at the Peabody Museum.

Saco City Hall, 300 Main Street — 1855

This impressive transitional Greek Revival–Italianate structure, designed by Thomas Hill, reflects the remarkable growth and progress of this important industrial center, whose population doubled between 1830 and 1860.

J.G. Deering House, 371 Maine Street — 1869

This large, high-style, brick, Italianate dwelling with attached carriage house is now used as the Dyer Library. Built by Joseph G. Deering, lumber magnate and Saco's leading nineteenth-century industrialist and philanthropist, this house is a local landmark and one of the finest of its type in southern Maine.

A.B. Seavey House, 90 Temple Street — 1890

An excellent, well-preserved example of the Queen Anne style, this house is completely documented in a full set of original plans drawn by J.M. Littlefield of Haverhill, Massachusetts.

SCARBOROUGH

Richard Hunniwell House, Black Point Road — 1702–3

The oldest house in Scarborough and one of the oldest in Cumberland County, this primitive structure was built by Richard Hunniwell, known as "Indian Killer" for his implacable hatred of the aborigines. Hunniwell was among the first settlers to return to Scarborough after its complete depopulation in 1690 due to Indian raids. He was killed in 1703.

Atlantic House, Kirkwood Road — 1850, 1877, 1911

Originally a farmhouse taking in guests in 1850 and operating ever since, the Atlantic House is very likely the oldest summer resort in Maine in continuous service. Greatly enlarged in 1856 into what could properly be termed a hotel, it predated by at least twenty years the beginning of the "summer hotel era" in Maine. Its popularity was such that in 1877 further expansion became necessary. Two large, 4-story Mansard wings were attached to the east and west ends of the old building. By 1911, the old center section began to show irreversible signs of age and in a tricky operation was replaced by a new, flat-roofed, 4-story structure. No other seacoast resort in Maine better represents in its history and traditions the development of the state as a mecca for summer visitors.

Winslow Homer Studio,
Winslow Homer Road — ca. 1870 (NHL)

Winslow Homer (1836–1910), an artist of rare talent and integrity, is noted for his Civil War paintings, landscapes, genre works, and particularly for his powerful paintings of the sea. He mastered both oil and water color, and his works in both media rank with the best.

Homer began his artistic career as an illustrator, but by 1876 he had decided to devote his life to painting. He settled at his brother's home at Prout's Neck in 1884 but soon moved into an empty carriage house nearby and converted it into a residence and studio. In this home overlooking the Atlantic he lived until his death in 1910. The small and rather modest Mansard-style building has changed little since Homer's day; the occupants, relatives of the artist, have kept his studio intact and display reproductions of Homer's work.

SOUTH BERWICK

Berwick Academy Historic District

The Berwick Academy Historic District derives its importance not only from the historic and architectural merits of the individual buildings it includes, but also from the significance of Berwick Academy in the educational history of Maine. In 1790, the citizens of Berwick, Wells, and York raised £500 in each town to help establish Berwick Academy. The 1791 structure was then built for housing and classroom space and functioned in those two capacities until the academy outgrew it in 1823. At that time, the oldest secondary school building in Maine was sold for $500 and was moved to Maine Street to become a private residence.

In the twentieth century, Berwick Academy enlarged its program to include the curriculum of a comprehensive high school and served the area as such. In the middle 1950s, a

Headmaster's House, Berwick Academy Historic District, South Berwick

serious attempt was made to strengthen the college preparatory course and to enlarge the school facilities. As part of this expansion, the Burleigh-Davidson House became part of the academy. This had been the home of John Burleigh, a prominent Maine manufacturer, representative to Congress, and trustee of the academy. In 1964, the original 1791 house was brought back to the campus of the academy to be the "oldest original frame schoolhouse in active use for school purposes in the United States." The Dunaway House, now the headmaster's residence, was acquired by the academy in 1968. This handsome Federal house of 1811 contains exceptionally fine French pictorial wallpaper of the 1830s.

Berwick Academy has long provided service to the town of South Berwick as a school for its children. After 1894, the Fogg Memorial Library was also opened for public use. Berwick Academy stands as a living monument to the history of Maine education and to the citizens who served their community by supporting it.

Sarah Orne Jewett House, Route A — 1774

The Sarah Orne Jewett House was built in 1774 by John Haggens, who sold it to Captain Theodore Jewett, Miss Jewett's grandfather.

Sarah Orne Jewett House, South Berwick

This excellent Georgian-style dwelling was built with a simplicity that increases its charm. The three dormers are nineteenth-century additions done in the Greek Revival style. It is typical of the fine houses built along the New England coast during the later eighteenth century, and it is of superior design.

Miss Jewett, one of Maine's most famous authors, occupied the house for much of her life and did most of her writing there. She died there on June 24, 1909.

The house is owned and maintained by the Society for the Preservation of New England Antiquities.

Hamilton House, Vaughan's Lane — 1787–88 (NHL)

Built between 1787 and 1788 and still standing in its beautiful and undisturbed setting, Hamilton House is a magnificent and little altered example of a large Georgian country

Hamilton House, South Berwick

house. Minor restoration work was done in 1950, and since then the Hamilton House has been open to the public as a furnished historic house exhibit. The Society for the Preservation of New England Antiquities has owned the house since 1949.

Colonel Jonathan Hamilton purchased this picturesque area in 1783 and had his house constructed there between 1787 and 1788. Hamilton was a merchant from Portsmouth, New Hampshire, but he lived in the South Berwick mansion from 1788 until his death in 1802. The house stood vacant from 1815 to 1839, and in 1898 Mrs. Emily D. Tyson purchased and restored the home. Her daughter, Mrs. Henry C. Vaughan, willed the Hamilton House and fifty acres of land to the S.P.N.E.A.

Counting House, Route 4 — 1832

This 2½-story, brick, Greek Revival industrial building is all that remains of the Portsmouth Company Cotton Mill. The interior and exterior of the building are handsomely decorated with Greek Revival detail; other details, however, are from approximately 1850. Like so many New England textile mills, the Portsmouth Company moved its Berwick operation south after the turn of the century.

SOUTH PORTLAND

Portland Breakwater Light, Portland Harbor — 1855, 1875

This Greek Revival structure was built in 1855 and abandoned in 1943. The circular tower of cast-iron plates fashioned as fluted columns with Corinthian capitals covering joints. Situated at the end of the breakwater, this uniquely styled lighthouse symbolizes Portland's maritime heritage. It also shows nineteenth-century Americans' desire to make essentially functional structures aesthetically pleasing as well.

WELLS

Early Wells Capes (nineteen houses) — Pre–1800

Among the communities first established in the state of Maine, only Wells, settled in the 1640s, lacked a harbor, river mouth, or other shelter suitable for extensive maritime activity. With little but an exposed beach along the entire coastline, Wells became a preponderantly agricultural settlement made up of small farms. While her neighbors de-

Early Cape, Wells

Mill House, Wells

veloped a certain prosperity in the seventeenth and eighteenth centuries, which was reflected in the development of town centers with several large and impressive houses, Wells remained a community of small, scattered dwellings.

During the worst of the Colonial conflicts at the turn of the eighteenth century, Wells was one of only two or three communities to avoid complete depopulation, but so great was the devastation that there are no structures that can be definitely dated earlier than about 1710. This is true also of the rest of Maine.

Throughout the eighteenth century, Wells continued as an agricultural area with relatively small landholdings and consequently a larger proportion of humbler dwellings, mostly Capes. Thus, because of its early date of settlement and its geography, Wells possesses a concentration of these "houses that built America" — and Maine for that matter — unmatched elsewhere in the state.

WESTBROOK

Cumberland Mills Historic District

The early story of the S.D. Warren Company and its success is largely the story of its founder, Samuel Dennis Warren.

Cumberland Mills Historic District, Westbrook

His career in the paper industry began when he went to work for his uncle's paper firm in Boston at the age of fifteen. In 1853, this firm branched out into paper manufacture; Warren and his uncle purchased a mill and its water privilege at Congin Falls, later Westbrook, Maine, for $28,000 in 1854. By 1867, Warren had bought out his partners and the firm became simply the S.D. Warren Company. The Cumberland Mills complex grew during the 1870s as Warren converted from rag paper to wood-pulp paper production. Slow sustained growth was the secret of the Warren Company's success.

Warren was a public-spirited, enlightened man who paid fair wages and contributed to local charities. His workers, however, were required to live in company housing unless they lived at home. Running water, electricity, a library, and a reading room were provided. During the strike-ridden 1870s and 1880s, Warren and his policies were held up as examples to other less concerned employers.

The Cumberland Mills Historic District is Maine's best surviving example of a nineteenth-century planned industrial community. Its buildings range from Squire Lewis's Federal farmhouse of the pre-industrial period to a Queen Anne–style meeting hall for workers. Architecturally, the most distinguished structures in Cumberland Mills date from the 1880s. During that decade, Samuel D. Warren employed Maine's leading late-nineteenth-century architect, John Calvin Stevens, to design an important group of houses and buildings.

Cumberland Mills Historic District, Westbrook

In 1881, Stevens planned the series of individual, Queen Anne, workers' cottages for S.D. Warren on Brown Street in Cumberland Mills. These were followed in 1882 by three of Maine's most elaborate Queen Anne structures: the Warren Block at Main and Cumberland streets, a community hall; the William L. Longley House, a residence for the S.D. Warren Company agent; and the John E. Warren House, a residence for S.D. Warren's son.

In 1886, Warren commissioned Stevens to design a street of Shingle–Style workers' cottages. Located off Brown Street, the new project was built that year and appropriately named Cottage Place.

The Cumberland Mills Historic District is significant because of its industrial history and architectural richness, but it is also a rare example of nineteenth-century urban planning and employer paternalism.

The Warren Block, Main Street—1882

The Maine architect, John Calvin Stevens I, designed this handsome Queen Anne–style business block; it was financed by and named after S.D. Warren, owner of Westbrook's large paper company. At a time when employer concern for the community was rare, Warren, with an honest mixture of benevolence and self-interest, provided numerous benefits to the area. He funded a church and parsonage, a school, and a library as well as the Warren Block, which housed four stores, several offices, a public hall, and a hall for the Odd Fellows and Knights of Pythias.

Westbrook High School, 765 Main Street — 1886–87

Designed by Frederick A. Tompson, this remarkable Romanesque Revival–Queen Anne style structure stands today as one of Westbrook's most significant architectural landmarks.

Walker Memorial Library, 800 Main Street — 1894

The Walker Memorial Library built in 1894 is a splendid example of the work done by Frederick A. Tompson, a well-known Maine architect of the late nineteenth century. As a library, it has provided a valuable cultural service to the citizens of Westbrook, a nineteenth-century mill town.

Frederick A. Tompson was a student and, later, partner of

Walker Memorial Library, Westbrook

the great Maine architect, Francis H. Fassett, in the years from 1886 to 1891. Under Fassett's influence, Tompson produced some of his greatest works, which include the Westbrook High School, the Union Mutual Life Insurance Building, and the Wilde Memorial Chapel in Portland, and the Walker Memorial Library of Westbrook. The Walker Library is an excellent example of French Chateauesque architecture, which is seldom seen in the state of Maine. It was built with funds bequeathed by Joseph Walker upon his death. Walker was a prominent businessman who made his fortune in the lumber business. This gift to the people of Westbrook stands as a tribute to two important men, the humanitarian, Joseph Walker, and the gifted architect, Frederick A. Tompson.

YARMOUTH

North Yarmouth and Freeport Baptist Meeting House, Hillside Street — 1796, 1825, 1837

Although twice altered (in 1825 by Samuel Melcher and 1837 by Anthony Raymond), this handsome structure, picturesquely sited at the crest of a hill, retains the best of its Federal, Greek Revival, and Gothic features in a highly successful amalgam of styles.

Mitchell House, 40 Main Street — ca. 1800

A fine Federal house with an unusually steeply pitched hip roof, this was the home of two doctors, Ammi R. Mitchell and Eleazer Burbank, both active in politics and community affairs.

North Yarmouth Academy — 1841, 1847

Russell and Academy halls at North Yarmouth Academy are typical of Greek Revival–style educational buildings that were erected in Maine towns before the Civil War. The construction of Russell Hall in 1841 was followed by that of Academy Hall in 1847. Both were built of brick, with granite and wood trim.

Russell Hall, North Yarmouth Academy

The two buildings are quite similar in design but differ in scale. Standing side by side, Russell and Academy halls are stately buildings that reflect the dignity and restraint of the Greek Revival. After nearly a century and a half, they continue to serve their original functions.

When they were built, Russell Hall was a dormitory and Academy Hall a classroom building for the thirty-year-old institution. The school also operated as a free high school for local students in the late nineteenth century, but later returned to fully private status.

North Yarmouth Academy survives as a typical small local academy. These two fine Greek Revival buildings form part of a strong tradition in mid-nineteenth-century academic architecture.

Captain S.C. Blanchard House, 46 Main Street — 1855

One of the most elaborate and finely detailed Italianate residences on the Maine coast, this building, with its ell and carriage house, was built by Sylvanus Blanchard, a highly successful shipbuilder. The design is by Charles A. Alexander, a talented and prolific architect who also executed the Chestnut Street Methodist Church in Portland.

Captain Reuben Merrill House, 97 West Main Street — 1858

Thomas J. Sparrow, the first native Portland architect, designed this Italian-style house in 1858. Done in wood, the 3-story house is an impressive example of a Maine interpretation of the Italian style. Captain Merrill was a well-known sea captain, who went down with his ship off San Francisco in 1875. Few changes have been made in the building, because it has never left the possession of the Merrill family.

Camp Hammond, 74 Main Street — 1889–90

The significance of this large Shingle Style house lies principally in its method of construction. This consists of a single exterior wall of heavy planks over timbers, with no hidden spaces or hollow walls. This so-called mill-built construction was used largely for fire protection.

Grand Trunk Railroad Station, Main Street — 1906

In Maine, where passenger service has almost totally ceased, railroad stations are among the most endangered species of buildings. Fortunately, the Grand Trunk Station in Yarmouth, now owned by the Village Improvement Society, has been handsomely restored and given new life, thanks to adaptive re-use. This is particularly fortunate because this neat little station is architecturally unique in Maine and stands on a historically important railroad route.

The Grand Trunk Station retains in modified form the large brackets supporting the extended roof overhang, traditional in Stick Style Italianate stations, which predominated during the last two decades of the nineteenth century. This building, however, has a much more steeply pitched hip roof, the north end of which descends to cover a curved apsidal form, found in no other Maine stations. The high-rising, granite-block wall base also lends the structure a stylish distinction unmatched in earlier small stations.

Grand Trunk Railroad Station, Yarmouth

YORK

Isles of Shoals Historic District, Kittery

The Isles of Shoals are a group of nine rocky islands, of which five are in Maine, that lie about nine miles southeast of the mouth of the Piscataqua River. This cluster of rocks and ledges became an important fishing station early in the seventeenth century. During the Indian wars, which began in 1676, these islands sheltered settlers fleeing attacks on their mainland villages.

In the eighteenth century, the Isles supported a flourishing whaling and fishing community, but the settlement had to be abandoned during the Revolution because of its vulnerability to attack by England's Royal Navy. After the Revolution, a small fishing village was re-established.

Starting in 1846, the Isles of Shoals became a summer resort for intellectuals and other visitors. Prominent artists and authors based themselves here in the late nineteenth and early twentieth centuries, making the Isles nationally known.

Today, the Isles of Shoals are largely uninhabited but have become important as a natural laboratory for the marine sciences.

Haley House, Smuttynose Island, Isles of Shoals Historic District, York. Photo by Douglas Armsden.

Stone Meeting House, Star Island, Isles of Shoals Historic District, York. Photo by Douglas Armsden.

Sayward House, York Historic District. Photo by J. David Bohl.

York Historic District

The York Historic District is situated in the extreme corner of southwestern Maine along the banks of the York River. The district actually comprises three distinct village areas: York Village, the oldest, dating from the seventeenth and eighteenth centuries; York Corner, a mainly eighteenth-century village; and York Harbor, architecturally an eighteenth- and nineteenth-century area.

The first settlers in York, then called Agamenticus, arrived about 1630. In 1641, the town became Gorgeana after the proprietor, Sir Ferdinando Gorges; in 1652, it was renamed York. The little frontier community prospered for a time, but from 1675 to 1713 the town was plagued by Indian attacks. With the end of these hostilities, York again prospered and grew. York residents worked in shipbuilding, lumbering, and farming. During the French and Indian War in the mid eighteenth century, many York men fought and died; others settled new frontiers farther east. York men

Emerson Wilcox Tavern, York Historic District.
Photo by Douglas Armsden.

also were active in the Revolutionary War and the War of 1812.

It was during this early period that two of York's most interesting buildings were constructed. John Hancock's warehouse was erected on the river in the mid seventeenth century, and the Old Gaol was built slightly earlier by order of the General Court of Massachusetts. Now open as a museum, the Old Gaol at York is the oldest English public building in the United States and now a National Historic Landmark.

During the early nineteenth century, York lost its designation as county seat and became just another small town. After the Civil War, however, a new era in York's history began. Summer visitors began coming to York to "get back to nature." First they boarded in local homes, then hotels were built for their convenience. Since then, the vacation industry has become one of the town's most important economic foundations.

Architecturally, York provides a broad spectrum: from simple utilitarian houses of the early eighteenth century, through the grander homes and commercial structures around the turn of the century, to those buildings erected by and for summer residents, and vacationing tourists. York has emerged as a charming village, rich in heritage and natural beauty.

McIntire Garrison, York

McIntire Garrison, Route 91 — ca. 1707 (NHL)

In the last quarter of the seventeenth century, Anglo-American communities quickly began to feature so-called "garrison houses." Today this term is often used to denote a 2-story dwelling with an overhanging second story. In the Colonial period, however, garrison houses were defined by function, not form. Thus, houses of all types were designated as garrisons — places of refuge and points of militia deployment. Garrisons were a response to the devastating Indian wars that descended upon Maine in 1676 and continued intermittently for nearly a century.

The McIntire Garrison, a National Historic Landmark, is the last of its type in Maine. The house is of sawn-log construction (7½ inches thick), with dovetailed corners, clapboard siding, gable roof, large central chimney, and overhanging second story. It is a rare survival from Maine's early settlement period.

John Sedgley Homestead, Chase's Pond Road — 1715–20

Because of ravaging Indian raids in the 1690s, virtually no documented seventeenth-century dwellings have survived in Maine. As a result, York County houses of the period of the John Sedgley homestead are among the earliest still standing. This well-preserved farmstead, located in a largely unspoiled area, has changed little during the 250 years of its existence.

Barrell Homestead, Beech Ridge Road — 1720

As originally constructed by Matthew Grover, the front portion of this house was a 2-story, hip-roof building typical of the period. After the 1841 alterations, it assumed its present massive appearance. It is distinguished as the home of the impulsive and eccentric Nathaniel Barrell, a member of the 1787 Massachusetts Ratifying Convention, and of Sally Sayward Barrell, Maine's first professional female novelist, who wrote under the name of "Madam Wood."

Old York Gaol, Lindsey Road — ca. 1720 (NHL)

One of the oldest public buildings in America is the Old York Gaol. Although long thought to date from 1653, it is now known that the earliest part of the building was constructed around 1720.

The earliest section of the Gaol is the fieldstone cell block,

Old York Gaol. Photo by Douglas Armsden.

measuring 30 by 18 feet, with walls 2½-feet thick. Part of the cell-block wall is exposed on one side of the building.

Throughout the eighteenth century the Old York Gaol was built upon and added to, creating the large and distinctive gambrel-roofed building that we see today. Since 1900, the Gaol has served as a museum administered by the Old York Improvement Society for the Town of York.

Old Schoolhouse, York Street — 1745, 1755

The residents of York Corner received permission to construct a schoolhouse in 1746. The one-room frame structure had an open fireplace at one end, a writing shelf, and only two windows. The exterior walls have narrow clapboards, and the roof is made of wooden shingles. In 1940, it was moved to its present location, and it is now a museum with figures in authentic costume.

John Hancock Warehouse,
Lindsey Road — Mid-Eighteenth Century

York's only Colonial commercial building, the Hancock Warehouse was built in the mid-1700s and restored in the 1950s. John Hancock owned wharves and warehouses all along the Maine coast, as well as several ships to transport his goods, but he was more successful in politics than in business.

Robert Rose Tavern, off Long Sands Road — 1756

When Robert Rose opened his tavern in 1759, the building was virtually new, although it was constructed on the site of a house built by John Banks in 1680 and may have retained some fabric of the earlier dwelling. Through more than two centuries of alterations, the straightforward lines of this rare mid-eighteenth century inn have survived.

Moody Homestead, Ridge Road — 1790

This house is important as the Maine structure most directly associated with the Moody family, who were prominent in the religious, political, military, and educational development of New England. In addition, it is a well-preserved example of a 2½-story, gable-roofed house with a double chimney arrangement.

STANDISH TO PORTLAND

Cumberland and Oxford Canal Historic District

The Cumberland and Oxford Canal was the only canal of any length built in Maine, but was one of many canals constructed throughout the eastern United States in the first third of the nineteenth century. It was designed to open the interior of southern Maine to development by connecting existing bodies of water with Portland Harbor and was planned to run from Waterford in Oxford County to Portland in Cumberland County. (The section of the canal in Oxford County was never executed, however.) Land surveying began in 1825; excavation began in 1828 and was completed in 1830; and the canal opened on June 1, 1830. The entire distance opened to navigation was thirty-eight miles. Eighteen miles of this made use of existing waterways: from Harrison at the head of Long Lake, across Long Lake, down the Songo River, and across Sebago Lake to Sebago Lake Basin. The district encompasses only the remaining twenty miles of the canal — the portion that was excavated. From the foot of Sebago Lake Basin, the canal followed a southerly and southeasterly route along the western side of the Presumpscot River to Westbrook, where it turned east across the contryside to Stroudwater, and from there it followed a course along the eastern bank of the Fore River to the foot of Clarke Street at the Portland waterfront.

The Cumberland and Oxford Canal flourished for twenty years until 1850, when railroads began to take away its business. The canal was taken over by the Canal Bank and sold in 1859 to private owners, who operated it until 1872, when it closed.

Most of the canal system is visible today. Wescott Lock, the aqueduct masonry, and the sluiceways and mill complex at Gambo Falls are in especially good condition. The masonry of several other locks is visible. The Cumberland and Oxford Canal is a valuable example of nineteenth-century engineering and transportation enterprise.

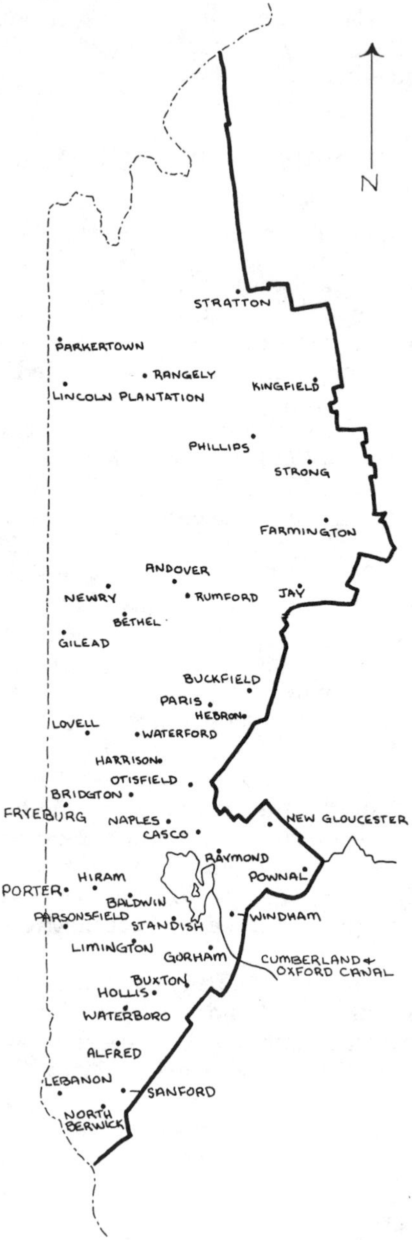
N
STRATTON
PARKERTOWN
RANGELY
KINGFIELD
LINCOLN PLANTATION
PHILLIPS
STRONG
FARMINGTON
ANDOVER
NEWRY
RUMFORD
JAY
BETHEL
GILEAD
BUCKFIELD
PARIS
HEBRON
LOVELL
WATERFORD
HARRISON
OTISFIELD
BRIDGTON
FRYEBURG
NAPLES
NEW GLOUCESTER
CASCO
RAYMOND
HIRAM
POWNAL
PORTER
BALDWIN
PARSONSFIELD
WINDHAM
STANDISH
LIMINGTON
GORHAM
CUMBERLAND &
OXFORD CANAL
BUXTON
HOLLIS
WATERBORO
ALFRED
LEBANON
SANFORD
NORTH
BERWICK

Western Region

ALFRED

Senator John Holmes House, Route 202 — 1802

Erected in 1802, this is an unusual example of a provincial-style mansion of the early nineteenth century. The fifteen-room dwelling was built around an enclosed court. Surrounding the house on three sides is a colonnade.

Senator Holmes was a noted lawyer and legislator who served as chairman of Maine's Constitutional Convention in 1819 and was elected her first senator the following year.

ANDOVER

Merrill-Poor House, Route 120 — 1791, 1896

Built in 1791, with alterations and additions executed in the 1890s, this large house is the oldest in Andover. It is distin-

Senator John Holmes House, Alfred

guished by the "Great Hall" added in 1896, probably designed by Stanford White. It has been in the Merrill-Poor-Chandler family for six generations. It was the birthplace of the railroad pioneers and promoters Henry Varnum Poor and John Alfred Poor.

Lovejoy Bridge, off Route 5 — 1868

Maine's shortest covered bridge is seventy feet long and was built using the Paddleford truss system. The wooden structure rests on granite abutments and spans the Ellis River to connect West River and East River roads.

Andover Public Library, Church Street — 1899

Originally built as a Universalist church, this structure is the last nineteenth-century building in Maine designed in the octagon tradition of Orson Squire Fowler.

BALDWIN

Valley Lodge, Saddleback Mountain Road — 1792

Built in 1792 by Ephraim Brown, one of the early settlers of Baldwin (then called Flintstown), the Valley Lodge is an interesting example of the adaptation and enlargement of a farmstead to suit the changing needs of a growing family. Originally constructed as a 1½-story, post-Colonial Cape, it was turned into a 2½-story Federal house, with an entirely new façade added a few feet out from the original front wall. Other additions were also made to the ell.

BETHEL

Broad Street Historic District

Consisting of twenty-seven buildings in virtually all the important nineteenth-century styles, this district includes Broad Street and the Common at its northerly end. The street began as part of the route from Bethel Hill to Norway during the early settlement of the town. In 1807, it was formally accepted as a town way and considerably widened to facilitate the training of militia, hence the origin of its name. The Bethel Common was originally the gift of Captain Eleazer Twitchell, who is generally considered the first settler of Bethel Village.

No building survives from the earliest days of the street's history — time and fires have taken their toll. The oldest surviving structure is the Dr. Moses Mason House, built in

Broad Street Historic District, Bethel

1813 and believed to be the first house painted white and built on a foundation in the district. The Wright cottage is the newest residence, dating from 1906. Most of the buildings on the street, however, were constructed in the middle of the nineteenth century and reflect the prevailing architectural styles of that period.

Undoubtedly, Bethel's golden age was the period when the Gehring Clinic attracted some of the most wealthy and brilliant people in the Northeast, particularly from New York society and Harvard University circles. Both the clinic and the Bethel Inn, as well as Gould Academy, located elsewhere in the community, profoundly affected Broad Street, making it a cosmopolitan island in an otherwise remote and largely rural region.

Dr. Moses Mason House — 1813–15

This handsome Federal house, a 2½-story frame structure, overlooks the Bethel Common. The main hall is decorated with murals by Rufus Porter and/or his apprentices. Porter was an important early American painter who popularized the use of local scenes and scenery in large-scale painting. The original owner of the house was a leading figure in Bethel; he was a doctor, postmaster, justice of the peace, congressman, sawmill owner, and selectman. The building is now owned by the Bethel Historical Society and serves as a museum and meeting place.

Gehring Clinic, Broad Street — 1896

Built in 1896, this residence is executed in the Queen Anne style, with elements of the Colonial Revival. The combination succeeds in creating a well-integrated house design. The owners of the buiding, Dr. and Mrs. John Gehring, were pioneer psychologists who operated a clinic in their home for the treatment of patients with nervous disorders. Because many of these patients were from the Cambridge intelligentsia, Bethel was once referred to as "the resting place of Harvard University."

BRIDGTON

Farnsworth House, Route 17, North Bridgton — 1825

Built by an early physician in the community, this hand-

Gehring Clinic, Bethel

some, late Federal house is particularly noted for its beautifully conceived interior woodwork.

William F. Perry House, Six Main Hill — 1870, 1874

Built in 1870 as a traditional Maine farmhouse with interconnecting dwelling, ell, and barn, this house was purchased and remodeled by William F. Perry in 1874. The blend of Italianate and Second Empire architecture is distinctive; the interior contains the traditional room arrangement with heavy Victorian decoration. William Perry was a leading industrialist in mid-nineteenth-century Bridgton. He owned and operated the town's largest woolen mill and made a fortune from blankets and uniforms during the Civil War. He also invented a turbine water wheel.

BUCKFIELD

Union Church, Route 140 — 1832

This is an outstandingly handsome and well-proportioned example of a late Federal period meeting house with transi-

Union Church, Buckfield

tional Gothic features. It was saved from destruction in the 1890s through the generosity of John D. Long, a Buckfield native who served as secretary of the navy under Presidents McKinley and Theodore Roosevelt.

BUXTON

Royal Brewster House, Buxton Lower Corner — 1805

This house merits attention as the residence of the American primitive portraitist, John Brewster, Jr., who lived here with his brother, Dr. Royal Brewster. In addition, it is an imposing example of provincial Federal-style architecture and the work of a local builder, Joseph Woodman.

Buxton Powder House, Route 22, Buxton Center — 1812–13

This small brick structure is one of only three War of 1812 powder houses known to survive in Maine. It presents clear evidence that military defense was still considered chiefly a local responsibility in the early nineteenth century.

Tory Hill Meeting House, Buxton Lower Corner — 1822

This fine example of a rural Federal church derives particular significance from its association with Kate Douglas Wiggin and her play, "The Old Peabody Pew."

CASCO

Friends Meeting House, Quaker Ridge — 1814

This modest structure on Quaker Ridge is the oldest meeting house of the Society of Friends in Maine. In 1814, the 1½-story building was divided into two sections, one for men and one for women, with a large shutter in the partition to allow communication. The fabric of the buiding appears to be entirely original, a remarkable survival.

FARMINGTON

Tufts House, Route 2 — 1810

Francis Tufts, one of the three original proprietors of Farmington, built this finely detailed Federal-style residence of bricks that he manufactured himself form local clay beds.

Jacob Abbott House, Main Street — 1819

This simple, 1½-story dwelling was the summer home of children's author Jacob Abbott and, for the last nine years of his life, his year-round residence. A pioneer in the education of the young, Abbott (author of *The Rollo Books*, the *Marco Paul* series, etc.) was among the first to emphasize the importance of early training and education in inculcating in children the proper sense of duty, industry, and moral worth.

The Old Union Meeting House, Farmington Falls — 1826–27

This is a rare example of a church whose exterior form derives from eighteenth-century architectural traditions, but which was built in the nineteenth century with Federal style details. The result is an engaging structure with major architectural significance for Maine.

Benjamin Butler, a noted carpenter and builder in the Farmington area, designed and built the Union Meeting House to serve many denominations; Methodists, Free Baptists, Universalists, and Congregationalists all used this church, one Sunday in four. Each of these denominations

Old Union Meeting House, Farmington Falls

eventually built its own church, and today the meeting house serves the Baptists.

The church has recently been completely restored, internally and externally, through a grant administered by the Maine Historic Preservation Commission.

Free Will Baptist Meeting House, Main Street — 1835

This late Federal-style building is one of the few early brick meeting houses in Maine. The first Baptist congregation north and east of Gorham was officially formed in 1793, but their meeting house was not constructed until 1835. Since 1900, the building has been used as a cheese factory, a Keeley Cure center, a stable, a fur depot, and a garage. The exterior, except for the garage door, is in excellent, original condition.

Nordica Homestead, Holly Road — 1840

This simple Cape Cod–style farmhouse was built by Edwin Norton in 1840. Seventeen years later, his sixth daughter, Lillian, was born there. When she was five years old, her mother, now a widow, moved the family into the village of Farmington. The farmhouse was sold in 1863, and in 1864 the Nortons moved to Boston.

Mrs. Norton intended that her daughter Whilemena be given serious voice training, but when Whilemena died young, Mrs. Norton turned her attention to Lillian. Following private lessons, she entered the New England Conservatory of Music and then went abroad to perfect her voice training. When she was twenty-one, she made her debut in Milan in the role of Elvina in *Don Giovanni.* At this time she Italianized her name to Giglia Nordica (Lily of the North), although she later changed her name back to Lillian.

Accompanied by her mother, Lillian Nordica spent ten years touring Europe. She made her American debut in 1891 at the Metropolitan Opera. Madame Nordica arrived as a star, but her new goal was to play Wagnerian roles. She studied under Wagner's widow and was one of the few sopranos ever to sing Wagnerian roles actually on key.

In 1911, the old Norton homestead was purchased by Lily's sisters. They presented it to her as a gift, and the three shared it during the summers until the diva's death in 1914.

Two large collections of "Nordicana" were acquired by the Nordica Memorial Association, which purchased the home in 1927. Since 1928, the house has been open as a museum.

Lillian Nordica, whose voice possessed liquid purity, exceptional range, and magnificent power, was a charming woman with a flair for the dramatic. Her fame as America's first and greatest prima donna was widespread.

Little Red Schoolhouse, Routes 2 and 4 — 1852

For over a century, this ungraded schoolhouse served the people of Farmington. Although a typical structure of its time, this frame building has an unusual arched ceiling. The schoolroom had benches, bookshelves, a teacher's platform, and a painted blackboard. The building was rennovated in 1898 and moved in 1937. It is now a museum and an information center.

Hiram Ramsdell House,
Corner of High and Perham Streets — 1858

Built in 1858 by Cyrus Ramsdell, a local brickmaker, this brick octagon house was probably inspired by Orson Squire Fowler's book, *A Home For All*. In 1868, the house was sold to Hiram Ramsdell (Cyrus's brother), a local merchant. Every façade has a different window treament. The back has a 2-story wooden ell. To the right are a glass hallway and an octagonal sunporch. Of the few octagonal houses in Maine, the Ramsdell house is certainly one of the finest.

First Congregational Church, Main Street — 1887–88

This Romanesque Revival Church, designed by George M. Coombs, is the most distinctive and best-preserved late-nineteenth-century church in northwestern Maine. Coombs skillfully combined impressive exterior design with a convenient interior plan for adjoining sanctuary and vestry. Since its completion, the building has retained its original integrity of design and decor.

Chester Greenwood House, Farmington

Chester Greenwood House, Route 27—1896

In addition to its architectural significance, this Queen Anne house is more particularly distinguished as the home of Chester Greenwood, inventor in 1872 of that important but humble adjunct to winter wear, the earmuff (or ear protector, as he named it). Inventor, handyman, and businessman, Greenwood epitomized the multi-talented nineteenth-century man, keenly interested in scientific development and convinced of the unlimited benefits of technology.

Merrill Hall, Main and Academy Streets—1888, 1898

One of the finest late-nineteenth-century academic buildings in Maine, this Romanesque Revival structure by

George M. Coombs, with its slightly older rear addition, was the first major edifice at Farmington State Teachers College, later to become the University of Maine at Farmington.

**Cutler Memorial Library,
corner of Academy and High Streets — 1901–3**

William R. Miller, a prominent Maine architect, designed this granite Beaux Arts library in 1900; the library was constructed between 1901 and 1903 using funds provided by Isaac M. Cutler. The exterior and interior are in excellent, original condition, and the lovely little library stands as a memorial to the Honorable Nathan Cutler.

FRYEBURG

**Squire Chase House,
151 Main Street — ca. 1767, ca. 1820, 1858**

The ell of this house includes the original home built by Nathaniel Merrill, one of the first settlers on the "seven lots" laid out by Colonel Joseph Frye in 1762. The foursquare Federal house was moved to the present site in 1824 by Stephen Chase.

A later owner added Italianate embellishments, including the cupola, overhanging eaves, and brackets, which form a very pleasing, if unusual, whole.

Benjamin Wiley House, Fish Street — 1772, 1790–92

This well-preserved farmstead incorporates in its ell one of the oldest standing buildings in Fryeburg. Architecturally, the massive house of 1790 is a prototype for the rural adaptation of early Federal design.

Hemlock Bridge, over the old course of Saco River — 1857

This 116-foot-long, wooden covered bridge spans the old course of the Saco River in Fryeburg. Built on granite abutments, this is the only surviving covered bridge over the Saco River.

GILEAD

Peabody Tavern, Route 2 — ca. 1800

An important stage and later railroad stop on the route from Portland, Maine, to Lancaster, New Hampshire, the Peabody Tavern was first owned by Thomas Peabody, who came to Gilead from Andover, Massachusetts, to settle in Peabody's Patent, as Gilead was first called. The patent was probably granted to Lieutenant John Peabody, Thomas's father, for services at Louisburg in 1758 and Ticonderoga in 1759, and as captain of a company during the Revolution.

GORHAM

Gorham Campus Historic District

The Gorham Campus Historic District is important not only for the architectural merit of each of its seven buildings, but

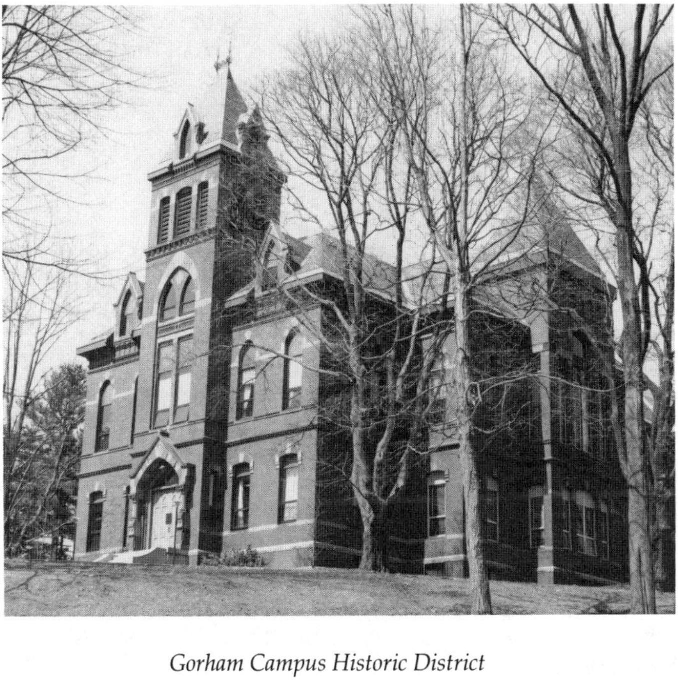

Gorham Campus Historic District

also for the interesting story it illustrates of educational development in Maine.

Incorporated in 1803, Gorham Academy began operations in 1806 (in the present Academy Building) as a men's school but began admitting women the following year. In 1835, the Gorham Female Seminary separated from the academy, which reverted to its original state. Known as Gorham Academy and Teachers Institute in 1847, the men's school was closed, and in 1850 the whole establishment became the Maine Female Seminary by an act of the state legislature. Men's enrollment was soon re-established, and in 1861 the whole became Gorham Seminary. In 1877, the seminary closed because the spread of public high schools had exhausted its pool of applicants.

In 1878, the Western Maine Normal School opened in the old academy buildings and the new Corthell Hall. The curriculum of the Normal School was expanded in 1911 to include the teaching of industrial arts. Kindergarten and primary-level teaching courses were included in the 1920s, and a third year was added to the program. By 1938, the course of study had increased to a full four years. In 1945, the school's name was changed to Gorham State Teachers College. The college became accredited in New England in 1960, and nationally in 1964. It is now part of the University of Southern Maine.

McLellan House, Gorham Campus — 1733

The oldest brick building in Cumberland County (and possibly the oldest in Maine) was constructed by Hugh McLellan, one of the first settlers in Gorham, of bricks made from the clay of a nearby brook. Completed in 1773, the house has been modernized many times and is now used as a dormitory by the University of Southern Maine.

Baxter House, South Street — 1805

Occupied for twenty years by Dr. Elihu Baxter, a highly respected physician and community servant, this finely detailed Federal residence was donated to the town by his son, James Phinney Baxter, father of Governor Percival P. Baxter.

Academy Building, Gorham Campus Historic District

Academy Building, Gorham Campus — 1806

This handsome structure was completed in 1806 for Gorham Academy, a college preparatory school for boys. The scale is large and ambitious, and the exterior detailing is carefully executed. An elegant Federal building, it continues to be an architectural focal point on the University of Southern Maine campus and in the town of Gorham.

Art Gallery, Gorham Campus — 1822

Formerly the Free Meeting House, this building originally had the same simple design as a Colonial meeting house.

Art Gallery, Gorham Campus Historic District

The single-story frame structure was constructed for the Handel Singing Society, which provided music for any group holding religious services in their building. It has been used as a town house, an interfaith chapel, and an art gallery for the college. In 1845, a classical pediment supported by four fluted Doric columns was added to form a portico in the Greek Revival tradition.

HARRISON

Barrows-Scribner Mill, Scribner's Mill Road — 1846-47

This early mill is unusually well documented. It is presently being stabilized and will be developed as a working up-and-down sawmill museum by a tax-exempt non-profit organization, Scribner's Mill Preservation, Incorporated.

HEBRON

Sturtevant Hall, Hebron Academy — 1891

Designed by Maine's most famous architect, John Calvin Stevens, Sturtevant Hall is outstanding among the four commissions he carried for Hebron Academy. Built at a cost of over $30,000, it was named after Benjamin F. Sturtevant of Jamaica Plain, the largest single contributor to the building fund. This well-preserved example of Romanesque and Colonial Revival architecture remains the dominant structure on the spacious campus.

HIRAM

John Watson House, Route 177 — 1785

This house is the embodiment of eighteenth-century Georgian architectural ideals, expressed in the forthright terms of rural New England. The fine 2-story structure was built in 1785 by a Revolutionary War veteran, whose first house in Hiram was swept away by a spring flood. The interior of the house is organized around a massive central chimney and contains simple but handsome early Federal woodwork.

General Peleg Wadsworth House, off Routes 5 and 13 — 1800–1807

This large but simple farmhouse was constructed in the early nineteenth century for General Peleg Wadsworth, Revolutionary War hero, prominent citizen of Hiram, and grandfather of poet Henry Wadsworth Longfellow. The house itself is unusually large, a central meeting room on the first floor has a ceiling high enough for the militia to use for drill practice during the winter. The entire farm is in unspoiled condition and is still being worked.

HOLLIS

"Quillcote" — Kate Douglas Wiggin House — 1797

The story of Quillcote is one of additions and alterations. The building has changed through successive generations from a basic farmhouse into a unique blend of new and old. As the home of a famous American author and as a comfortable aggregation of architectural styles and tastes, Quillcote is a structure of broad significance.

Quillcote became the home in later life of Kate Douglas Wiggin, distinguished educator, author and lecturer, who is perhaps best known for her beloved children's book, *Rebecca of Sunnybrook Farm*. Having purchased the house in 1905, she named it "Quillcote," meaning house of the pen.

JAY

Holmes-Crafts Homestead, Route 4 — ca. 1820

This 2-story, hipped-roof, Federal-style dwelling can be definitely traced back to 1820, but some reports state that it was built in 1803. It is a fine example of sturdy Federal-style architecture that has managed to survive to the present. The timbers were hand-hewn, the floors are made of wide pine boards, and much of the original hardware remains.

North Jay Grange Store, Route 17 — 1895

America's last grange store, one of thousands at one time, closed in 1976 after almost a century of operation. The North Jay Grange was formed in 1874, the tenth in Maine, and set up a cooperative store in 1882, but it was not until after 1895 that the group combined their grange hall and store in a new, 2½-story, frame building. The twentieth-century cooperative store operated as it did in the nineteenth century, with a molasses barrel, a wheel of cheese, and an almost unlimited supply of agricultural goods.

KINGFIELD

Amos G. Winter House, Winter Hill — 1896–98

Winter's Inn at Kingfield is a significant example of Colonial Revival architecture, which is most unusual for the remote area in which it is located.

The house was built for Amos G. Winter, a wealthy grain merchant of Kingfield, who also operated the local general store near the house. Winter's wife was an aristocratic

Amos G. Winter House, Kingfield

woman from New York City who entertained frequently and desired a residence of refined elegance.

Winter was a close friend of Freeland and Francis Stanley, architects and inventors of the steam car. It is recounted that, upon returning from a hunting trip in the 1890s, Winter and the Stanley brothers were casting about for some activity to occupy the afternoon. After some thought, Freeland suggested building a house on the hill, and it was then that rudimentary plans were formulated as to approximate size, number of rooms needed, and living spaces to be created. Freeland Stanley returned to Boston with the rough sketches and, with the help of his brother and associates, final plans were drafted.

The engineering propensities of the Stanley brothers were evident. The original heating system was designed around a furnace that had once been a railroad engine boiler. A steam-driven elevator was planned but never completed.

This sophisticated and elegant building in relatively humble surrounds is of unusual interest.

LEBANON

West Lebanon Historic District

West Lebanon was first settled in 1747 by John Canney (Kenney) of Dover. By 1765, there were twenty to twenty-five families settled in town. The Meeting House was raised in 1754, and a permanent Congregational minister, the Reverend Issac Hasey, a graduate of Harvard, was called and ordained in 1765. In 1767, the town was incorporated and named Lebanon, which replaced the Indian name of Tow-woh.

The village developed in the late eighteenth and early nineteenth centuries, when the first permanent settlers sold many lots and divided the ministerial lot. Increased travel and commerce converged at the fork in the main highway. The present roadways, replacing the old wheel-paths to the river and the center, were laid out in the early 1820s.

Since the last century, the village of West Lebanon has survived nearly unaltered. No commercial structures disturb its serenity, and, with the exception of one house built in 1915, no new dwellings have been erected. The village's individual houses, along with its academy and its church, have retained their beauty, durability, and convenience.

Although its agricultural basis has disappeared, and with

West Lebanon Historic District, Lebanon

it the general store and tavern, its charact
same. It is this character that both visitors an
ognize and appreciate. The comfortable ci
the now-residential village remain — te
nineteenth-century rural community.

Old Gristmill, Little River Road — 1774

Joseph Hardison's Gristmill of 1774 is significant as a rare rural industrial building of the eighteenth century. The Maine Historic Resources Inventory shows only one earlier gristmill in the state, the Perkins Gristmill of 1749 in Kennebunkport.

LIMINGTON

Limington Academy, Route 117 — 1854

The Limington Academy building of 1854 is an exceptionally strong and forthright semi-peripteral, Greek Revival Temple–style structure, which still serves its original purpose as an educational building within the community of Limington. Its splendid lines make it an outstanding landmark in an essentially rural setting.

Founded by subscription in 1848, Limington Academy first held sessions in 1851 in the village district schoolhouse and later in the Masonic hall and other locations. In 1853 a lot was purchased, and the following year the present building was erected at a cost of $2,102.05. The bylaws of the academy board state that its object was "to establish an institution for the promotion of Science and Literature and wherein youth may be instructed in the higher branches of education usually taught in the Academies of this state."

In 1895, the trustees of the academy voted to receive all qualified students of the town upon application, and some years later the institution became a public high school. With a new high school next door to it now, the old building provides classroom space for elementary grades but is still in the ownership of the trustees.

Limington Academy

LINCOLN PLANTATION

Bennett Bridge, off Route 16 — 1901

This wooden bridge rests on granite-block shore abutments at either end of its ninety-two foot span over the Magalloway River. Built for the convenience of farmers living close to the New Hampshire border, the bridge was designed on the Long truss system.

LOVELL

Knight's Olde Country Store, Route 5A — 1838, 1844, ca. 1850

This grouping of three attached structures is a fine example of vernacular, Greek Revival, rural, commercial architecture in a setting little changed since its construction. It remains the shopping center of the community, which it has served under a long, well-documented series of merchants and tradesmen.

NAPLES

The Manor House, Route 302—1797

This handsomely conceived, brick-ended, early Federal-style house is particularly remarkable for its rather remote location. It was built by George Pierce, a proprietor's agent and one of the earliest settlers in the region.

Sam Perley Farm, Perley Road—1809

This simple but distinctive Federal-style farmhouse, named not for its builder but rather for his son, is part of a generous farmstead beautifully sited on a hill in a remote part of Naples Township. Its significance lies both in its architectural merit and in its association with the Perley family, leaders in the community from its inception. Thomas Perley of Boxford, Massachusetts, was one of the original proprietors of Bridgton (part of which was taken to form the town of Naples in 1834); his son Enoch was one of the early settlers in 1776, who accumulated more than two thousand acres of timberland; and his son Thomas, a major in the militia, built the present house. Thomas's son, Samuel, was a progressive farmer, president of the Cumberland County Agricultural Society, trustee of the Maine State College of Agriculture and Mechanic Arts (now the University of Maine at Orono), and four-term state legislator, serving in both houses. At the time of his death in 1881, he was Naples's most prominent citizen and well known throughout the state.

Songo Lock, Songo River near U.S. Route 302—1830

This canal lock was built in 1830 of stone masonry with wooden gates as part of the Cumberland-Oxford Canal from Portland to Harrison. For two decades, the canal supplied an efficient trade route, but the increased use of railroads made the canal less attractive to farmers and merchants. Until 1896, it was still used during log drives. The Songo Lock was rebuilt in 1911 for water-level control, and it is still used by private boaters.

Isaac Parsons House, New Gloucester Historic District

NEW GLOUCESTER

New Gloucester Historic District

The significance of New Gloucester lies in the fact that it was one of the few well-settled inland towns in Maine during the last half of the eighteenth century. The wealth of fine late-eighteenth- and early-nineteenth-century homes in the New Gloucester Historic District attest to its early prosperity as an agricultural community. Few villages in Maine have as many substantial 2½-story dwellings of the period in their original natural setting.

The township of New Gloucester was granted in 1735 to sixty citizens of Gloucester, Massachusetts, who named the area after their town. A number of families soon built log houses and a sawmill. But a new war with France broke out in 1744 and continued until 1751, during which time the community was abandoned because of Indian attacks.

In 1753, some of the inhabitants returned and built a blockhouse to serve as their home, fort, and church. Slowly the community rebuilt its ruined cabins and sawmills. In 1756, a road was cut to North Yarmouth on the coast, and two years later the first gristmill was constructed.

With a good beginning before the Revolution, New Gloucester grew rapidly after the war. The town was incorporated in 1794. From the early 1790s until 1805, New

Gloucester served as half-shire town with Portland for Cumberland County. This further helped to develop the community. Many of the houses now standing in the historic district were completed by the first decades of the nineteenth century.

Since its founding in the mid eighteenth century, New Gloucester has been primarily a farming area. For more than two hundred years, the farmland and the houses have blended to form a distinctive and enduring picture of rural Maine.

Shaker Village Historic District (NHL)

Brought to America from England in 1774, the United Society of Believers, more commonly known as Shakers, remains today as the oldest American communal religious organization. Its search for perfection, not only within the individual but within society, led eventually to the estab-

Third floor of meeting house, Shaker Village Historic District, Sabbathday Lake

Sabbathday Lake Shaker Community: dwelling house (foreground), Trustee's office (background). Photo by John McKee.

lishment of twenty-three Shaker societies in eleven states. The community at Sabbathday Lake, Maine, founded in 1783, is the largest and most active of the two remaining Shaker groups. Within its thirteen buildings, clustered near the northern shore of the lake that gives the village its name, there survives a tradition of workmanship, rapidly disappearing from the American scene.

Of the remaining buildings, nine predate 1850. The community's meeting house, designed by Moses Johnson of Enfield, New Hampshire, was built in 1794. The walls of the plain and unpretentious meeting room are lined with pews unadorned except for the rich Shaker blue paint that can no longer be duplicated. Ten long beams overhead serve as the only support for the building's two upper stories. The meeting house now holds the nation's oldest Shaker museum in continuous existence. Founded in 1931, it contains exhibits illustrating all phases of Shaker life and work and serves as a living memorial to the early Believers, who in loving consecration put their hands to work and gave their hearts to God. Of outstanding interest are its exhibits of starkly beau-

Meeting House, Shaker Village Historic District, Sabbathday Lake

tiful and high functional Shaker furniture and of early hand-woven textiles, as well as outstanding collections of tin and woodenware. Examples of the unique inspirational drawings produced during the 1840s and 1850s are also on display, along with several pieces of Shaker art in the early American primitive tradition.

Other buildings include a central brick dwelling of 1884, a store, a work house, barns, and various shops.

NEWRY

Sunday River Bridge, Sunday River Road—1870

Of the nine covered bridges remaining in Maine, the Sunday River, or Artist's, Bridge, is the most picturesque. It spans the Sunday River, but it is called the Artist's Bridge because, over the years since its construction in 1872, many artists have traveled to Newry to paint it.

Sunday River Bridge, Newry

The 100-foot-long bridge was built on granite-block abutments, using the Paddleford truss system of construction. Because of the swift current of the Sunday River, several bridges were swept away before the present bridge was constructed.

Although the bridge was built in halves assembled separately on opposite shores, when erected it settled into place correctly and firmly. It has been kept in good repair for the past 110 years and, although it was retired from use in 1955, it is still preserved for its historic and aesthetic values.

Lower Sunday River School, Sunday River Road — 1895

This modest schoolhouse, within earshot of Dug Hill Brook at Sunday River, is a remarkable survival of a late-nineteenth-century rural school. Though closed over thirty years ago when Newry became part of a larger school district, it has been kept in excellent repair, the result of its later use as a Sunday school and community center. Despite these varied functions, the school retains its turn-of-the-century atmosphere with the help of its original furnishings. Many school museums strive for years to achieve the appearance of authenticity; through some stroke of luck the

Lower Sunday River School, Newry

Sunday River District, District Number 1, has survived looking very much as it did some seventy years ago.

One of the last one-room school buildings in northern Oxford County to remain intact, it represents a now-faded era in rural education. Its unaltered interior provides a realistic view of a Maine school as it looked three-quarters of a century ago.

NORTH BERWICK

Thomas Hobbs, Jr., House, Wells Street—1763

Another important example of mid-eighteenth-century rural domestic architecture, this one-room-deep house was for many years a well-known hostelry, when it was the social center of North Berwick. Hobbs, a veteran of the French and Indian wars, offered food, drink, lodging, and, according to his account book, sizable amounts of powder, shot, and flint. Still a private residence, "The Hostelry" is a well-preserved late Colonial structure.

Old Morrell House, Bauneg Beg Pond Road—1763

This 2-story Colonial farmhouse was built in 1763 by Winthrop Morrell, a Quaker, and remained in the Morrell family until recently. It was purchased in 1974 by its present owner in a state of considerable dilapidation and beautifully restored.

Hussey Plow Company Building and Museum, Dyer Street Extension—1831

This small and simple structure served as an office building for the Hussey Plow Company, founded in 1835 by William Hussey. From very humble beginnings, this industrial enterprise has emerged today as the highly respected Hussey Manufacturing Company, still a family business, now under the leadership of two of William Hussey's great-great-grandsons.

Mary R. Hurd House, Elm Street—1894

Among the most impressive examples of the Queen Anne–Eastlake tradition in Maine architecture, this house stands as a memorial to its builder, Mary N. Hurd, a remarkable woman and benefactor of North Berwick for over seventy years.

OTISFIELD

The Nutting Homestead, Gould Corner—ca. 1796, 1820

This early-nineteenth-century farm complex has been occupied continuously by five generations of the Nutting family. Nathan Nutting built the original, Cape Cod section of the house in 1796; his son, Nathan, Jr., built the attached Federal house for his brother, Lyman, in 1820. This fine example of a rural farmhouse, expanding with family growth, attests to the adaptability of early Maine settlers.

PARIS

Paris Hill Historic District

Steeped in history and rich in architectural resources, the Paris Hill Historic District is spectacularly located on the crest of a hill 831 feet about sea level and commands a panoramic view of the White Mountains. Settled in the 1780s by the family of Lemuel Jackson, the area was divided into smaller lots in 1800, and the village grew rapidly. In 1805, it became the shire town of Oxford County, and the county buildings, as well as most of the residences built at this time, still remain. These fine Federal structures and those in the later Greek Revival style combine to give the village an impressive and dignified early-nineteenth-century tone, largely unspoiled by later intrusions. The growth of the community slowed after 1860 and virtually ceased in 1895, when the county seat moved to South Paris.

During its years of prominence in county government, Paris Hill attracted many significant families. Over the years, four elected Maine governors, three speakers of the Maine House, three presidents of the Maine Senate, twelve U.S. representatives, two U.S. senators, and one vice president have been born or have lived in Paris Hill. Hannibal

Old Jail, Paris Hill Historic District

Cyrus Hamlin House, Paris Hill Historic District

Rawson House, Paris Hill Historic District

Hamlin (1809–1891) was born in the Cyrus Hamlin House and served in the United States Senate, was elected governor of Maine, and later became vice president in Abraham Lincoln's first administration. Albion Keith Parris, whose law office still stands beside the Hubbard House, served in the United States Senate and was five-time governor of Maine. Enoch Lincoln and Sidney Perham also served as governors of Maine for three terms each.

The buildings which stand today on picturesque Paris Hill are living monuments to the vigorous nineteenth-century shire town of Oxford County. Surrounded by open land — fields, woods, and orchards — the village is set apart in time and space, preserving its unique character and integrity.

Robinson-Parsons Farm,
Town Farm Brook Road — ca. 1795, 1803

Although part of the ell of this farmhouse may date from the 1790s, it is the main brick-ended structure that is significant as a fine rural Federal dwelling. This larger building was erected after the births of Stephen Robinson's five daughters. Eventually, five more daughters and a son arrived, so it is little wonder that a hinged partition was installed between two large second-floor bedrooms to provide room for dancing and social events.

One of the Robinson daughters married John Parsons, and the farm passed to that family line. It has stayed in the Parsons family ever since.

PARKERTOWN

Vail Site — Prehistoric

The Vail site lies under Aziscohos Lake in the northwestern boundary mountains of Maine, near the borders of New Hampshire and Quebec. Aziscohos Dam was completed in 1919, and the reservoir waters behind the lake rose to cover all but the edges farthest inland of the site. When the lake level drops and the former Magalloway River recedes to its original channel, one can see that the site occupies a slight slope at the edge of a rolling river floodplain, just before the valley rises steeply to the surrounding mountains.

but fragments of broken tools from some of the loci fit tool fragments from a locus at the other end of the site. Moreover, the remnants of fireplaces have been recovered near the centers of the stone-tool loci. It is surmised that these oval distributions of stone tools are the last remnants of a series of huts or tents that were pitched along the valley site.

The site has been carefully excavated by the Maine State Museum. Most exciting is the discovery of an area that has been called the killing ground in the middle of the valley floodplain, adjacent to what may be an old stream channel. The killing ground has yielded about a dozen fluted points in a long scatter along the south side of the channel. The killing-ground points are either complete or represent the broken, pointed ends of spearpoints. There are no stone tools or flakes from the killing ground, in stark contrast to the debris around the valley-side loci. In addition, most of the fluted points from the hut or tent locations are either complete or represent the broken proximal (hafted) ends of spearpoints. At least one of the broken pointed ends from the killing ground fits to make a complete spearpoint with a broken hafted-end fragment from one valley-side tool scatter.

Thus, for the first time in the Northeast, we have a complete picture of a very short occupation, perhaps a seasonal one in these mountains, with a limited number of tents and one successful hunting area within sight of the campsite. From the distribution of the points on the killing ground, and because of the lack of other stone tools, like butchering knives or resharpening flakes, we can say that the prey were small animals, perhaps caribou or horses, rather than large mammoths, and that they were probably ambushed as they crossed the river.

PARSONSFIELD

Captain James Morison House, South Road — 1785

Built by a Revolutionary War soldier of some distinction, this post-Colonial inland residence in rural Maine is particularly distinguished by the fine, well-preserved murals in the halls and stairwell, executed and signed by Jonathan D. Poor, a pupil of Rufus Porter, in the mid-nineteenth century.

Blazo-Leavitt House, Route 160 — 1812–17

This expansive high-style Federal homestead reflects both externally and internally an advanced level of woodworking technique. It is believed that the exceptional woodwork was the work of ship's carpenters from Portsmouth who were left unemployed by the Embargo of 1807.

Porter-Parsonfield Bridge, Route 160 — 1876

Three granite blocks support this 152-foot-long wooden bridge. Designed on the Paddleford truss system, the bridge spans the Ossipee River.

PHILLIPS

"Maine Woods" Office, Main Street — 1848

This extremely rare example of a wooden, Gothic Revival, commercial structure is also significant as the former office of the "Maine Woods," an internationally known journal dealing with hunting and fishing in Maine.

PORTER

Old Meeting House, 1.8 miles north of Route 25 — 1818–19

The Bullockite sect (followers of Baptist clergyman Jeremiah Bullock) erected this frame, clapboarded meeting house between 1818 and 1819. The open interior, with its three-sided gallery and box pews, is almost completely original. The exterior has been renovated with a new roof and a fresh coat of paint. The building is now dedicated to the memory of Porter's pioneer ancestors, who constructed and used it.

POWNAL

Jacob Randall Homestead, Lawrence Road — ca. 1800

This very fine example of rural, Federal-style, brick domestic architecture was built by an early settler in the region, who erected a grist and saw mill and became a prominent figure in the community for many years.

RANGELEY

Rangeley Public Library, Lake Street — 1909

The Rangeley Public Library is a small structure of unusual charm and grace exactly suited to the ambiance of this early summer resort region. Built entirely of native Maine materials and designed by Ambrose Walker of New York City in a modified Romanesque Revival style, it is sited on a side street that runs down to the shore of Rangeley Lake.

As with many other summer colonies, Rangeley drew to it people accustomed to cultural facilities, particularly an adequate library. In 1907, a library association was formed, and, after a brief but successful fund drive, land was acquired and the library building begun. Dedication exercises were held on August 12, 1909.

RAYMOND

Nathaniel Hawthorne's Boyhood Home, Hawthorne Road — ca. 1800

Once known as "Manning's Folly" because of the extravagances of its period wallpaper, eight fireplaces, and Belgian glass windows, the ten-room home of Richard Manning was also the home of his nephew, Nathaniel Hawthorne, between 1813 and 1825. Remodeled several times, the building has since been used as a tavern and, for the last 142 years, as a meeting house.

RUMFORD

Strathglass Park Historic District

History shows that, in 1900, the new breed of industrialists had yet to demonstrate a strong interest in workers' welfare

Strathglass Park Historic District, Rumford

and housing. A notable exception to this rule was Hugh J. Chisholm, entrepreneur and prime mover in the development of the Rumford Falls industrial area and the Oxford Paper Company.

At the turn of the century, Rumford was a boom town, and the burgeoning mills and shops drew a flood of workers into the area. At first, the skilled workers lived in boardinghouses provided by the various manufactories, and the day laborers, mostly Italian, occupied sod huts and other primitive dwellings.

Chisholm, seeing the dramatic housing shortage and the need to attract a stable and qualified work force, determined to provide housing of high quality and a pleasant living environment. He conceived the idea for a unique project: the establishment of a parklike area with attractive brick duplex homes surrounded by lawns and with wide tree-shaded streets. To design the buildings, he retained the services of Cass H. Gilbert, the noted New York architect.

For his park, Chisholm selected a convenient and desirable location across the river from the mill. In all, fifty-one brick units were built between 1901 and 1902, providing 102 dwellings. After three quarters of a century, the good condition of these structures attests to the quality of their construction.

First choice of these new houses was given to workers recommended by their foremen. Rents were minimal, enough to cover maintenance and amortization. Many services were supplied, including snow removal, sanding, lawn mowing and rubbish disposal. The charge for electricity, conveniently provided by the Chisholm-owned Rumford Falls Power Company, was a mere one dollar per month.

During 1948 and 1949, the Rumford Falls Realty Company divested itself of Strathglass Park by sale. No profits were ever recorded by the company, and occasional deficits were met with funds from Oxford Paper Company.

Strathglass Park is a remarkable example of enlightened industrialist paternalism. The durability, quality, and attractiveness of the buildings is mirrored in the way they have been maintained during twenty-five years of private occupancy.

Historic Resources of Rumford

In 1882, Hugh J. Chisholm and Waldo Pettingill purchased large tracts of land at Rumford Falls on the Androscoggin River. The first industrial building was constructed there in 1892, and the Rumford Falls Power Company was founded.

Strathglass Building, Historic Resources of Rumford

Within the next twenty years, growth so phenomenal took place there that national attention was attracted. What had been a remote, rural countryside now reverberated with the noise of machinery. The Oxford Paper Company was founded, and a small city grew almost overnight.

The four buildings included in Rumford's historic resources were constructed between 1906 and 1916. The commercial architecture of these buildings is more decorative and opulent than would be expected in a typical Maine industrial community, but they represent Rumford's ambitions and high expectations in the early part of this century.

The Rumford Falls Power Company Building, constructed in 1906 in the Beaux Arts style, was built by the company responsible for Rumford's remarkable development.

Another Beaux Arts–style building, the Strathglass Building of 1910, was built to house department stores and a hotel.

The Mechanic Institute of 1911 was erected in the neo-Classical Revival style to house the benevolent and educational association formed for the mill workers. It is now the community center.

Harry S. Coombs designed the Municipal Building in the Colonial Revival style in 1916. This structure and the others in downtown Rumford reflect the aspirations of a community that viewed the future with abounding confidence.

Deacon Hutchins House, Route 5—1802

Architecturally, the Deacon Hutchins House is a fine restoration of a very early nineteenth-century farmhouse, whose ample proportions reflect the social status of the first owner. Hezekiah Hutchins, who came to Rumford from Hampstead, New Hampshire, in 1801, was a founder and the first deacon of the Congregational Church at Rumford Center, moderator of the town meeting, collector and constable, and justice of the peace. The primary significance of the house, however, lies in its stunning frescoes by Rufus Porter (1792–1884), a remarkable painter and natural philosopher, which adorn the front parlor.

SANFORD

The Emery Homestead, 1 and 3 Lebanon Street — 1830, 1862, 1908

Added to by various generations of the Emery family, this complex of attached structures marks the location of the original settlement of Sanford. It is still owned by members of the family, which has contributed substantially to the life of the community over the years.

Thomas Goodall House, 232 Main Street — 1871

The Thomas Goodall House of 1871 is a good example of a Victorian mill-owner's residence. Designed in the Second Empire style, the home received Colonial Revival modifications at the turn of the century. Goodall was the industrialist who transformed Sanford from an agricultural village to one of the most important textile-manufacturing towns in the state. An enlightened employer for the times, Goodall supplied a recreation hall and public library for his workers.

STANDISH

Daniel Marrett House, Route 25 — 1789

Built as a typical Maine farmhouse in the late eighteenth century, the Marrett home was given Greek Revival decoration in the mid nineteenth century. Marrett, who came to Standish as pastor of the meeting house in 1796, did much of the finish work himself. The simplicity of the Marrett house and the integrity with which it has been preserved place it among the finest examples of rural Maine architecture.

"Old Red Church," Oak Hill Road — 1804–6

The First Parish Meeting House in Standish was built between 1804 and 1806 to replace the old meeting house in the center of town, which had been irreparably damaged by a group of drunken soldiers. The land upon which it was built

Old Red Church, Standish. Photo by Harold Warren.

was donated by the Reverend Daniel Marrett, who had been ordained as pastor in the community in 1796. He dedicated the "Old Red Church" in 1806 and remained as pastor until 1829. Shortly thereafter, a rift developed over the issue of Unitarianism. In 1834, the congregation split into an Evangelical Congregational church and a Unitarian church. The Unitarians used the "Old Red Church" until 1860.

STRATTON

Oramendal Blanchard House, Main Street 1892

Stratton, the largest village in the township of Eustis with a population of about four hundred, is still more or less a frontier town in a remote section of western Maine. The only residence of particular distinction in the community is

Oramendal Blanchard House, Stratton

this remarkable and very unusual Queen Anne house built in 1892 by Oramendal Blanchard.

Blanchard was the most important figure in Stratton at the turn of the century. He owned the local sawmill in what was still a very heavily timbered area. He was also the owner of the local water and electric companies, when these services became available. His position was such that the principal residential street was named after him.

This house is *the* landmark of the community and, with its peculiar tower, is a rare example of its style.

STRONG

Porter-Bell-Brackley Estate, Lower Main Street—1866

The Porter-Bell-Brackley Estate, built in 1866 and located in Strong, is among the best examples of the Italianate style of architecture in Maine. The highly detailed and beautifully proportioned residence is the equal of any to be found in either urban or coastal areas. It is all the more striking in the small remote community of Strong.

Porter–Bell–Brackley Estate, Strong

Originally, this house and another, virtually its twin, were built by Alexander and James Porter, prosperous mill men in the region. Their principal enterprise was a match factory, later a toothpick factory, which survives today as the Foster Manufacturing Company.

The James Porter House eventually became a hotel, which burned in 1971. Alexander Porter unfortunately succumbed to certain "temptations of the flesh" and lost his business and most of his property. Fortunately, he had transferred ownership of the house to other members of his family, so that they were able to remain there until it was sold to the Bells and later the Brackleys. This handsome estate survives today in excellent condition, virtually unchanged.

WATERBORO

Elder Grey Meeting House, North Waterboro — 1806

A simple and extremely well preserved structure dating from the first years of settlement in the area, this meeting house was named for one of its first pastors, who served the community for over forty years.

Barn at Gage–Rice House, Waterford Historic District

WATERFORD

Waterford Historic District

The Waterford Historic District comprises a cohesive and compatible grouping of eighteenth-, nineteenth-, and twentieth-century buildings. It is located on the western shore of Keoka Lake (formerly Thomas Pond) in the central part of the Waterford Township and occupies an area known locally as "The Flat," because of its level terrain in the midst of a hilly region at the foot of Mount Tire'em. As in most rural villages in Maine, the houses and other buildings are generously spaced. Within the last century or so, Waterford has undergone very little change and looks today very much as it did in the mid nineteenth century.

The town of Waterford was first surveyed in 1775. The first settler at Waterford "Flat" was Eli Longley, whose property encompassed the entire historic district. About 1793, Longley built a log dwelling, but so many calls were made upon his hospitality by passing travelers that he

Ambrose Knight House, Waterford Historic District

opened a public house in 1797, which, considerably altered, is now the Lake House. A man with an eye to the future he planned for the village that he knew would spring up and laid out the common, which remains today, though reduced in size.

The Waterford Historic District is significant as a remarkably unchanged and well-maintained nineteenth-century village, reflecting in its quiet dignity the slower pace of a departed era.

WINDHAM

Parson Smith House,
River Road (corner of Anderson Road) — 1764

This large 2½-story Colonial house is finished in clapboards and has an offset chimney at each end of the house. Parson Peter Thatcher Smith built this house himself two years after his ordination in Windham. He lived in the house until his death in 1826. In 1952, a descendant bequeathed the property to the Society for the Preservation of New England Antiquities, which maintains it. The home is in excellent, nearly original, condition.

Suggestions for Further Reading

Beard, Frank A. *200 Years of Maine Housing: A Guide for the House Watcher*. 2d rev. ed. Augusta: Maine Historic Preservation Commission, 1981.

Blumenson, John J.G. *Identifying American Architecture: A Pictorial Guide to Styles and Terms, 1600–1943*. Nashville, Tenn.: American Association for State and Local History, 1977.

Bradley, Robert L. *The Forts of Maine, 1607–1945: An Archaeological and Historical Survey*. Augusta: Maine Historic Preservation Commission, 1981.

Bradley, Robert L. *Maine's First Buildings: The Architecture of Settlement, 1604–1700*. Augusta: Maine Historic Preservation Commission, 1978.

Burrage, Henry S. *The Beginnings of Colonial Maine, 1602–1658*. Portland, Me.: Marks Printing House, 1914.

Hatch, Louis G. *Maine: A History*. New York: The American Historical Society, 1919.

Meyers, Denys P. *Maine Catalogue*. Augusta: Maine State Museum, 1974.

Morris, Gerald E., ed. *Maine Bicentennial Atlas: An Historical Survey.* Portland, Me.: Maine Historical Society, 1976.

Sanger, David. *Discovering Maine's Archaeological Heritage.* Augusta: Maine Historic Preservation Commission, 1979.

Thompson, Deborah, ed. *Maine Forms of American Architecture.* Camden, Me.: Down East Books, 1976.

Whiffen, Marcus. *American Architecture Since 1780: A Guide to the Styles.* Cambridge, Mass.: M.I.T. Press, 1969.

Williamson, William D. *The History of the State of Maine from Its First Discovery, A.D. 1602 to the Separation, A.D. 1820, Inclusive.* Reprint. Hallowell, Me.: 1832.

Willoughby, Charles C. *Indian Antiquities of the Kennebec Valley.* Augusta: Maine Historical Preservation Commission, 1980.

Index